Praise for Dutiful Daughters

"An eclectic and evocative collection of first-person narratives by women who serve as the primary caretakers of their elderly parents. Gould, a visiting scholar in Women's Studies at Northeastern University, has collected 22 moving and provocative essays examining the many emotions felt by those caring for aging parents. From the diversity of voices and experiences, a number of common themes emerge. Among them is the healing that can occur between daughter and parent as the roles of dependency are reversed. . . . *Dutiful Daughters* provides a powerful, intimate overview of circumstances likely to touch many of our lives." — *Kirkus Reviews*

"[T]his unusual book of first-person essays by women writers is timely and engaging. Appearing just as policy-makers reassess Medicare and Social Security, it documents the private side of aging and caregiving. Each of the 22 stories told here is different. . . . As a result, this is a wonderfully varied exploration of the complicated emotional and spiritual issues that emerge for parents and daughters as their bodies and relationships age. It will likely be read by aging parents and their caregiving children alike." — *Library Journal*

"*Dutiful Daughters* offers a critical place for engagement about what it means for women to care for our aging parents, and what it feels like to confront the associated loss, grief, and eventually, death. Twenty-two women speak about their experiences in complicated and poignant ways; there are no answers, but there is much exploration, more than a little humor and heartbreak, and the beginning of a bridge across so much silence. . . . *Dutiful Daughters* is necessary testimony and an open door." — *Sojourner*

"[*Dutiful Daughters*] is a portable support group . . . with testimonies from 22 women caring for their parents. The stories detail the trials and rewards of this time." — *MetroWest Daily News*

Dutiful Daughters

Caring for Our Parents
as They Grow Old

Edited by Jean Gould

Seal Press

Cover design: Clare Conrad
Cover photographs: (top center) Dennis Wise (Barbara Pickett and Rosemary Norton); (left to right): Dick Luria/FPG; Edward Carreon (Clarence Maurhan and Dr. Deborah Newquist); Sandra Butler and her mother; Dennis Wise (Irene Vitulli and Gasperina Di Maio).
Text design: Laura Gronewold
Fonts: Ex Ponto and Weiss

Library of Congress Cataloging-in-Publication Data
Dutiful daughters : caring for our parents as they grow old /
   edited by Jean Gould.
      p.   cm.
   ISBN 1-58005-026-3
      1. Aging parents—Care—United States. 2. Daughters—United States—Family relationships. 3. Caregivers—United States Biography. 4. Adult children—United States Biography. I. Gould, Jean, 1939– .
   HQ1064.U5D87   1999
   306.874'0973—dc21   99-16445
                                                                               CIP

Printed in the United States of America

First printing, September 1999

10   9   8   7   6   5   4   3   2

Distributed to the trade by Publishers Group West
In Canada: Publishers Group West Canada, Toronto, Ontario
In the U.K. and Europe: Airlift Book Distributors, Middlesex, England
In Australia: Banyan Tree Book Distributors, Kent Town, South Australia

To the memory of my father
Thomas Leo Colgan
1900–1951

Acknowledgments

Good independent presses are the jewels in publishing today. If a writer is lucky enough to work with one like Seal, where professional relationships involve mutual respect as well as collaboration, she is lucky indeed. I am grateful to publisher Faith Conlon for her continuing commitment to document women's experience in all its forms. Jennie Goode, my editor, helped shape the anthology with a seasoned perception and a keen intelligence. Her availability and encouragement have been vital. Kate Loeb did a fine job gathering and organizing the resource materials listed at the end of the book.

Dutiful Daughters was nurtured and informed by the more than two hundred writers who shared experiences with aging parents. Some even thanked *me* for the opportunity to transform their thoughts into writing. It was an honor to read their work. The writers whose essays appear here have been an editor's dream. Their flexibility and patience throughout this process have been outstanding.

Energetic discussions on this topic with Mercedes Anderson, Marguerite Bouvard, Heidi Keller Moon, Helen Nayar, Joan Nolan, Kathy Power, Marlene Samuelson and Marget Sands have been provocative and insightful. Sue and Dan Hamer made their Wellfleet home the ideal place to read manuscripts by providing just the right blend of conversation and solitude. The work of Marilyn Gardner of the *Christian Science Monitor*, Richard Knox of the *Boston Globe* and the Children of Aging Parents organization was enormously helpful. I am grateful to all.

The loving support of Irving Gould and Deborah Colgan are gifts beyond measure.

Honor thy father and thy mother: that thy days may be long upon the land . . .
— Exodus

On my honor, I will try to do my duty to God and my country, to help other people at all times, and to obey the Girl Scout Law. — *Juliette Gordon Low*

I had the habit of obedience, and I believed that, on the whole, God expected me to be dutiful. . . . My mother's whole education and upbringing had convinced her that for a woman the greatest thing was to become the mother of a family; she couldn't play this part unless I played the dutiful daughter. . . .
— *Simone de Beauvoir,* Memoirs of a Dutiful Daughter

Contents

Introduction

*J*acaranda blossoms fluttered blue-purple the Florida afternoon that the seeds for this book took root. I had been making the trip from Boston three or four times each year following my mother's retirement. This time I was more eager to see her than usual, since she had been recovering from an arm injury for some weeks in an "assisted living" facility. Without knowing it, I had joined the millions of adult children—mostly daughters—actively involved in the care of aging parents.

I remember now that the building, a house in a residential middle-class neighborhood, brought the word "ordinary" to my lips as I approached. Next door, a woman in red shorts weeded her garden. A postman put letters in mailboxes on the other side of the street. And there was the porch my mother had described to me, where she often sat smoking with the other residents.

But here imagination and fact collided. The comfortable outdoor furniture was actually an old sofa and shabby armchairs. In the doorway, a puffy middle-aged woman brushed by me, saying that unless the state raised her hourly rate she would quit; later I learned she was a court-appointed guardian for a man whose family had abandoned him. And although my mother had told me that the other residents were stroke patients, I clutched my purse to my chest as their vacant stares asked me for something they couldn't name. *The place was not perfect, but it would certainly do.* These were the words of the daughter—my sister—who lived nearby and had assumed responsibility for her care.

The drum of TV commercials followed me from the empty living room, through a narrow hallway, to the kitchen with its table already set for the evening meal. Just beyond was the door to my mother's room. Lying fully dressed on a single, unmade bed, she held out her arms when I entered. During the next minutes, as I took in the plum-colored bruises on her face, we rocked each other a bit, just as always. Cockroaches skittered along the baseboards. She had fallen, she said, and since there was no call bell in her room, she had lain on the floor all night waiting for help. Moreover, she had been living here several months, not several weeks. Yet I had spoken to her almost daily, had talked with her doctor, my sister and the director of this place. How could this have happened?

She didn't want to bother me, she said now, slurring her words. Newspapers cluttered the room. She wanted to go home but was too tired to arrange it, she told me. I discovered that although she had no specific medical diagnosis, at least seven different medications had been prescribed. And while the doctor told me he saw no evidence of it, my sister claimed our mother had "severe dementia."

We held hands and ate Hershey's Kisses without speaking for what was probably less than a minute. When a man identifying himself as "the toe clipper" entered without knocking, I screamed at him to get out.

I had a strange urge to photograph the scene: the intruder with what looked like a shoe shiner's stool, the daughter's mouth contorted in its shouting and the elderly woman awkwardly arranged against a flat pillow in a flowered case.

If she had it to do over again, my mother often said, she'd be a general in the armed forces. She became an accountant instead and organized figures rather than soldiers. How could I imagine a time when she was not in charge?

This was, after all, the young widow who managed to educate two children on her own, the woman who helped me when I myself became a single parent. She had lived in New York with Grace Kelly, returned to college for a liberal arts degree in her sixties, traveled to India on her own when she was seventy-five. Certainly at eighty-nine she had slowed down. But dementia?

The time had come, my sister said, to take control of our mother's financial affairs. But after she and her husband moved to Florida two years before, several unsettling incidents about money occurred. I can't die soon enough to please some people, my mother said now and again.

At four o'clock we heard residents taking their places for dinner. They have nothing else to do, she told me. The staff was very kind to her, she said, but she suspected that the director, who claimed to be a nurse, knew nothing about health care. The white bread and gray soup I saw on my way out completed the nightmare. When she was fifty-three, my mother ended what she often spoke of as the happiest time of her life—her years in business—to move to Florida to take care of my grandmother. I wondered if I would have to do the same.

Scheduled for a three-day visit, I stayed for two months. And that was only the beginning. Alone and without a passport, I had entered a country whose customs, rules, language and attitudes were foreign to me.

I had generally identified myself as a problem solver, comfortable with collaboration and decision-making. But I knew nothing about the differences between assisted living facilities and retirement homes, nursing homes and home health care, advanced directives and health proxies. I didn't know that to be eligible for rehabilitation under

Medicare, a person has to be hospitalized for three days first. And how on earth did there get to be a job called toe clipper?

As I investigated resources, made files, consulted friends, found websites on the Internet, I discovered one of the major secrets of American life: *Those who care for aging parents feel like failures—and the resulting sense of shame is so pervasive that it prevents the expression of reasonable dialogue and emotions.*

Depression, social isolation and guilt are well documented among caretakers, and scientists have found evidence of immune-system impairment as well. How does the caretaker take care of herself? Can we set limits without guilt? What are the dimensions of commitment? These are complex issues. While not an illness, aging is terminal. We cannot save our parents or prevent their decline. And the knowledge that one's best efforts can have value in the process without altering the result is hard won.

On the other hand, the opportunity for re-engagement with a parent can foster new perspective, intimacy and mutual respect. Gerontologists tell us that helping the elderly review their lives enables them to take stock of both setbacks and successes in a gentle way, one more suited to closure than correction. That kind of ongoing dialogue may sweeten the prospect of old age for caretakers, as we develop an awareness that the sum of a life can be greater than its disappointments, that one can find relief in letting go and that the actual experience of old age may be different from what we imagine.

This is a volume that for the first time gives permission to daughters of the elderly to explore these issues, to share their experiences and to know that they have meaning. Each of the twenty-two essays presents a unique view, as writers recount their efforts to come to terms with the requirements of their parents' aging. This invisible work is the fastest-growing unpaid profession in the United States. More than twenty-two million households—one in four—are involved in caring for an older person. According to the National Alliance for Caregiving, the typical caregiver is a married forty-six-year-old woman with a full-time job and a high school diploma. Indeed, four out of five adult children who care for their aging parents are daughters. Typically they provide eighteen hours of care each week for four and a half years.

Additionally, when women are called upon to care for parents, they often are in the midst of transitions themselves; their children may have recently left home or they may be retiring and developing new careers and interests, just as the time allotted for such redefinition is eroded by new caretaking responsibilities. And since it has become common for women to bear children into their forties, there may still be infants or teenagers also needing attention. In this book, these events generally occur off-stage; yet they remain an important part of the story, raising questions about the conflict between the right to selfhood and the nature of responsibility, and why these might be seen as mutually exclusive. What does it mean to put a life on hold for an indefinite period?

The scope of this collection is limited to the experiences of women. Clearly some sons accept responsibility for the welfare of their parents, but daughters are still the ones expected to know intuitively what's required and how to act, and to do it silently and without credit. Studies show that men are more likely to manage parents' financial resources, facilitate moving, sell property. This is an unfortunate reminder of the cost of rigid gender roles. Women are not valued for unpaid work, and men are denied the opportunity to be of service. Moreover, those of us who have spent a lifetime struggling to break free of these boundaries now find ourselves again trying to be the "good girls" we were scripted to be when we were children.

When I set out to collect material for *Dutiful Daughters* using the foreign country metaphor, I imagined an adventure akin to exotic travels abroad. Unfamiliar language and customs could be learned and systems could be negotiated. In my arrogance, I suppose I believed that I would find willing, knowledgeable guides. But this country of aging parents is largely uncharted territory, providing no suitable analogies. That life spans are longer, that family members live geographically distant, that both partners in marriages work and are having children later—these are only the most visible circumstances to mushroom in the late twentieth century. The morass of social security, Medicare and Medicaid policies, the growing acceptance of institutional care, the skyrocketing financial costs also have yet to be factored in to form working solutions. And old age is big business; it's often difficult to separate the profit motive from social responsibility. Local councils on aging and state departments of elder affairs can hardly keep up with their mandates, much less arrange systems of support for the children of those they serve. Theoretical perspectives abound; adequate hands-on support and service do not. And although this book is not intended to deal directly with these issues, they provide the context in which daughters find themselves.

The courage of these women who risk transforming powerful experiences and feelings into written words is heroic. When a subject is so integral to one's sense of self, the writing is neither easy in its process nor ordinary in its product. In their depth and scope, the pieces in this collection follow no prescribed pattern. There are no sound bites like "sandwich generation," "role reversal" or "adventure," which serve only to oversimplify and often to pathologize. There are no easy formulas for self-care, for saying goodbye, for the expression of tenderness and grief. These stories document a wide range of daughters' experiences: from humor to devastation, love to rage, desperation to serenity, denial to acceptance, exhilaration to contemplation of one's own aging. Most of all, they express the determination of daughters to find places in their families of origin that make sense, to know that they have done their best and to forgive themselves when they have not.

Spirituality, whether in organized form or in valued connections with nature, plays a prominent role in a number of these stories. When Sheila Golburgh Johnson's father moves to California to be near her after his wife dies, he develops solid connections with the Jewish community there and ultimately offers her an unexpected legacy. In "The

Minyan Connection," she integrates a disturbing childhood experience with a rabbi and the compassion of her father's new congregation, closing the gap on her earlier life, permitting the comfort she denied herself in adulthood to rise slowly and enfold her.

Place also appears significant, as daughters recall leaving home, returning, then leaving again. In "To Kill a Deer," Debra Marquart drives her parents from Montana to North Dakota, where an unexpected event and the treachery of winding mountain roads echo their relationship past and present. Transformed from teenage black sheep to successful musician, writer and university professor, Marquart is ready to take charge when they are stranded far from home. But her equanimity is challenged when her parents refuse to recognize the competent adult she has become.

Managing geographical distance presents major difficulties common to many caretaking daughters—whether this involves arranging local supports for parents, dealing with the intensity of visiting or attempting to get a sense of current conditions from a faraway telephone voice. In "Sheer Grace," Bonny Vaught recounts an exquisite patience, as she herself is ill and unable to travel to see her ailing father. Relying on a cousin, a close friend and eventually her husband, the process and outcome develop beyond what she expects from the strain of separation.

Cultural expectation and custom often play a role in a daughter's decision to care for a parent in her own home. "Kin care for kin until the very end," writes Florence Ladd ("Life with Mom"), describing what appears to be an optimal situation made possible by her own superior organizational skills, her determination to lead a balanced life and her mother's financial independence. The arrangement requires constant adjustment as circumstances change, but it's one Ladd finds manageable, particularly when compared to other options.

Some writers wish better lives for their parents, especially that their mothers were freer from traditional roles and had the options their daughters enjoy today. In "Margie's Discount," BK Loren fantasizes about her Parkinson's-afflicted mother, whose main focus in life has been getting a good retail bargain: "She is eighteen again, and suddenly she can choose to be married or not; she can choose to have children whenever and if ever she wants; she can walk over to this rack and pick up a college degree . . . she can go to this case and decide if her marriage is working out. . . ."

On the other hand, when powerful parents insist on independence, this can wreak havoc with daughters who strive to protect them. When Kathryn Morton ("Autonomy of the Hovercraft") attempts to take her mother for a doctor's appointment, the two of them struggle over a loaded gun as her mother, herself a physician, refuses to go. Despite the commotion a hovercraft creates over rough ground or high waves, it gets to its destination. This is Morton's mother, an eccentric and lovable parent, whose qualities that make her most uniquely herself are ultimately honored by her daughter. As the author walks that fine line between her mother's wishes and her own common sense, she offers effective caring and devotion amid the many obstacles that face her.

Each of these stories has the potential to evoke controversy as readers identify with writers and imagine their own attitudes and actions in the situations described. When parents' lifelines grow shorter, veering now this way and that, beyond our control and theirs, decisions loom larger and may need ever more careful measuring. In "The Promise," Diane Reed faces this head-on as she struggles with whether or not to abide by her mother's wishes about dying. This essay points to the desire to ease suffering and to the loneliness of the daughter's condition, as Reed makes good on her obligations.

While the intensity of situations such as that above can consume a caretaker, the perspective of writers who find themselves at the beginning of the journey with their parents and those who are able to take the long look back is an essential part of this collection. Some years after her mother's death, Wendy Fairey ("Her Hair") reflects that "the relationship has softened." Contemplating her own aging at a college reunion, the writer acknowledges that she is better friends with her mother since she died: "She used to be very difficult. But now she's so much more reasonable." In an essay combining wit with basic truths, Fairey finds the relationship clearly has a different look to it as she grows closer in age to her mother.

Memory also can frame current exigencies so they are more tolerable. As Marion Freyer Wolff deals with her demanding father ("You Always Come Too Late and Leave Too Early"), she poignantly remembers that it was he who rescued her from the Holocaust. Even as she confronts him with his lack of consideration, she notes a great sadness in his eyes and retreats, allowing compassion to replace her anger.

Loss hurts. As a parent ages and loses physical capabilities, a spouse, friends or a home, the ability to parent may also wane. And those of us who still seek approval may find ourselves in the unaccustomed position of having to give it. As time for resolution runs out, childhood wounds can resurface and seem to be occurring in the present: "You never gave me a birthday party." "I wanted braces on my teeth." "You didn't come to watch me in the high school play." Or, "You never said you loved me."

In their rage at feeling unaccepted and unseen, children can direct their feelings of rejection into aggressive displays of power. Physical abuse then is just a whisper away. Sometimes the relationships are too damaged to be repaired. It is striking that even those daughters who report the most serious neglect and abuse continue their attachments in some form. In "A Bridge of Sparrows," Maija Rhee Devine permits her mother to live with her and her family in Wyoming but refuses to have direct conversation with her. The shame of their earlier lives in Korea proves unforgivable.

More often, children seem able to set their grievances aside. Even as there is usually one daughter who takes major responsibility and keeps others informed, siblings generally make an effort to cooperate. For those who have had positive relationships, the chance to give something back can be welcomed. But in truth, for most of us, attitudes

Jean Gould   xix

toward parents fall into uncertain categories of ambivalence. When Patricia Gozemba ("Cookie and Me") hears her father announce his acceptance of her lesbianism after years of silence on the issue, she is overwhelmed and pleased. But did he have to wait so long?

We do not ever become our parents' parents. Possibly we become the repository of some of their accumulated experiences; possibly we involve ourselves in their physical and/or financial well-being. But their power to move us endures. As we consider our responsibilities to them, scrutiny of the connection becomes as inevitable as aging itself, when circumstances force us into close and sometimes uncomfortable proximity.

At this writing, my mother lives in her own apartment in a retirement community. Now ninety-one, she does the *Times* crossword puzzle each morning, plays bridge most afternoons and manages her own affairs. She has given up driving but not cigarettes. Shortly after the time I helped her escape from the place where I initially found her, the facility burned down. In the year that followed, I lost thirty pounds as I immersed myself in her care and recovery. For the several months that she lived with us, she was able to get off all prescription drugs and straighten out my sister's bookkeeping. Although my husband and I had hoped, indeed lobbied, for her living with us permanently, she returned to Florida, citing the warmer climate and independence.

In the course of these years, we have made good use of the opportunity to review and revere our bond. Somehow, without saying so directly, we forgave each other's imperfections. I no longer spend one week each month in Florida as I did at first or encourage a move to Boston. We speak at eight o'clock most nights and I visit frequently.

My sister continues to participate in the way she sees fit. Despite our differences, I have to believe her intention is to do what she thinks is right. Remarking once on her impatience and lack of compassion, she told me that I had always been "the tender one," "the diplomat" in the family. But in my mind, there is no competition for best or worst daughter. We do what we can.

Most of us are less noble and more human than we hope. The banner of expectations inherent in the role of the good daughter—the dutiful daughter—flies too high for many to touch. Public testimony legitimizes what we do and can validate others who experience it through us. The writers whose essays appear here are exceptionally talented in their ability to draw us into their worlds and to make us stand taller for having done so. Together they speak beyond personal experience to strength and to vulnerability, but most particularly to the spirit of fidelity and endurance. As daughters share what they have learned and continue to learn, they teach us how to age *with* our parents, while we discover again and again that we are the experts on caretaking, both real and perceived, and that our most valuable resource is one another.

Jean Gould
Natick, Massachusetts
April 1999

Dutiful Daughters

Autonomy of the Hovercraft

KATHRYN MORTON

$\mathcal{B}$y the time I found where the gun was—hidden under a plastic produce sack—Mom was clamoring through the bedroom door, grabbing for the gun and hitting me. She was eighty-three, frail, tiny, quavery and furious. The gun in my hand felt like a toy, like one of the Hopalong Cassidy revolvers I had worn in childhood when this room had been my bedroom and the curtains, made by Mom, had cowboys on them. My brother and I used to drive a stagecoach from the front end of our top bunk here, while the bottom bunk was tented around for a tepee or a miner's shack. Beginning each year when the breeze and mockingbirds would wake us in the mornings and continuing till mosquitoes got bad in August, the window had been an escape route to the "corral" out back where the swings were tethered.

My revolvers had been shinier than this one, larger and more fearsome. Getting the little black thing untangled from the plastic sack, trying to remember it was dangerous, I held it straight up, as in keepaway. This did not feel any more real than a game, except to Mom. Then, over us both loomed my six-foot-six brother. Even in the cowboy

3

days he used to do what he wanted and have first choice of toys. He now took the gun off the top of the pinnacle of hands, saying, "Now, Mother, that's not safe. Mother! Mother, it's not *safe,*" speaking patiently and dispassionately as one might in taking matches from a child. But to Mom the gun *was* safety, her assurance against the insufferable. It could defend her against burglars, but more important, it was her always ready, one-way ticket Home. Not for her the ragged, dragged-out dying of the helpless.

Removal of the gun was only part of Brother's plan for Mom's welfare this day. He had an agenda and, unlike last week, he would not let himself be sidetracked this time. This time we would not spend hours trying to fix the latest TV sets or VCRs, as we had a week ago when Mom turned every query about her failing health into a plea that if we wanted to help, we should do something about the maddening machines. We had obsessively tried to show her how to change channels without going into "menu." Each newcomer to the house, Brother, me, his wife, my husband, my son, would take the new set out of the packing carton and taped-up plastic wrapper and again (and again) try to prove that it actually *did* work—so long as, when you were trying to get the closed captions to stop writing Spanish, you didn't accidentally pre-program the set to be an alarm clock. We had rummaged among the assortment of remote controls and owner's manuals, none of which seemed to fit any appliance at hand, while Mom corrected us about what was wrong, referring to the three VCRs and TV sets variously as "the Sony," "the new one," "not that one, the other one" and "that piece of crap." Dan Rather glowed orange, channels changed their locations and tapes wouldn't play all the way to the end. Murders had disappeared from the *Masterpiece Theater* recordings of "Miss Marple": Bunny no longed died in the same episode as Captain Longberry. A taped TV concert of Kiri Te Kanawa now stopped in the middle of the last song, and "The African Queen" was missing its beginning credits.

The TV table is in one of the many dark corners of Mom's house.

To help whoever was having a go at reconnecting the set to one of the antennas, Mom would hold the flashlight to save electricity. Alternatively, to save flashlight batteries and yet illuminate the high-tech, invisible buttons, she would run an extension cord with a shop lamp. And whatever one was doing, she would provide instructions on how not to do it because it wouldn't work, she'd already tried that. During one such day, two con men, both named Cliff, had showed up. Under threats, they had come grudgingly to discuss returning six hundred of the twelve hundred dollars Mom had given them for a pair of toaster-sized "air purifiers." When the larger Cliff became abusive, Brother unfolded himself from the chair, rising and rising like a cumulonimbus warning. Cliff looked at Cliff and one of them signed a refund check with trembling hand. The bank teller took it without question minutes later. That was last week.

This time, the defective equipment to be investigated was Mom's own. At one o'clock an echocardiogram was scheduled four blocks away at the hospital where Mom used to be on staff—till they took her name off the In/Out list for failing to hospitalize her quota of patients. No fan of hospitals then or now, she was not the one who had made today's appointment, and she had no intention of keeping it. She had had it with doctors. She knew what was wrong with her, and whether her judgment was terrible or not, it was hers, it was her own. She would not be told what to do in her own house or with her own life. If we were going to be unreasonable, she would just show us that her autonomy was unimpaired. Even though we might deprive her of her gun, we could not deprive her of free will. Lacking the gun, she would just give herself a heart attack to prove her point. But to achieve this end, she needed to disconnect the VCR so she could carry it down the front steps into the bitter March air and run far enough up the street for the exertion to kill her. The cables were tangled. Neither Brother nor I offered to hold the flashlight. Brother put his hand on the VCR so she wouldn't knock it on the floor while she wrestled with the pliers, and then he took her hands. "Get her coat," he said in a soft voice as though the the comment was casual and not in fact an absolute order. Then to her, at first reasonably but with gradually increasing volume, he became huge. As she fought to free her hands, his discourse went from today on, expanding globally: "Mother, sit down. We are trying to help you. All we are doing is trying to help you. Why can't you ever listen to anybody else? Why do you always have to . . . ! You never . . . always . . . can't ever . . ." His equal in navigating time, she charged him with having turned bad in kindergarten when he'd started running around with that brat next door and talking back and refusing to mind. I got her coat and we all sat down to listen to her relate the saga of our lives till one o'clock.

Brother has not come to visit often in recent years and never for more than part of a day. Once or twice a year he will drive the four-and-a-half hours from the town where he is on the medical school faculty, as he has today. He will usually do some tree pruning or heavy lifting for Mom and give her something he has meticulously devised or carefully sought out as special, coming from his area of interests that he thinks she might be interested in too, but seldom is. They'll chat to crossed purposes until they are disputing what had or had not happened in the 1950s, and then he'll drive home again, listening to his favorite novels read on tape in German or Russian. Last week he came on Tuesday, bringing his wife. While he dealt with televisions, then went home again, she stayed over and arranged for the echo-cardiogram, masking that activity with hours of cleaning. The cleaning had filled the ninety-gallon city garbage can with what appeared to be trash, but Mom could now itemize the excesses—perfectly edible, barely sprouted potatoes, jar lids that fit something, cardboard boxes and magazines that could be burned to help warm the house. The next day, Brother returned, bringing his own TV set—old enough to have visible knobs, no remote and a thirty-day return policy that had expired years ago. This week he has come back to ensure that Mom gets to the hospital.

I was responsible for starting all these visits of his. In December I had called him because Mom was sick. She was losing weight, from one hundred five to one hundred and sliding. He had been planning on making the trip in August, October, over the Christmas break. He shouldn't wait too long, I wanted him to know. After I called him, we began e-mailing two and three times a day, his questions, suggestions, demands, plans and, much to my surprise, his encouragement and gratitude. We have had little contact since the cowboy days. He has a talent for saying things that hurt; I, years ago, got good at making him want to say them. But over the Net this winter we conversed about how to circumvent Mom's furious autonomy and get her into a doctor's care. We exchanged quips and analyses. He sent explanations of physiological processes. I sent him what I know about Mom's motivations and the stumbling blocks—both natural and handmade—that keep her from following a simple course of action. We exchanged news of our children. He recommended books.

Unaware of the developing plot, Mom dwindled toward ninety pounds with no intention of seeing a doctor, turning her free will over to some patronizing fool who would just want to order a lot of expensive tests, totally ignoring anything she would say to explain her symptoms and their cause. No. No doctors, no hospitals, no tests, nobody telling her what to do.

At first she had felt too weak to sit up for as long as even a prompt doctor would take. Nauseated, she found food repulsed her, except for red grapes, root beer and potato chips. She would sometimes eat other things if I brought them in small packages, fresh and at random—pizza, sweet and sour pork, peanut brittle, a ripe pear. Any food, however small the portion, of course exacerbated her irritable colon. Because of that, she would not come to my house—I have only one bathroom, what if somebody was using it? Besides, my house is not hers. She wants her own turf. In January she decided she had vestigial cholera from bad water decades ago in Spain. On and off she considered cancer but always changed her mind. Whatever it was that was wrong, food poisoning, a stomach flu or something worse, it reduced her from being a chain saw–toting back yard farmer to being a virtual invalid. Housebound, frail, insomniac, she faced infirmity, cursing like a sailor.

Scatological terms that she had always damned as repugnant now were the staples of her vocabulary, right along with the theological imprecations that I had grown up on. Every third sentence now started with brimstone and ended in the outhouse. Plain cursing she had learned in medical school. Those ready invocations of the Almighty and the underworld and the charges of illegitimacy of assorted people, she had explained many times, were derived from the influence of "the boys who all talked like that." In the fall of 1935, Oklahoma University's medical school admitted one hundred and twenty-five "boys" and two women. At midterm the other woman, Katherine Bailey, flunked out. Unlike Mom, Katherine Bailey didn't have to work at an eight-dollar-a-week WPA job to support herself, and she probably had more than one meal a day and surely did not sleep behind a curtain on the stair landing of a noisy boarding house. We know that her luxuries extended to include owning her own copies of textbooks. We know this because of one of the scenes told and retold from the saga of those years, when Mom hung on by the skin of her teeth while others far more able and with far more advantages unaccountably sank. In the scene, Katherine Bailey, in tears, is forever trying to give Mom her almost-new *Gray's Anatomy*. Mom is forever taken aback at the wrong-headedness of the offer. However kind the intention, Katherine ought to resell the book for almost as much as she had paid for it. Such a volume was just too expensive to give away to somebody who wasn't even kin. Mom had an old, used copy, and anatomy hadn't changed that much—not like chemistry and pharmacology.

In the 1940s and '50s when my brother and I were growing up, we called *Gray's Anatomy* "the muscle book" because it had pictures of breasts in it, and we weren't going to mention that word in describing a tome that clearly possessed dignity, perhaps even sanctity. So it was, euphemistically, the "muscle" book. From time to time, Mom would heave it open and flip to the right pages to show us why an elbow won't bend both ways or where the ring I had swallowed was wending its way through pink and purple parts of me or how the ridges of our chests are made like a row of bars we live inside or where the heart is—not really on the left but just off-center in the middle and not heart-shaped at all. The print was small; the multicolored pictures, authoritative. I knew then and know now that my own innards are more jumbled up and murky. But this is what we are supposed to look like inside. This is how complicated we are and how clever, how wonderfully clever.

Then Mom would tell us about anomalies she had encountered dissecting cadavers in school or doing "posts" on those who died in hospitals where she had worked: the woman with one long U-shaped kidney, the man with the second fibula, an old lunatic who had been institutionalized after a fight and at death turned out to have a broken-off knife blade in his head. And there were all the people who had died of something other than what the death certificate said, twenty-five to thirty percent of them listed wrong, and the statistics have not improved. There were unsuspected aneurysms, gangrenous innards, tumors nobody had spotted, blockages and kinks and quirks and lapses, all sorts of fascinating stuff: "The body is fascinating, and when you look at it, it's a miracle that it works at all; it is all so cobbled together, no two people alike." She would show us her hands, how the veins in one made a whole different pattern from that of the veins in the other, or in ours. Still, whenever I look at the backs of my hands, I feel like a tightrope walker, heady with the perilous knowledge that the rope is made of frangible threads.

The anatomy book had an extravagant aroma. Mom dismissed the smell as "just formaldehyde" absorbed during so many dissections. But the aroma of the formaldehyde that I eventually encountered in high school biology bore no similarity to that winey, musky scent. Only during the 1960s in Europe, looking at a reliquary in which a saint's finger bone was garlanded with coral and pearls, did I ever encounter incense like it—that whiff of the sanctity of the human miracle.

I didn't mention that aromatic discovery to Mom. She has no use for religion: "It's all wishes and lies. You can ask all you want, but nobody's listening; there is no God," she tells me when she thinks I am too involved with my Sunday school students. She used to pray in childhood over and over that her own mother not die of one of her fainting spells. Mom now dismisses her juvenile folly at misdiagnosing what must have been anxiety attacks or migraines—never a mortal threat, but scary enough to send a child fleeing for a magic remedy. Prayer had "nothing" to do with the fact that Grandmother lived to ninety-two in Mom's round-the-clock care.

In the late 1930s Mom had again been foolish enough to pray, when she herself had encephalitis. She prayed that the blinding pain would stop. With the seventeenth spinal tap, the doctors in the hospital where she worked found the pneumococcus. Pneumococcic encephalitis was ninety-nine percent fatal then, before antibiotics. They tried out one of the early sulfa drugs on her, Neoprontisil. When Mom's temperature came down to one hundred and nine, the attending physicians began to think she might live. How many times has she told me about lying with her eyes bandaged, figuring how to make a living blind, and then about the day when she was better and the bandages were removed. She looked out the window at the yellow cottonwood trees, their leaves drifting in showers of gold. "But God had nothing to do with it." That was luck and human research, neither of which is to be counted on. They had been inadequate to save my father from his stroke and my son from lupus. You can't count on God, and you certainly can't count on doctors. You have to just count on yourself.

I think that some people almost can. They have so strong a will that they ride on the force of it, levitated above the impossible, repudiating gravity because they have simply and unilaterally decided not to fall. A hovercraft rides on a tornado-like blast of air that separates its weight from the ground. Mom's like that. Near her, you are knocked dizzy by the noise and the vortexing dust, and you may think, "Surely, it doesn't have to be this hard. There has got to be an easier way." I am the younger child and the girl. I still live half a mile from the house I grew up in, in which I got married and in which Mom and I sang to my father as he stopped breathing at the end of a hard, long dying. I am simply the one nearby. I tie my hair back and face the tumult.

Like now. Like this winter. Making food runs that only sometimes resulted in getting any food into Mom, pleading with her to come home with us the day that, while talking to my daughter, Mom spaced out and began searching the house for paintings of fruit. I have averaged five hours a week on the phone, mostly listening to bodily complaints and grievances that date back to the 1920s and before, about the jealous older sister who was the thirteenth of the sixteen children. Mom was fourteenth. Birth control did not exist for dirt farmers in the days when Oklahoma was becoming a state. Mom spent her childhood protecting the fifteenth child, a brother, from the town bullies who had real barbershop haircuts and expensive, store-bought peanut butter for their sandwiches. The sixteenth child died within two weeks of birth from diarrhea when, dry of breast milk, Grandmother had tried to feed him cow's milk without knowing to boil it to reduce the size of the curd. In all, seven of the sixteen children died before the age of five—diphtheria took two in one week. Mom's sense of life's injustice came early. The decades collapse as she tells of the young neighbor who turned away yesterday without waving, though surely he must have seen Mom just inside the closed window, and he is linked to the deadbeats who would run up debts at her father's store while their horses fouled the streets, and the people in '48 who said my dad was a Communist for his work with the Progressive Party, and the anonymous midnight callers in '58 when we were among those suing the governor to make him open the public schools he had closed to prevent integration. Sometimes, without getting caught and chastised for being a Pollyanna or for showing a rude lack of interest in her news, I can ask a question to change the subject or to resurface us in today's world. Sometimes, as though weather had shifted, she will remember the good.

In January, while Brother and I were planning medical care, Mom got to feeling better and one day decided that she would see a doctor to have him check her for diabetes. She had recently decided that was her ailment. It took but a week of trying to eat low-sugar foods when she wasn't hungry anyway to make her want to rule out diabetes. She looked up an internist nearby, made an appointment and then called to tell me what she had done and to ask me to take her. The doctor did a thorough work-up, found her heart enlarged, her liver enlarged, a mass in her abdomen. He ordered a battery of blood tests, a chest x-ray and an abdominal CAT scan. In whispers, he expected to confirm a malignancy. Wrong.

The CAT scan turned up clean. The liver function tests were unexciting, the blood tests reasonably normal. Whatever Mom had or had had, she didn't have anything the doctor tested for. He wanted to do follow-ups, an echocardiogram to check for congestive heart failure, a stomach-emptying test to seek an answer to the food aversion. Nope. No more. Her ribs had been exquisitely tender to his touch during the physical, the internal exam had been excruciating, diarrhea from the CAT scan juice was thirty-six hours of "torture." She had been docile through all the ordeals, during which I had been an "angel" for being there. Afterwards, she was back in Tabasco mode, and I had no vote from now on. She had had enough doctoring. It wasn't diabetes, "or so *he* said, if you could trust what *he* said." In any case, before the test results came back, she had decided for herself that it wasn't diabetes. As for cancer? Huh! She had never considered cancer a threat, since she could always just blow her brains out.

She fired the doctor, fired off salvos of vituperation in his general direction at regular intervals and began ordering seeds and bulbs from the gardening catalogues. Brother was less mercurial and more convinced of the values of medical know-how. He had received the family gene for determination, and the gene found its expression in today's agenda. She *would* have the echocardiogram if he had to carry her kicking and screaming the four blocks, for which he was both prepared and capable.

Sleight of hand is my mode. I slipped outside with the gun. My husband was waiting. Ready to chauffeur us to the hospital, he had been spending the time rehearsing for his upcoming part in a little theater murder mystery. Thus it was that he was the only one of our generation who knew how to unload a real gun. He unloaded it and put it in the car's trunk. He went ahead to the hospital to have a wheelchair waiting and ready. It took Mom half an hour to decide that she would not fight, that she would let this happen, this pointless test her fanatic children believed to be so important. I told her the test would not hurt. I was wrong. I did not realize how tender her ribs were and that the technician would push the probe up hard against them so that Mother would catch her breath, seething in pain, barely able to breathe for the thirty minutes the test would take. For that half hour a nice young woman probed and pushed, Mom wept and gasped, and I watched the inside of my mother's heart on the TV screen, messier and meatier than the textbook picture, not unlike an ultrasound fetus, *whh-whush, whh-whush*. Doppler radar showed, in red static, the blood flowing away and, in blue static, the blood flowing toward the probe. Yellow eddies sometimes fringed the valves' edges. Mom, lying the wrong way on the cot, could not see this, which at one time she would have found so fascinating as to obliterate her awareness of pain. By the time it was over, she was too weak to sit up. We kept a hand on her, rolling back down the hallway toward the car and home, where she locked us all out and took a nap.

In the following days, Mom became convinced that she had congestive heart failure, indignant that nobody had ever considered this obvious diagnosis that accounts for so much of her trouble—the bad bowel from inadequate blood flow, the constant fatigue and weakness, the confusion. She was undaunted when the echocardiogram report said that, in fact, her heart is sturdy, the valves competent, the blood flow strong. She has her diagnosis, and it is her own. In view of it, she has begun to give herself permission to take life a little easier and to hang up quicker on people who make her mad.

Brother went home. Within two months, his TV set with the visible knobs would no longer get any station. Mom gave it to the people down the street in exchange for one they were selling in a yard sale, which went dead in two days, was picked up by a repairman who said it had suffered delayed damage from a power surge that must have occurred in some recent lightning storm. He could fix it, he said. We asked if his name was Cliff when he changed his phone number, disappeared, and when traced, said the set could not be fixed but that he could replace it for a couple of hundred bucks. The replacement lasted two weeks before Mom called my son to come and get it out of her house and out of her life. I then went to the store and bought whatever combined TV-VCR had the simplest controls. When it went dead, my son revived it by pushing the reset selection on "menu."

After holding her weight at ninety pounds for several months, Mom is up to ninety-four again, eating what she feels like. I have a case of Ensure that my brother brought her and that she says she gags on. It is ready in case she decides a food supplement would be a good idea. The flower bulbs she ordered came and came up. Their blooms were her daily news for weeks. She is trying to get the place cleaned up and cleared out so I'll have less to face when she "bumps off." Relieved to have diagnosed herself with congestive heart failure, she's confident that a nice easy attack will take her, sparing her the slide into dementia like her mother's or the catastrophe of paralysis like Dad's. She won't even have to use the gun. (We gave it back to her when she threatened to buy a new one. We tried first to get the firing pin removed, but neither gun dealer could do it without considerable delay. The second dealer, however, suggested taking the fronts off the bullets. In the chambers, the shells looked OK. It took Mom a week to discover the ruse and to replace the shells with live ammunition again. She figures that for all the years she has had the gun, the bullets have been dummies and that her children were dummies to be afraid of a gun that wasn't in fact even loaded, till now.)

Mom called today to tell of finding an 1885 grade-school speller in the attic and began to rhapsodize on how amazing television and videotapes are—all those pictures, people talking, moving, any time you want to see them, because of waves coming in through the air, little wires connecting the parts. "What an amazing thing. Don't you think so, really?" she said. She has had another birthday. Brother called, but they got to arguing about what she had done to his TV set and she hung up on him. She had just sent him the money she had taken out of a savings and loan bank that had merged against her advice—he could buy several new TV sets.

I call her daily and stop by every few days and take hot French fries from the burger place, watermelon, some of the latest soup. I look around at the rearranged clutter. She pulls me to the door and says goodbye if I start "messing around trying to clean and getting things all out of order."

She will die, probably after the year 2000, because she wants to wait and see what people call it. She will probably not blow her brains out nor succumb while portaging a VCR, but death will happen. I'll go through her house then, the piles and boxes and trunks and sacks and racks and shelves of things she is still keeping because they might come in handy. I know there are clothes that date back to childhood—mine and hers (some of them the same clothes). And there are all the letters my father wrote her from the army, and later when he was away in Houston handling the Humble Oil account, and later when he was in Canada painting pictures for the Price Paper Company. He wrote wonderful letters. Somewhere among the boxes are letters between my grandparents, and there is my grandfather's certificate from President Cleveland giving him title to the land he won in the Oklahoma Land Rush in 1889 and farmed for forty years and died on.

These things are somewhere in rooms full to the rafters with anonymous junk. I'll go through it all, crying that kind of cry that is like rain washing down a window—no point in trying not to. Sometimes the sniffles will catch and turn into a wail. I know from the deaths I have already cleaned up after that you can't tell what will hit you, knock you blind, unable to breathe, unable to be silent. It's usually little things, not the wedding license or the family photographs. It'll be yard goods that didn't get made into a dress, the tag from a rose bush with advice on how to prevent blackspot before it starts, a boat turnbuckle still needing a cotter pin, something unfinished. It'll come. And after I've thrown out bins of trash and have given away boxloads of clutter, I'll find in front of me *Gray's Anatomy*. What will I do with it, falling apart, its spine now fractured, its magical scent gone? I'll look through the pictures, read the long Latin names of our parts. Her parts will have reverted to the stuff of clouds, leaving a little residue of ash. I am to take her ashes and mix them with my father's ashes and my dead son's and spread them together on a sunny south-facing hillside in the mountains of North Carolina. They will be in a warm, beautiful place forever together. And I am instructed not to mourn. But I have never been as obedient as she thinks I am.

To Kill a Deer

DEBRA MARQUART

*L*ater everyone would agree it was the least likely time to be encountering a deer. The two young guys in baseball caps who stopped to help us on the freeway said it, as did the highway patrolman who came to fill out the report after the two guys in baseball caps went to the next town and called for help.

The old man who came with the tow truck seemed equally perplexed. He removed his greasy cap and scratched his head, as did the manager of the body shop where our car was eventually towed. Everyone agreed that a deer should not have been on that stretch of highway during that time of day at that time of year.

We'd left Bozeman before dawn, full of the coffee and pancakes my sister's husband had risen early to make us. I took the wheel in the semidarkness, glad to be done with the three-day visit. I imagined the sun barely kissing off the flat eastern horizon of North Dakota—the place where we hoped to be by nightfall.

Montana was movie-beautiful that morning. By the time we reached Livingston, the light began to fill in the horizon. We sped through the passes, flanked on either side by the giants of the road—the Gallatin Range spreading long and wide to the south, the huge blueness of the Big Belt Mountains to the north and in the distance the sharp crag of Crazy Peak.

We noticed the Yellowstone River snaking beneath us, crossing and recrossing the freeway, as if to escort us out of the state. At every mile marker a view presented itself like a tourism postcard begging to be snapped. I fully expected Brad Pitt to appear over the ridge as Tristan riding an untamed stallion, his sun-bleached hair trailing behind him in the wind. Montana was green and gorgeous that day. It was strutting around, ready for its close-up, and we were sick of it.

My father is sitting in the back seat holding the nitroglycerin pill under his tongue to quiet his racing heart. He has spent his life working the unspectacular farmlands of central North Dakota that look like they've been laid out with a carpenter's level. Something about the mountains makes him short of breath.

I'm in the driver's seat with my right arm slung casually over the wheel, trying to assume that confident-driver pose I've seen my brother Rick take on so naturally whenever he drives a car. I hum lightly under my breath and speak only in forced monosyllables, just as Rick would do if he were here. I stare straight ahead and drive, taking my eyes off the road long enough to watch my father in the rearview mirror.

This is the fourth trip I've made to Montana with my parents, so I know that his condition will correct itself when these dramatic elevations level out to the mundane flatness of the central plains. Then he will lean back in the soft upholstery of the Oldsmobile, take a deep breath and say, "At last, God's country," in a voice ringing with sheer disgust over being lured away from the quiet splendor of North Dakota. If he had his way, he would never leave home.

In his old age he remains forever uninterested in places like Florida, Arizona and Hawaii, locations which I've tried to convince him would be fabulous for retirement. This is partly selfish. In the United States, North Dakota boasts the coldest winters and the hottest summers. According to the National Tourism Bureau, it's the least visited state in the union. In December on my Christmas break from the university where I teach, the last thing I want to do is get on the road and head north, north and ever northward into more fierce snow and cold.

"For once," I beg, "can't someone I'm related to live in an exotic climate?" But pleas like this go unheeded by my father. Since retiring he's kept himself enormously busy with small but critical tasks, like checking the downtown post office box at eight o'clock sharp every morning, just to make sure the town postmaster is still doing his job, and toodling out to the family acreage once a day to see how many farming mistakes Rick might be making.

And he has other pressing engagements—the twice-a-day coffee appointments he must keep with all the other retired farmers in town who spend their mornings and afternoons in the corner cafe, sitting at tables in their clean overalls, chewing on toothpicks, talking about the crops and harassing the old waitress who has never, in her entire career, received a tip from any one of them. That done, he returns home to his La-Z-Boy where he naps sporadically, watches cable with the remote in his hand and waits, like the Buddha, for the world to come to him.

It's only when we, his moved-away daughters, shame him with news of our various children, weddings, graduations and anniversaries that he is forced to visit us in the neighboring states we've flown to. Once away from home, he's determined not to be impressed by anything he sees.

About Mount Rushmore he said, "So it's a bunch of faces in a rock. We've got plenty of rocks at home." Although he's never visited the Grand Canyon, I imagine his response to it would be, "A big hole? We drove two thousand miles to see a hole?" About Europe he would wave his hand in dismissal and say, "Ah, everything is so old here."

Every spring for the last four years we've made this trip to Bozeman to visit my oldest sister. My parents are the tourists; I'm the daughter-driver. It's a concession I've made in my thirties to compensate for the wildness of my teens and the intractability of my twenties. Every spring when the school year draws to a close and my desk is scattered with unfinished drafts of poems, revisions of stories and student portfolios to grade, I receive the first Montana inquiry.

"Of course, we could drive ourselves," my mother will say to my answering machine in the polite, breathy voice she uses when asking for help. And soon after that I will call back, open my crammed calendar and settle on a date for the trip. The day I turn in my final grades, I get on the road and drive the first seven-hundred-fifty-mile leg of the trip by myself from Iowa to North Dakota. From there we take my parents' car and head west into big sky. The first year we made the trip, my very nice husband went along, but now he knows all of us a lot better and can't be convinced to do that anymore.

Once on the road, I submit myself to their whims and routines—start out before sunup, mandatory pie stops in the late afternoon, pee breaks allowed only at locations preapproved by my mother. At first it seems strange to hear my old name, Debbie, which no one has considered calling me for twenty years. But I don't try to correct them. My mother still refers to me as "the baby" when she introduces me to people, a habit I was never able to break her of no matter how nasty and unbabylike I became. So I mind my own business and drive the car, drinking in as much of the sagebrush and rolling foothills as I can without putting us in the ditch.

Every year, no matter how I prepare myself, I'm surprised by the first sight of mountains. As a born and bred flatlander, I seem destined to be forever in awe of mountains. In central Dakota, we sometimes joke, the only hills we have are the inclines the Feds created when they built the off-ramps for the freeway. Once in the mountains, I try to convince my father of the beauty of the place.

"Look there, Dad," I'll say, pointing to the nearest eight-thousand-foot peak. "See how that one just pierces the clouds?"

He scans the horizon quietly, his nose turned up at the idea that this could be big sky country ("You wanna see big sky. I'll show you big sky").

Soon my mother catches on and fills in the silence with small enthusiasms, things like, "Isn't that something," or "Gee, I never noticed that before."

After some time my father will raise his hand and point his knobby middle finger at the mountain. He doesn't point at the peak, however, but to a small area at the base of the mountain where someone has managed to squeeze in six rows of spring wheat.

"I see they got a few acres in there," he will say, admiring the thin yellow stalks waving in the wind. This is the farmer's view of Montana. If you can't run a plow over it, what the hell good is it? "What a waste," is the most-repeated phrase I hear from him as we drive.

My mother is in the passenger seat folding and refolding the maps. This is something she will do until we get home. But what's to check? We've all made this trip several times, and from Bozeman to Bismarck it's a straight shot—I-90 to I-94, then we're home. Even Lewis and Clark found the way without much trouble.

Still, she feels compelled to give us updates: Livingston, one hundred, Billings, one seventy-five. By her calculations, we will make lunch in Miles City by noon exactly. She loves the symmetry of this and reminds us every fifteen minutes that Miles City is the exact halfway point between Bozeman and home.

I know that when we arrive at Miles City we will eat at the same truck stop where we've lunched every time we make this trip. I no longer take issue with this. One year when I suggested to my mother that we try the 4Bs family restaurant on the other side of the overpass, she was thrown into such a frenzy that I've never mentioned it again.

My mother is trim and tight-lipped with a curl-and-comb hairstyle that reminds me of the smooth, rounded shape of a football helmet.

Most of the ladies in our town wear their hair this way, I suspect, because they all go to Connie, the town beautician. When I prompt her to try a cut more fitting to the shape of her face, she says, "This is just so easy."

Style is not one of my mother's priorities. Her life is driven by the twin purposes of precision and economy. As a child of the Depression, she was raised to despise waste of any kind. In the spring and summer she wears white and red pantsuits; in the winter and fall she wears navy blue and red pantsuits. All the pieces in her closet are interchangeable, and she never buys anything that must be dry-cleaned.

She goes to bed late, gets up early, keeps a spotless house and wrenches as much as she can out of each day. "I like to make things with my hands," she will say, showing off the row of cabbages she's grown, the batch of cookies she's baked, the cotton blazer she's sewn.

As her most extravagant and accidental daughter, I have not registered very often on my mother's Richter scale of achievement. With a failed career as a rock musician (where I squandered my twenties), one bad marriage and no children to recommend me, I have gone so far into the red with her that everything I do meets with suspicion. Even in my late thirties, I can't count on my career as a writer and a teacher to salvage myself in her eyes.

Both she and my father are full of nervous inquiries about my work. For example, whether I am "on break" or "unemployed" during the summer when I'm not teaching is something my parents often quiz me about. When I make the point that the summer is a good time for me to catch up on my research, they remain unconvinced. This seems like fuzzy logic to them.

When I try to explain that my writing *is* my research, it comes out sounding like one of those nebulous excuses you concoct as a teenager when you're asked to account for a missing block of time: *Yeah, the library, that's right, I was at the library.* They worry and wonder, how could I possibly have that much to write about?

They're equally perplexed by my teaching load—how can I get

by with only teaching three days a week? Once when I called home to tell them I'd been hired for a better teaching position and now would only have to teach two classes a semester for the next few years, my father got silent for a time and then nervously asked, "Are you able to get in a forty-hour week, then?"

When I explained that with my "research" I worked well over a forty-hour week, he was still unsatisfied. Thinking I had strapped myself into another hopeless situation, he tried to be helpful, finally coming up with a solution. Maybe I could ask them, he suggested, if they'd let me teach a few more classes?

Here I'm reminded of a story Jay Leno told about his mother on the *Tonight Show*. After he replaced Johnny Carson on late night, he was anxious to impress his mother with the lucrative deal he'd just signed. Trying to give her an idea of the elite millionaire's club he'd just joined, he bragged to his mother about some of the actors he'd be rubbing shoulders with, people like Sylvester Stallone and Bruce Willis.

Why just that week, Leno boasted, Arnold Schwarzenegger was coming on the show to promote his latest film. Then he made a big point of mentioning that Arnold's contract for his latest role was reputed to be upwards of twenty-three million.

"I guess that's not bad pay," Leno said, "for three months' work."

"Yes," his mother replied quickly, "but what does he do for work the other nine months of the year?"

Take away most of the zeros, and this is how incomprehensible my career path has become to my parents. Tenure-tracks, sabbaticals, Fulbrights ("If you got it, would they really make you leave the country?")—hopefully my parents will go to their graves blissfully unaware of all the dead ends and potholes on that road.

Once again, I return to the policy of my youth—the less they know about my life, the better. Still, it's been lonely out here in the world without them. This spring I am buoyed by the release of my first book of poetry—something solid to show for all my troubles—and by some gossip I've received from my second oldest sister in

Minnesota who says that, in her opinion, my status in the family has been upgraded from "outcast" to "rebel."

My sister, an artist who went back to school in her late thirties to get a degree in nursing, has since diagnosed all of us. In our family we now have attention-deficit disorders, chronic thyroid problems and congenital heart conditions where we once only had vague, paranoid feelings that something about us was terribly wrong.

My mother, in turn, has been pegged by my sister as a classic obsessive-compulsive personality. I consider this diagnosis as I watch my mother page endlessly through the little black book she keeps with her when she travels. In this book she has jotted down vital details about all the stretches of highway she has ever traveled.

High on her list of things to note are gas prices, good food stops, cleanliness of restrooms and easy access on and off the freeway. In it she has sketched aerial perspectives of all the on- and off-ramps she has ever taken. An engineer from the D.O.T. couldn't have done a finer job.

If an exit does not appear in her book, she is reluctant to take it. She means to avoid any of those roads that veer wildly to the north and never return you to the freeway, or those off-ramps that clover-leaf into endless circles, causing you to lose your bearings. I suspect she fears we might go so far afield that we will end up in the French-speaking part of Canada, or some bad neighborhood in Los Angeles where we will be mugged, car-jacked and never able to find our way home again.

Watching her pore over the drawings and notes of her black book, I am reminded of my own book. All during this trip, I've waited for some indication that my parents have read my book of poems. Two months earlier, I had signed a copy, packed it into a padded envelope and held my breath as I dropped it into the mail slot. That was the last I heard of it.

When I got to their house, I looked around for it. Would it be displayed on the coffee table, or maybe nestled in the magazine rack, dog-eared from so much use? But it was nowhere in sight. I went in search of it, eventually finding it in the bookshelf in my mother's sewing room, wedged between the town Centennial Book and the Betty Crocker recipes.

All week the silence about the book worried me. I began to wonder if they had found the one nasty poem I wrote about my mother—the one that my friend calls my teenage-mother-hate poem—that begins with the lines:

> *when I think of her*
> *I think of silence*
> *my mouth growing tight across my face*
> *after she has told me*
> *not to sing in the house.*

The poem goes on to depict an emotionally killing relationship between a mother and a daughter. I remember my palms sweating and my teeth grinding the night those words appeared, as if written by another hand, in the pages of my notebook.

In the poem, the girl dreams that the family home is stormed by street gangs, rock bands and Nazis who "trash the furniture, raid the refrigerator" and "have their women in her bedroom." In the end, the girl hides "upstairs, trying to be quiet" while the intruders are downstairs, tearing the mother "limb from limb."

If my parents have read the poem, I wonder, will they ask me what it means, and if the "I" in the poem is me, and if the "she" is my mother? And how will I answer them? Will I reel out a teacherly explanation, scolding them that one should never assume the "I" in a poem is the author?

Before I shipped the book off to them, I tried cutting the poem from the book with a razor blade, excising it so cleanly that its absence would not be noticed. But I quickly found that removing the poem meant that the first page of another poem would have to go with it, which meant that I would have to take the second page of that poem too, causing me to have to eliminate still another poem. In total I found I would have to extract nine pages from the book—a gap so flagrant that even they would notice.

My sister, the newly trained nurse in Minnesota, finally calmed my fears, assuring me that our parents would never read the book, because they'd be "too grossed-out by the cover," which was a wild Peter Dean painting of three women emerging from water with their breasts bared. Her prediction may have been accurate. So far I had heard no mention of the book—not on the twelve-hour drive to Montana, not during the two days in Bozeman.

Instead my mother crammed all available air time where a genuine conversation may have taken place with endless chatter about the volunteer work she'd been doing at the Catholic Church. Listening to her, I began to realize that her mind runs on an endless tape loop, like Muzak, repeating hourly the five or six things she knows for certain that week.

On the way home, for example, she becomes fixated on the evergreens—the way they grow "straight out the side of the mountain." She repeats this observation roughly every seven miles, and I agree with her each time, answering with a light "uh-huh" whenever I hear her breathy voice rise in the car, all the while scanning it for tone, waiting for that slight inflection that indicates she might veer off into anger or disapproval.

"Two hours to Miles City," I whisper into my shirt sleeve as we pass the industrial smoke stacks that mark the outskirts of Billings. By nightfall, I will have them safely home. To pass the time, I imagine my burgundy-colored van, with all its fluid levels topped off and ready to go, sitting in my parents' driveway, patiently anticipating my return so that I can hop in, turn the key, point its nose southeast and never look back.

It's ten in the morning. My eyes are already drowsy with sleep, but I will not yield the wheel. I crack the window open for fresh air and pop myself on the side of the head a few times to wake up.

My mother sits in the passenger seat with her white vinyl purse tucked neatly under her legs. She reaches down every few minutes and touches it with her fingertips to make sure it's still there. Once we clear Billings, I press down hard on the accelerator, set the cruise to eighty and push into the open road, letting the Oldsmobile swallow up miles.

I saw the deer a second before we were upon her, time enough to tap the brake and release the cruise, but not long enough to warn my passengers or fully slow the car. She moved through the green, the grass thick and high around her. Then she stepped delicately through the opening and onto the edge of the pavement. There she hovered in the emergency lane with her tail end turned toward us.

In a field to the right, sunlight reflected off a shallow creek. Perhaps she had sheltered there the night before in the small stand of trees winding along the water line. She seemed to be taking in the day, the cool velvet of her nose sniffing out the crisp morning air. She looked to her right, where the creek flowed lightly over rocks and the open field stretched into infinity. She looked to her left, to the twin lanes of worn pavement. Then she twisted her neck and looked long down the road to where our car was screaming toward her.

Don't do it, I thought. She seemed to look straight at me behind the wheel. Her eyes were black and luminous and filled with a kind of dew. "Don't even think about it," I said.

She swayed to the right for a moment and looked to that endless rolling prairie that waited beyond the ditch. Then she turned and stepped left into the driving lane, the tawny brown of her body growing large in the windshield, meeting with the powerful front bumper of the Oldsmobile, the hood crumpling up, pieces of fiberglass flying to the side as we pushed through, her body lifting up and glancing off, finally coming to land in the grassy median between the east- and westbound lanes.

Behind us as we slowed, a group of cars rushed by, their tires crushing debris and scattering chrome and fiberglass down the road and into the ditches. Feeling the front end wobble, I touched the brakes lightly and angled the car into the emergency lane. My mother put her hand on the dashboard; my father sat forward in the back seat as we slowed, the radiator already blowing a thin plume of steam. Everything in the car was silent for a moment.

My first thought was of my father. Would his heart survive this? I glanced at him in the rearview mirror. He was sitting up, breathing easily, more alert than I'd seen him in days. He caught my eyes in the corner of the mirror.

"Are you OK?" I said to his reflection. He nodded, yes, with a stunned expression, almost as if to say, Wow, that was some ride.

"I didn't even see it coming," he said.

"I knew it," my mother said from the passenger seat in a wavering voice. "I knew we shouldn't have left home." She seemed on the verge of crying.

"Are you OK, Gladys?" my dad said to her, putting his hand on the front seat headrest.

"I just had a feeling something bad was going to happen," she said, rocking in her seat and clutching at her pant legs.

"Are you OK?" I repeated, looking at her. Physically, she appeared unhurt.

"My car," she began to cry, putting her face in her hands and rocking in her seat. "My beautiful car."

"Oh, Mom," I said, thinking about all the other turns this accident may have taken, "that can be fixed." I pulled the car to a complete stop and turned off the ignition.

"The most important thing," I said, "is that we're all OK." Right about then I would have appreciated an "are you OK?" from her.

"I bought this car with my own money," she answered in a cry. "It was the only new car I ever had."

"Oh, Gladys," my dad said from the back seat, "we'll get it fixed."

"It'll never be the same," she said, pointing to the steam that was still rising in a thin wisp from the radiator. She nervously undid her seat belt and grabbed her purse off the floor. Outside cars were whizzing by without even slowing down to see if we needed help.

"How are we going to get home?" She said in a voice that sounded lost and childlike. She pulled on the handle and the passenger door cracked open, letting in a rush of wind.

"We'll figure it out," I said. I had no doubt we would. For seven years I was a road musician, touring in old buses, trucks and vans on a less-than-zero budget. I'd maneuvered my way through more roll-overs, accidents and breakdowns by the age of twenty-five than most people experienced in a lifetime.

"We'll have to get it fixed," I said in a disgusted voice. "We might have to rent a car and tow it."

"Tow it," she screamed. "We're over five hundred miles from home." She pulled out her wallet and began digging through it. She pulled a driver's license, an insurance certificate and a roadway assistance card from the neat slots of her billfold. "You know what that would cost?" she said.

"Could I see those?" I asked, taking the cards from her hands and scanning them for information. Immediately I saw that my parents were insurance-poor. Although they had a great deal of money from selling the farm to my brother Rick, it was clear they had bought the cheapest policies they could find. For accident coverage, they held a minimal policy from State Farm with a five-hundred-dollar deductible and no emergency tow services.

They didn't have AAA, like everyone else in the country, but "Oldsmobile Roadway Assistance." I checked the paperwork, scanning through the list of twenty-five exclusions, provisos and caveats, the most significant of which was the requirement that the car could only be towed by an authorized Oldsmobile dealer. Otherwise, claims would not be honored. In this way we belonged to the Chrysler

Corporation forever.

My mother began to pull out all the plastic cards in her wallet one by one, as if an answer lay there. Her hands were shaking as she sifted through the pile—a Social Security card, a lifetime membership to Sam's Club, an Amoco gas card and a garden-variety MasterCard.

I thought about my own wallet, stashed on the floor of the back seat. Inside it was my own secret line-up of cards—a Gold-Plus AAA card, a Preferred Gold MasterCard and a Platinum Visa. Forget *Don't leave home without it*, I thought. Hello, *Anywhere you want to be*. A slight rush went through my body. I felt the numbness in my legs that comes after the danger has passed. I knew I could get us home. The only challenge was how quickly and efficiently it could be done.

"We need to get some help," my mother said. The contents of her purse were spilling over her lap. She kicked open the passenger door with her foot, and her hankies, lipsticks and compacts rolled onto the pavement.

"Oh, Gladys," my father said. He reached for his windbreaker as she jumped out of the car.

"Just wait a second." He slipped his arms into the sleeves. I reached into the back seat and grabbed my coat. The breeze that had seemed cool and refreshing from the inside of the car was now blowing hard and cold on the outside.

By now my mother was in front of the car, hanging on the edge of the pavement without a coat. She was waving her Oldsmobile Roadway Assistance card at passing motorists as if the sheer sight of it would cause automobiles to go from ninety to zero in five seconds flat. It wasn't working. Cars were switching to the left lane and zooming by as if to avoid this wild-haired lunatic.

"Why won't they help us?" my mother screamed in the wind. She stepped into the driving lane and raised her right arm as if she was hailing a taxi. All the cards from her wallet fell to the concrete.

"Gladys," my father said with alarm. He rushed to where she stood. I followed behind, picking up the glass, chrome and fiberglass pieces as I went along.

"Move back," my father yelled, waving his hands at my mother. He bent to pick up the cards as they blew down the highway. "You're going to get run over."

I finally caught up with them. "Why don't you guys get in the car?" I said. In my arms I held pieces from the Oldsmobile's front end. I put them down in a pile. "I'll stay out here and try to get help."

"No," my mother moaned, a cry raging in her voice. "Why won't they stop and help us?"

I circled around to the back of the car, picking up more debris—the bent rims and bits of glass from our headlights. I returned all the pieces to the pile.

"They won't stop for all three of us," my father said over the wind. He pulled my mother toward the car. She finally yielded to him, but not before leaving the Oldsmobile Roadside Assistance card with me.

As soon as they were inside the car, a beat-up Chevy pickup slowed down, pulled to the side of the road and snaked its way toward me in reverse with its back-up lights shining. Inside it were the two guys with baseball caps who quickly agreed that they would drive to the next town and call the highway patrol. I told them what had happened. I pointed down the road to where I thought the deer had landed.

"If you bag it," the one guy asked, "do they let you keep it?" He eyed the median nervously, as if he was considering coming back and loading up the carcass himself.

"I don't know what they'll do with her," I said, looking down the road.

"Maybe they'll feed it to the wolves," the other guy said.

Then my mother opened the car door and stepped out of the passenger side, her white shoe setting down on the pavement. "Don't forget to tell them," she said, holding on to the car door for support, "that it has to be a tow truck from an Oldsmobile dealership."

After the two guys in baseball caps drove off, on their way to make the phone call for us, I knew that we'd have a long wait. I spent the time cleaning up the rest of the debris, running back down the highway a hundred feet where a few large pieces of fiberglass lay in the middle of the road. I waited for the lanes to clear, then I charged across to the median.

I found the deer lying flat and completely still on her right side, her left eye staring blankly to the sky. I thought about how, for a moment before she disappeared from my view, just as the car lifted her off the ground, I saw her eyes one last time. And it seemed they registered shock and recognition, as if she'd always known we were out there, somewhere, speeding by on the edge of her world.

There was a coolness in the air I hadn't expected. I pulled my coat tight. I bent over her in the grass. She looked like she had not moved or struggled in that spot, like she was dead when she landed. I hoped that was so.

I thought about something a friend told me about the writer Barry Lopez—how he stops when he sees roadkill on the side of the highway, and he blesses the animal and asks for forgiveness. I considered doing it but found that I could not. Something inside me would not say I was sorry.

One thing you discover after you hit a deer is that nearly everyone else in the world has, or has almost, hit a deer. And when you try to tell your story to someone, they will interrupt you with their own I-hit-a-deer stories.

Theirs may be more or less dramatic than yours, but they've had more time to formulate the plot, so they will rush ahead in the telling and leave you behind, holding a jumbled collection of details that you have not yet neatened into a story. In this way, for a time, you will go away from the experience of hitting a deer frustrated.

That day, after I cleared the debris from the road, I returned to the car and told my parents that I'd found the deer. I assured them that she was dead and that she hadn't struggled.

"I don't care about the damn deer," my mother said. "All I care about is my car."

I turned to look at her in the passenger seat. She had smoothed her hair down with a comb and applied a fresh coat of lipstick; it ringed her lips in a bright O. Her purse was at her feet again, packed up and all in order. For a second I had the urge to push my fist hard into her mouth, but I did not.

We spent forty-five minutes sitting in the car, waiting for the highway patrol, repeating the four or five things we knew for sure—how no one saw her coming, and that we'd been very lucky, how it could have turned out much, much worse and how it was no one's fault. Outside the wind blew and cars rushed by. The sky grew larger with every passing minute.

When the highway patrolman arrived, he asked to speak only to me, since I was the driver. I gave him my AAA card, my parents' insurance certificate and my driver's license. He offered to give me a ride to town because the tow truck would only accommodate two passengers. My mom and dad agreed to stay with the car.

When I got to the dealership where the car would be towed, I knew I had about twenty minutes to devise a plan. I asked Jeff, the manager, if I could use a phone. He put me behind a desk, and I set to work, dialing numbers. I had all the cards laid out in front of me, calling insurance companies, inquiring about rental trucks. My idea was that we would strap the car into a tow dolly behind a rental truck and get on the road. We would be home a few hours later than planned, but we would still get there by evening.

I made careful notes, and I calculated costs. All told, it came to about two hundred dollars, a small sum of money in my estimation, which I had decided I was going to pay if the insurance companies would not cover it. I did all this in twenty minutes and was beginning to feel quite proud of myself.

I was sitting with my feet up on the desk, thinking about a scene in an old movie called *The Hawaiians*. The film is an adaptation of a

James Michener novel, and stars Charlton Heston as an imperialist settler of Hawaii, famous for having introduced the pineapple to the island.

In the movie, Heston's character becomes hugely wealthy and lives alone with his son in a large, plantation-style home. The mother of the boy has been dead for years, her portrait occupying a place of honor above the formal dining table.

For the most part, the movie is unmemorable, but there's a scene that's always stayed with me. Near the end of the movie when the son reaches his late teens, he grows restless with being the heir-apparent to the pineapple fortune and yearns for true adventure. There are a couple of heated scenes between the boy and the father, until Heston, an old sea baron himself, realizes the problem and arranges for the boy to set sail as a ship's mate.

The next day, seeing the boy off at the pier, the father knocks the kid on the side of the head and says, "Son, take care of yourself." He grabs the boy's shoulders and stares at him face to face, as if he can't believe the boy will soon be a man.

"I will, Pa," the boy says obligingly and kicks the dirt.

"And if you get into trouble," the father begins, but then he stops himself. He has all the power and wealth of the world at his disposal.

"If you get yourself in trouble," he begins again, turning away from the boy and starting the long walk down the pier. The camera lingers on the back of his short-cropped riding jacket, as he yells behind him, "Well, just get yourself out of it, that's all."

When I was seventeen my parents drove me to the junior college I would be attending and dropped me at the front door of my girls' dorm with a few boxes of my clothes, records and books. The goodbyes were not tearful. I was the youngest and most problematic of their five children, and perhaps they were just glad to be on their own for the first time in twenty-five years.

I suppose I stood on the steps and waved goodbye to them as they drove off, and I'm sure they waved back. They're not the kind of people who wouldn't wave back.

The day we hit a deer, I looked out the window of the body shop and waited for my parents to appear in the tow truck. I was anxious to show them all the survival skills I had acquired since they last knew me. Soon the truck pulled into the lot with the Oldsmobile trailing behind. It seemed strange to see the wreck so far from the freeway, all trussed up and traveling through the city as if on display.

"Ooh," the body shop manager said, wincing when he saw the car. "That's bad."

My parents climbed down from the tow truck and walked across the parking lot. They appeared small to me then, like kids getting off a school bus at the end of a day full of word problems and pop quizzes.

They came through the door with a beaten look on their faces. I rose quickly behind the desk and introduced them to Jeff. He had taken on our problem as if it were his own and had helped me with phone numbers and arrangements.

Jeff scratched his head and talked to my parents for a moment, agreeing that, "No, the car sure doesn't look like it could be driven home," and adding, "Gee, it sure was strange that a deer was out there on the road at this time of the day."

My parents nodded. My father looked at him with glazed eyes. "We didn't even see it coming," he said for the fortieth time.

"Well, here's the idea I have," I said, stepping from behind the desk. I began to spell out the plan, giving them details and dollar amounts. I could finalize the arrangements within half an hour, I told them. Then Jeff would mount the car on the tow dolly, and we'd be down the road.

I stopped breathlessly.

"Did I mention," I said, "that I'm willing to pay for all this?"

It's not like I expected them to jump up, clap their hands and squeal "Oh, goody, goody, goody," like a couple of four-year-olds. What I wanted was a sigh of relief, the recognition that the crisis was over.

Debra Marquart　35

Then I noticed that my mother was shaking her head. My father was silent, looking out the window, perhaps not hearing anything I had said. I looked at Jeff; he was standing in the corner watching the scene.

"Mercy, no," my mother said in a wary voice, as if I'd told her some very bad news. "Oh, no," she repeated, her voice soft and wobbly.

I then realized that the plan had too many moving parts for her. Right there in the body shop, she was considering the possibilities— what if the car came loose, floating backwards on the freeway, causing a twelve-car pile-up that would be followed by just as many lawsuits. What if the rental broke down and then we'd be stuck in some strange town with a broken-down truck and a wrecked car.

"Oh no," my mother repeated. Then she turned and walked toward the telephone.

"Let's call Rick," she said. Right now he would be in the fields working late into each night, trying to get his crops planted in time to beat the spring rains.

"Rick could come and get us," my mother said, liking the sound of it already.

I looked at Jeff, but he didn't say anything. He drew a deep breath, raised his finger in the air and began to move toward the door that led out to the body shop.

"Tell you what," he said, stopping with his hand on the door. "I'll give you folks some time to talk in private."

I couldn't blame him. Who wouldn't like to move through a room, and with one simple turn of a knob, be rid of a family and all the hurts and history they carried with them?

"Call Rick?" I said in disbelief as soon as Jeff was gone. Granted, Rick owned a Suburban that could tow us, but I couldn't believe what I was hearing. Every day my father drove out to the farm and dogged my brother, quizzing him and cautioning him—are you keeping up, how much did that cost, don't buy that tractor, stay ahead of the weather, don't let the bank get ahold of you. And now they were proposing that we pull him out of the field for two days during spring planting to come and save us.

"We're over five hundred miles from home," I said to my mother. It felt good to be the one reminding her of this. "It would take him ten hours just to get here."

"We don't have any choice," my mother said. She walked over to the desk and dialed the number to the cellular phone in Rick's tractor.

"Rick," she said after a moment. "We had a little accident." She paused while Rick said something on the other end. "We're all OK," she said, "but the car is wrecked."

And now her voice got very high and watery. "And we were wondering," she said, "if you could come and get us."

And so it was decided. My brother would arrive late that night with his Suburban. We would all stay in a motel, and in the morning he would take us home, driving a confident ninety miles per hour with the wrecked Oldsmobile hooked to the back bumper.

That afternoon, when everything was settled, we got a ride to a Comfort Inn on the south side of town. Once in the lobby, I stepped up to the front desk. I had spent half my life on the road, checking in and out of motels. This was something I could do.

"Two rooms," I said and opened my wallet. "Preferably non-smoking." I pulled out the Platinum Visa. It felt good in my hands as I snapped it onto the counter.

"Oh, no." My mother stepped up behind me and looked for a moment at the silver card tucked under my fingers. "We're all family." Then she smiled at the girl behind the counter. "One room will do just fine," she said.

"I'm happy to pay for this," I said. At that point, all I wanted was a bath, a bed, thirty-five channels of mindless sit-coms and a few hours of quiet.

"You can't afford this, honey," my mother said. "You know you're not working right now." She pushed my credit card to the side and pulled a stack of crisp bills from her wallet. With her thumb, she began to peel off twenties.

"Let her spend her money if she wants to," my father said with a wheeze of exhaustion. He was near the front door, looking out the window at all the cars in the parking lot.

"We should be way past Miles City by now," my mother said in a confidential tone to the girl behind the counter, as if motel policy required that we must explain why we needed a room.

"Really," the girl said. She was counting the cash, mouthing out the amounts under her breath as she set the twenties in piles.

"Yes," my mother said, taking the girl's response as a sign of interest. By this time I'd moved away from the front desk and was hiding near the continental breakfast nook. Still her voice followed me.

"We should have been almost home by now," she said, "but our daughter hit a deer with our car."

"A deer?" the girl said. There was shock in her voice.

"Our son is coming to get us," my mother said, as I rounded the corner to the vending machines.

"We didn't even see it coming." I heard my father step up to the counter and say for the forty-first time that day.

And I was way down the hallway, almost to the stairwell, when I heard the girl behind the counter begin to tell my parents about the time that she almost hit a deer.

Taking Leave

CAROLINE JACKSON

$\mathcal{I}$ sit parked in the driveway and take in the house. It's long before light and the car is frigid, the windshield rimmed with crystal. Wisps of my breath twirl briefly in front of my face, then dissolve into the darkness. The breaths are short, shallow. I've only been up half an hour, but already feel scooped out, exhausted.

The house looms before me. By day, it's a rambling, joyful colonial. For now, it's a dim mountain that fills my entire field of vision. Two smaller, deeper shadows accent its base, the wrought-iron benches that flank the front door. The carefully tended shrubbery is eerily at rest, shrouded by the ebbing night. These trips back have been more frequent since my divorce. Call it regression, call it a craving for the comforts of what was home for the first half of my life. Whatever, they are getting less and less comforting.

I long to start the engine, get the heater going, hit the road. But I hesitate, knowing I should go back for a proper goodbye. The cheery words I left on the kitchen counter swim before me in the dark: "Another great Easter. Thanks for everything. Love you."

Finally I feel for the ignition and fit in the key. The engine jumps-to, overloud. Its roar is like a reprimand for my sneaking away. I watch the upstairs anxiously for a light, am grateful the house stays locked in sleep. I had taken special pains while getting up. The tiptoeing, the groping in the dark, the careful turning of knobs before easing doors closed. He needs his sleep, I told myself. The truth is, it's getting too hard to say goodbye.

There were signs. Not blatant like on the last visit. Not the surprise of the shambling gait or the bleary eyes retreating into parchment pleats. Not the confident physique suddenly an uncertain husk. Not the fissured memory.

"Route 13, Dad, Route 13! Have you forgotten how to get downtown?"

"They've changed it, moved it. The stores are all different." The voice was petulant. He was preparing to mount a defense. That, at least, was the same as always.

At first nothing seemed changed. The house was locked tight when I arrived even though it was midday. No point in ringing a bell that wouldn't be heard, so I carefully navigated his labyrinthine setup for access. He goes over it with me on the phone before every visit, and I always feign admiring surprise. The hidden button that activates the garage door opener. The stairs at the back leading down to the basement door, the only one ever left unlocked. Then the grope through his shop. Don't go for the light switch, you might get the lathe or saw. If you make it that far there'll be the stairs to the first floor. The last hurdle is the door at the top. You need to know that the knob turns the wrong way and that it won't open without a sharp kick in a particular spot.

I'm used to the stifling overwarmth of the house, the dense air pocketed with stale-bread smells. And the urge to rush around flinging windows open is long gone, quelled by the sagging cardigan he now wears buttoned all the way up.

The next morning an unknown something summoned me from deep sleep. It took a few hazy minutes to realize what woke me was silence. Gone was the high-pitched cadence from the basement, the hymn of his bandsaw as it touched wood. For as long as I could remember, he would be up at first light, eager to get going on this table or that bowl, waking a grousing household. The anthem came to me as a whine. It penetrated all the way to the top floor bedrooms, spewing motes of sawdust in its wake. Every day would begin with my grumbling about twanging ears and peppered nostrils, a schtick as routine as orange juice. This new stillness was unfamiliar, almost eerie. I wasn't sure I liked it.

I didn't notice the handrail until the day after, in the stairwell just where the steps turn the corner at the bottom. It looked new, the wood's rawness lately refined, its brass fixtures gleaming overbrightly. None too straight, though. Not installed with the precision of the old days, with that sure hand and exacting eye. He could always make anything, fix anything.

He spends more time in the den now, lying on his battered old couch. The TV is on like always, but he snoozes to the drone of talking heads or the weather channel. I love to lie there too, after he's gone to bed and the screen is gray and silent. I drink in the essence that infuses the balding corduroy cover—a rich mingling of Prince Albert, warm skin, whiskers. His younger days float back to me, the self-made man, side-show strong, electric with rapid-fire wit and fierce intelligence. When I was a teenager I pored over his high school yearbook. Captain of the football team, president of the student council, the strapping boy who'd dropped out to help out on the failing farm had caught up fast. I'd been amazed by his sheik-like good looks, the olive skin and dark eyes, so odd for his heritage that was equal parts Scots and German.

Hot was what my kids would call him. My own father! No wonder my mother had fallen at first sight—his first day back in school after the two-year halt—he liked to tell the story again and again. A new, much larger school where you had to go from room to room to classes. He found the milling throng around him unnerving and was afraid he wouldn't find his way, make a fool of himself. Then, in the midst of the swirl of bodies ahead, one turned. A girl. She smiled at him, *the most beautiful thing. I fell in love on the spot, and I'm as in love with her now as I was then* is how he would end the story every time. The family knew the line by heart, chiming in every time. He has been silent on the subject since she died five years ago.

The inscription under his yearbook picture declared: *Just like all other mortals. No better, no worse. Just funnier.* They got that right. He could deliver a bon mot as effortlessly as a pratfall, provoke a laugh from whomever, whenever he wanted. A saving grace, as it happened, because his temper was not to be toyed with. When I was little, early storm warnings would clear the room. First his eyebrows drew together and his mouth hardened. Then his whole face darkened. I'd run, grab the nearest pillow and cover my head to ward off the shouts soon to come, shouts that made me burn from the inside out. He never had to spank me. "The look," that black glower, was enough to silence me, to leave me in tears. I vowed I would never marry a man with a temper like that, a shouter. But of course I did. My father, however, apologized. Over and over, much later, after the heat was off. But it still made all the difference.

"Sorry, sorry, sorry. How could I? It's not you, you know."

I didn't know. He never named the demons, and I couldn't ask. I simply accepted the dark look, the explosions, the yelling. That's what fathers did. Besides, it wasn't the whole package.

Arms like hawsers swoop down and scoop me up. Up, up I ride, all jubilant expectation. Treetops unfurl over his shoulder like a dappled green umbrella. Then the ramrod trunks, the bank, the calm khaki-colored water basking in the shade. This time I let my eyes follow the shoreline. They carry me beyond the deserted cove, out to the shimmering river. It's dotted with islands, more than a thousand it's said, so many you could never count them all. I imagine stepping stones to the edge of the world. I think of the giant tankers that slide soundlessly between them in the middle of the night.

I put my stubby arms around his neck and snug into his chest. His pale skin touches mine, damp and warm. He's soft on the surface, solid underneath, like the seat in the bay window back at the cottage. I can feel his heart beating.

He backs into the water slowly, smoothly, like he's in the living room dancing with my mother. "I want you to see where we're going." He starts this way every time.

"You look funny without your glasses," I giggle, "like somebody else." But he's as familiar as bread.

We move further into the water, him talking quietly all the while, his mouth close to my ear.

"Don't be afraid. It's just like always."

We've done the routine every day since we arrived, but this time there's a difference I can't name. The glitters on the water, brighter. The cries of the gulls, sharper. Cool water laps at my ankles like a friendly puppy.

He ruffles the water with one hand like always, leaning down, balancing me on one arm. The splashes on my back tickle. I want more. He ladles handfuls over my shoulders. The tingling surprise makes me laugh out loud.

When we're in halfway he commands, "OK, pollywog, wiggle your toes, like last time."

The coolness rises higher. Soon we're neck deep, the two of us swaddled by the quiet water. This is the part I love best. Gently bobbing, weightless, from the neck down a formlessness shaped and reshaped by the swirling water. I look around, to the left the calm of the empty cove, to the right the mute, graying cottages along the river, getting smaller and smaller as they march away.

"Hang on," he takes his arms away. Then with one mighty push he's floating, making slow eights underwater with his hands. "I'm the raft and you're the paddler, just like I showed you yesterday."

I take my arms from his neck and do what he says. And wondrously we move. We move further than ever from the shore. I know the water is deep now, over our heads. But I don't care. Beneath me he feels solid and safe.

He hasn't stopped the stream of words, reminding me of practice in the bathtub, how to hold my breath, blow it out through my mouth, slowly, bubbling the water. Just a little at a time, until I know when to come up for air.

Suddenly I sense a falling away, and just for a second, make to grab him. "C'mon, sweetie, you remember," he urges. "Use your legs like scissors. Cut that water, hard."

I do. They rise, and my feet follow. A miracle.

He paddles off. I float free. Then in a frenzy of fluttering feet, churning arms and sputtering water I'm moving forward. Propelled by a buoyant mix of muscle and elation, I am almost swimming. Soon I realize I'm in control and the thought relaxes me into an easy rhythm. I become aware of the water sliding over my shoulders. It slips off like silky farewell fingers, tangling in my legs until I kick them away, leaving them behind swirling sadly. Now I know to stop fighting, to share strength. And in the giving over, the water becomes my friend.

I falter only once. "Don't leave me," I shout suddenly.

"Just a little way," he calls back, "I have to." And did he say "for now"?

His work in those days, the days of the Second World War, took him away a lot. But he was there when it counted. When air raid sirens closed my bedroom drapes, I saw soldiers behind them, the top half of a helmet, the tip of a bayonet appearing over the valance. But I knew the safe crook of a strong arm was just down the hall. Even later, when I was not so little, he wasn't far away. Ditched by a sock-hop date? I knew who'd be on call. Mornings after too many boozy fraternity parties his *So, did you wash away your problems?* made me put on the brakes. *Your freedom is more important* was all he said when my divorce settlement dwindled into lawyers' pockets.

By the end of the second day I could see he spent most of his time looking for something to do.

"How's the Ken Follet I got you for Christmas?"

"The what? That book?" An embarrassed chuckle. "I can't recall enough of the chapter before to make sense of the one after."

"How about taking a walk with me?"

"Later maybe. The knee, you know. "

He simply seemed not to be interested in much of anything.

Except for tidying. He was compulsive about picking up. Newspapers would be in the recycling bin as soon as they were put down. I got into the habit of sitting on the sections I wanted to save for later. Sometimes he stood over me while I worked the crossword. I sensed a silent dare, *Go ahead, stall over a tricky clue.* Surprisingly, I did. The defiance, though small, was unbidden, new. No matter, he managed to outlast me.

He declared the dishes were now his job. This was fine with me, except he couldn't wait until I finished. My plate would be whisked away while I was still chewing the last mouthful. He'd ferry the plates one at a time outside to the garbage for scraping, wash each one thoroughly and rinse it before it went into the dishwasher.

The third day, Easter Sunday, we were greeted with snow. Not just a few lazy flakes, but a true snowstorm that plunged us backward to the deadness of deep winter. An indifferent sky swiftly buried the tiny baubles of purple and gold studding the lawn, the frail green shoots spiking up through heavy mulch.

"Some Easter," he remarked as we stood together at the living room window. "Winter has gone on too long."

His eyes were fixed somewhere in the whirling void. They were unreadable, showing neither joy nor sorrow, acceptance nor anger. I wanted to say something, but didn't know what words would bring him back. I longed to put my arm around his shoulder, imagined holding him, stroking his back in that long-ago way I had with my babies. But he had never been much for physical displays of affection. And I was afraid of the sharpness of his bones.

Later, the entire family, from toddlers on up, gathered as usual for ham and chaos. Two of his granddaughters announced they were pregnant. "Where will we put everyone next year?" he chuckled. I wondered if my children would have children, if I would ever be surrounded by the joyous, melancholy tumult of holiday gatherings. A cheerful accumulation of board games, stuffed toys, shoes of assorted sizes and overlooked jellybeans kept him busy picking up during the day. But in the winding-down evening, after most of the company departed, he had to look hard for clutter. Would he ever tire of wandering from room to room?

In supper's peaceful aftermath, my favorite cousin and I were still at the table, lost in talk. It was her husband. His mother had died last year, and he still wasn't his old self. My cousin sounded out her worry. She had read every book and article on the subject of grief, she said, and things weren't going according to plan. One of her charms was that she still believed if something was typeset and bound it had to be true.

"He still seems like a lost child. Nothing seems to work. He's done denial, worked through anger, bargained, shaken depression—but he hasn't really accepted."

"Yes, well." I started, then stopped, afraid of being preachy.

Why is everyone expected to fit into tidy theories, I wondered as I watched my father hustling plates and forks to the kitchen. I'd never believed, didn't want to believe, emotions could be reduced to easy formulas. Besides, no matter how old you are when your parents die, you're an orphan, and you shouldn't have to be reasonable about it.

Suddenly *bam bam bam* cut in like an angry gavel. We looked up, incredulous. It was my father's fist, pounding the tabletop. The noise reverberated like an aftershock.

"You through?" he gruffed, eyeing my empty plate.

The sound detonated something behind my eyes. My mouth flew open and words blasted out.

"Not yet!"

I sat stunned. It had been my voice, all right. But how? Where had it come from? In my whole life I had never answered him back. Now just two words changed all that. They weren't even true.

The stinging words hung between us. Little, bland words, now huge with our history. For once he didn't have a comeback. But his silence and stance were a challenge, a thrown gauntlet that forced me up from my seat and to the kitchen for grapes I didn't want. I left the empty plate to hold him there, a reprimanding eye. Sitting down again, I made a show of arranging the grapes on it. I took my time, not looking up, not speaking. I chewed them slowly, gleefully discovering there were pips to be tongued out and delicately removed, one by one. Finally he retreated huffily to the den. Only then did I walk the plate to the kitchen, wash it, dry it and put it away.

You could call it a hollow victory, except I didn't feel victorious.

The others left last evening. But I stayed over, rising this morning in the dark for the four-hour drive back to New York. I love to drive in the hour or so just before sunup, to savor the backroads landscape at leisure before I hit the interstate. My route winds through the undulating farmland of my childhood. Its contours haven't altered in the years of my travels back and forth, but it never looks the same twice. There are predictables, though, and I revel in them. Knowing where I can pull out and pass, where I can flatten the pedal, where to hold back. There isn't a rut or bump I don't expect. The road is still a narrow two-laned macadam, showing its years. The center line, once bright school-bus yellow, now appears only here and there, speckly and pale. The shoulders are long gone, just bits of paving crumbled into parchy, stone-strewn ryegrass. A generation of strangers now occupies the faded houses and barns. There are satellite dishes in side yards where well pumps used to be. A cluster of glossy mobile homes has sprouted on the old Hallelujah Campground.

I look at fields shackled under yesterday's surprise snow, the white-blanketed houses frozen in sleep. But I know next trip will show me green—alfalfa-spiked clover, tasseling corn. There'll be barking dogs and snortling pigs, the gleeful shouts of summer children.

I think back to the house and wonder if he's up yet, if he has found my note, that note I meant and didn't mean. I'll call as soon as I get to New York, soothe, smooth, make everything all right. How is it I always look forward to seeing him, then can't wait to get away. The thought prompts a smile. That's what my friends say about their grandchildren.

The ramp for the interstate appears. I turn and aim south on the highway unfurling ahead. The rest of the trip is by rote, allowing my mind to float. It's as if there are two of me in the car—the driver, the passenger next to me. The speedometer reads sixty-five, then seventy. I feel lighter, more buoyant, with each jump of the needle. Finally I relax into a steady seventy-five and settle back. Road signs rush by, green with white borders. They come faster and faster as my humming wheels churn out the highway. *New York 185, New York 130, New York 95*. The large white characters, blurred and dancing, mark the miles I'm putting between where I am now and what's behind. I sigh as I see the distance I've come, how far I have yet to go.

Margie's Discount

BK LOREN

*M*y mother loves a good bargain. We're in the designer section of the department store where she worked for two decades. She says, "Don't you like this one better?" She holds up a blouse.

I counter with another blouse. "This one's the same but it's ten dollars cheaper."

She tucks her own find under her arm and approaches me. She looks at the label, then the price tag. She holds high the blouse she picked out. "This is a *Liz*," she says, in the same way I might say, "This is by Shakespeare." My mother points to the seams, explaining the underground world of designer clothes to me. "*Liz* clothes last forever. And look, this used to be fifty-six dollars and it's marked down to twenty-five, *plus* my discount."

"Do you get a discount here?" I say, teasing her because "Plus my discount" has been her mantra for the past two hours of shopping, as it is her mantra whenever we shop here.

"Yes, I get a discount," she says, in the same way I might say,

"Officer, I did not run that red light," with indignity and a hint of doubt, even though I really did not run the light. She adds, in a whisper, "And I get an extra fifteen percent on my VIP card."

My mother wears hats, has a virtual stockroom of shoes (bought on sale), and lives in a mobile home made of vinyl and formaldehyde. She's built a little like a tree, if the tree could be a redwood and a willow simultaneously, with a strength and rootedness accumulated over time, with a pliability and grace that allow her to bend with care for those around her.

Although I can't put a finger on what it is, there's a quality to the expression on her face that pinches my emotions. It's an expression that remains even when she's relaxed. One eyebrow is higher than the other, and it is sharply arched; the other brow curves softly, the eye underneath it more open, more innocent. This asymmetry gives her the constant look of confusion. Not the confusion of one who does not understand the world, but rather of one who understands but perceives something is wrong. The expression has been there since she was a child. I've seen it in old photos: Margie and her brother, Bill, standing by the dairy cart; Margie and Bill proudly holding a stick with two or three trout dangling from it; Margie holding her handmade rag doll; and later, Margie holding her first child, her second, her third, her fourth. She is my mother, the woman with the eyebrows unevenly arched, the eyes that suspect everything and are simultaneously innocent in every moment.

This month is my birthday. Though I am nearing forty now, my mother will shower me with gifts, and as I unwrap them, she will say, "Guess how much I paid for that?" I will not need to guess high in order to satiate her appetite for bargains. She will have given me the best of the best for the least of the least. She will look at me with the eyes that tell two stories. She will say, "Open this one next."

❧

I don't remember when bargains overtook my mother's consciousness. She was free of the condition when I was a kid. My earliest memories are of her rising in total darkness, putting on tights and a T-shirt, and exercising. I sat on the sofa with my legs curled into my chest and watched as she raised her arms to the ceiling and touched her toes, once, then again. She did back bends and knee bends. She sat on the floor, stretched her legs into a V, and held out her hands.

"Row with me," she'd say. And I'd lower myself from the too-big sofa, sit on the floor, stretch my legs out, place my feet on the inside of her knees. She'd grasp my hands, and we'd row back and forth, around and around. From this position, my mother could touch her chest to the floor. She didn't do push-ups on her knees. She ran three miles a day before Nike told her she needed a special shoe to do so. She did all this in the silence before dawn. By eight a.m., she looked like anybody else's mother, smearing peanut butter on two pieces of Wonder bread, licking grape jelly from her thumb, patting meat and bread crumbs into a loaf for dinner, wearing an apron, opening the screen door halfway to check on me or to wave hello to another kid's mom. I'm continuing her ritual these days, not the bargains, but the workouts. I get up at five, put on my sweats, and lug my gym bag to the car. When I arrive at my mom's place, she's sitting on the porch, the half-light of dawn shadowing her, making her look even smaller than her five-foot-three frame. She waves from beneath the eaves, and comes out, wearing, today, a red tam cocked to one side of her head.

"You don't have to wait outside for me, Mom," I say. "It's dark."

She says, "I wasn't waiting long. I heard your car."

As she slides into the car, I think of the avocets. I've been riding my bike to a marshy pond where they stand in the bent morning sun, their long, amber necks sometimes shadowed, sometimes gilded in the light, their black wings like precise pencil etchings on their white shoulders. I think of them not because my mother resembles them in any real way, but because she is graceful and quiet beneath her body that appears to some to be growing awkward with age, her mind that will not still from worry.

She says, "I know what you're thinking. You're thinking I'm deaf in one ear, so I couldn't have heard your car. But I did. You always drive in on my good side." She points to her hearing ear.

"Are you riding the bike today?" I ask.

"Yes," she says. "I went ten point eight miles last time. I'll go eleven today."

In the gym, I take my place on a treadmill behind my mom's stationary bicycle. I watch as her feet pedal in circles, and as I run, I can feel the rain that fell on us the day we rode mountain bikes in Crested Butte when she was sixty. My memory keeps clicking backward, her odometer, forward. I close my eyes, let my memory go. But shortly, my mother pokes me. "I did it," she says. She's standing beside me, pointing to the bike odometer. "Eleven miles."

"Good job, Mom." I stop the treadmill and follow her to the weights. We look like retired boxers, our sweaty towels hanging around our necks. She places the pin under the sixty-five pound plate. I spot her. I watch her left arm tremble, her right arm remain steady as she lifts.

"That's the same weight I lift, Mom."

"You better work harder, then," she says. She laughs and spots me as I lift.

Though my mother is strong, there are two challenges that inevitably defeat her. She cannot allow herself to sleep more than five hours a night, and she cannot remain quiet when she's feeling an emotion. That is not to say she speaks about the emotion. Rather, it goes like this: After we work out, it is tradition to have tea and toast at my house. As we enter, my mother sees a photo of my grandmother, her mother, on my coffee table. "Is that a picture of Mom?" she says.

"Yes. I was going through old photo albums."

My mother pauses for some time, both physically and verbally, then referring to her mother's premature death, she says, "I never got a chance to thank her." She stands motionless in one spot.

"She knew," I say. "Like you know how much I'm grateful to you."

Her eyes well up. She looks at the living room carpet, zeroing in. "Is that spot from one of the dogs?" she says. She walks quickly into the kitchen, returns with a wet rag, kneels down, and starts scrubbing. It takes me five minutes to convince her to join me in the kitchen. "I'll be in in just a minute," she says, her voice cracking. After tea is served and the toast is hot and buttered, her bent body rounds the corner. She's fighting the emotion still; I can tell by the way she focuses on the rag and talks incessantly.

"I think I got most of it. You might check it later. When things are wet you can't tell for sure if they're stains or . . . " She takes a seat by the window, her audible stream of consciousness like a river during spring runoff.

"I got a positive response from the editor I told you about," I say.

"The one in New York?" she says.

"Yes. I'm going there Friday."

"Going where?"

"New York."

She stares out the window. She looks hard at the horses in the field behind my home that used to be her home. She looks as if she is trying to remember something. She fails.

"Why are you going to New York?" she asks.

I reiterate. She remains quiet and places her right hand on her left to still the tremble.

The doctors tell my mother she has the heart of a child, sixty strong beats a minute at rest, one-fifty on the cardio machines and she's not even maxed; she was eating sprouts and yogurt when the rest of America was drowning in mayo and iceberg lettuce. The doctors tell my mother,

"You're in great shape." She comes home and says, "I don't have Parkinson's. The doctor says I'm in great shape."

"You can be in great shape and have Parkinson's." I bark this sentence at her like a Doberman, then I hate myself for being the one who must remind her of her disease. Occasionally, I hate her for having it, then I hate myself more, and it goes on like this until I accept the world for exactly what it is: unfair, mean, graceful, luscious and magically illogical.

My mother defends, "They don't even know what causes Parkinson's, so how can they know I have it?" She is also magically illogical.

It's been three years since her diagnosis, three years since she first sat at my kitchen table and lost the thread of an easy conversation, her face staring and expressionless, her arm shaking, her eyes that tell two stories narrowing now to none.

Before my mother moved out of this home and into the vinyl-formaldehyde box of my father's choice, she had a garage sale. She sold things dear to her for reasons I could not understand. She said, "I got this Hummel for only three dollars. And this original oil painting for twenty." I could not tell if it was the object she loved most or the bargain marked by the object. She sold these things for a significant profit. I'm talking thousands of dollars.

This weekend she is having another garage sale. It will be at her new home, the formaldehyde palace (apparently formaldehyde is essential to the construction of "manufactured homes"), and the mobile home park (called "Holidaze Homes," for seniors only) is sponsoring the all-tenant sale. She spends weeks getting ready, pricing items, doing nothing less than a stock inventory.

When the day arrives, everything is priced and recorded on a tally sheet. At six a.m., people start knocking on her door, and she is ready; she steps outside and lifts the plastic wraps from the sale tables, unveiling a masterpiece. You could mistake your shopping experience in my mother's carport for a pleasant day at the local outdoor mall, the way the dresses hang elegantly on the makeshift racks, the way the jewelry is still in its original box, velvet, satin, lush, ten dollars firm, but she'll take five. She misses her days in retail, you can tell by the way she greets each garage-saler individually, by the way she prepares each purchase in bubble wrap, places it in a box, and says, "Thank you. Enjoy!"

Inside, my father sits in his La-Z-Boy. He has been sick recently. His kidneys have failed and his heart pumps like a locomotive just to push a hairline of blood through the dark and narrowing tunnels of his veins. In addition to cleaning, cooking, doing laundry and shopping, my mother now has to bathe, shave and dress my father; she has to give him his insulin shot. She washes bloodied sheets. "I am not a nurse," she says. And my father, a military man to the bone, has devised a ritual around administering his shot. The syringe must sit on the counter for five seconds before throwing it away. The insulin bottle must never touch porcelain. The angle of needle insertion must be twenty-two and a half degrees (by his calculations), no more, no less. My mother wears tie-dyed scarves, rainbow socks and Doc Marten sandals. Neither my mother nor my father is malicious or mean; they are simply as made-for-each-other as Rush Limbaugh and Shirley MacLaine.

My father rises from his La-Z-Boy at ten a.m. and calls my mother in from the sale. "I need to take my shot," he says. Then he disappears into the bathroom. Moments later, I go inside to ask my mother how low she will go on her pewter collection. As I enter, I watch her place the hypodermic needles on the counter. Her body quivers like a tree in a sharp, undecided wind. "Is that right?" she asks, and my father nods, yes. He says to her, "Don't do too much, today, Marge." He says to me, "I worry about her. She's not well, you know. She needs rest." His concern is real. An hour later he rises from his La-Z-Boy, pokes his head outside, finds my mother in the middle of a group of people, collecting money, socializing, saying, "Thanks, enjoy!" and my father says, "Marge, are you going to make lunch?"

Five years ago I took my mother to Sea Ranch, a quiescent stretch of beauty nestled in the redwoods along the Pacific Northwest coast. We rented a small house with an ocean view, and daily we walked through shaded woods laced with ferns and mossy creeks that meandered, like us, toward the sea. At the base of the steep hill a collection of boulders demanded we scramble on all fours to reach the sea. I thought my mom would turn back, but she laughed when I doubted her agility. She scrambled ably, showing less fear than I.

At night, as the California sun turned to cool, gray fog, we made popcorn and hot chocolate and watched old black and white flicks: Bogey and Bacall; Tracy and Hepburn. "It's a shame about Katharine Hepburn," my mother said. "Her Parkinson's."

My mother has always been good at pity. I have not. "She handles it well," I said. "She still takes parts in plays. She exudes strength in spite of it." My mother nodded, her eyebrows growing more asymmetrical as she watched Kate in all her glory.

Last week, we returned to Sea Ranch, a sort of rendezvous to see if what we had gained there the first time—peace of mind, rejuvenation—was still available to us. My mother did not walk down to the ocean on the wooded trail this time; she did not scramble over the rocks. And I did not pity her, but instead, found a new path to the same ocean.

Instead of watching old movies, we lay in front of the picture window and watched the sky turn to night. Twice she saw what she said was "a star stuck in a black hole." "See the way it moves so quickly— like a race car bumping up against the edge of that black hole."

When I said I did not see the black hole, my mother described it.

"It's like a donut, or a bagel, and that crazy star is moving so quickly, but the black hole is keeping it in."

I looked up. The sky, to me, remained only an endless theory of possibility; the stars were so lush it was difficult to separate one from the other; they blended together and milked the sky with light, only the brightest among them adding texture and points. I didn't see the star stuck in the black hole; I didn't see it desperately trying to get out.

When I returned home, I researched, again, the symptoms of Parkinson's. I learned it is more than a tremor, more than a crooked body that cannot easily find a point of balance. It is a smorgasbord of symptoms: memory loss, disorientation, hallucinations, and eventual schizophrenia. Like a smorgasbord, however, the person with Parkinson's does not necessarily have all of these symptoms; each symptom exists as a mere possibility.

Throughout the trip, though, my mother saw UFO-like stars trapped in black holes. She listened to foghorns one evening when there were no ships in the bay; she remembered, in detail, things that had never happened, and, on occasion, she failed to recall what did take place. On the way back into San Francisco, a city in which she lived for several years, she asked, "Do we have to go over that bridge?"

While at Sea Ranch, we ventured out into the world of commerce on only a few occasions, and my heart ached as my mother searched for souvenirs, trinkets, anything to help her remember the event. But it was more than memory loss that drove her. She shopped here with the same urgency she displayed when buying bargains at home. When we returned from a day at the ocean, she clung to her new sweatshirt the same way she held to her discount at the department store, as if her experiences would be lost if not made tangible, as if her discount illustrated, in no uncertain terms, the amount of love she felt for her family and friends—if only she could give them what they were worth—if only she could grasp and hold on to what she was worth. But she could not.

It occurred to me then that in no other time in history and in no other place but America would I have this experience of losing a parent so slowly, so ethereally, so painfully in exactly this manner. In my mother's day, *choice* meant three makes of automobiles (if you had the money), one brand of tennis shoe, two brands of coffee and marriage at eighteen. Today, the definition of choice would not fit on this page, nor in this volume. Overwhelmed as she is (as we all are) with the ease of fulfilling her external desires, she seems to have mistaken them for her dreams—or perhaps she has simply learned to mistrust what she dreamed.

Suddenly it makes sense to me that my mother wants desperately to get more than she paid for; in what other realm of her life has she ever been given such a break? In what other realm of her life has she ever been marched into an arena and told, "This can be yours, or perhaps you'll choose this"?

I fantasize this happening for her now: She is eighteen again, and suddenly she can choose to be married or not; she can choose to have children whenever and if ever she wants; she can walk over to this rack and pick up a college degree, a few "self-improvement" courses, or a selection of art classes; she can go to this case and decide if her marriage is working out; she can go to counseling if it is not, and if it still does not work, she can choose to make it on her own. At some point in her life, she can choose to live by herself if she wants; she does not have to live under her parents' roof, then under her husband's roof, then under her children's roof, and when that is all over, she does not have to spend every ounce of spare energy she has caring for her husband, keeping her vows because she is loyal and good, and so is he. I fantasize that she is Katharine Hepburn, that in spite of her place in history, her gender, her class, she was able to make choices, and she chose well, and because of choosing well, she can go gently into that good night—or, if she chooses, she can howl against the dying of the light. I fantasize that the black hole has finally released that crazy star.

But this is one of the accomplishments my generation has made: the overwhelming ability to choose. Because I live it, I have never truly recognized it, and recognizing it now, I want only to be able to deny that it was ever otherwise, because we all want to believe, in America, that our fates are cut by chisels we hold in our own hands, that circumstances do not limit, that time and culture do not dictate. But they do. My generation has nothing if not choice. But what void will we feel at our deaths? What easy pill will ease our pain, or slow time enough for us to question who our daughters and sons are, who we are, who our parents were? Though the world itself may end in either a whimper or a bang, an individual's life does not. In America, it ends like a metronome whose ticking we did not hear, at least until the last measure of the song.

I hear my mother's metronome ticking, and I want nothing more than for the music to grow louder, to drown out the easy comforts that quell her desires and overshadow her authentic dreams.

Five days after our return from Sea Ranch, there is a knock on my door. I open it. It's Mom. She's dressed in jeans and T-shirt, and her hat of the day is a ball cap with her short pony tail hanging out the back hole.

"There's a sale at the department store," she says. "They've been bought out. This is the last sale where I will get my discount."

I know the gravity of the situation. I know what not getting that discount will mean, what it will do to her self-esteem, and silly as I seem to myself, I harmonize with her desperation about the loss. I gather my wallet and comb my hair. As I get ready to go, however, I am suddenly pleased. This "no discount" may offer a time for my mother to discover her worth in something other than dollars and cents. It will open a space, perhaps, for her to see that I would love her and remain by her until death (and beyond) if she gave me only an ugly rock for my birthday—if she gave me the gift of her presence, if she gave me only the gift of life and the good mothering that followed. I want to hold up my Liz Claiborne next to these winnings and say, "Thanks," not for the clothes.

On the way to the department store, my mother unfolds, like the village storyteller, the decline in prices she witnessed firsthand (she went to the store before she came to my house). "*This* jacket was on the two-dollar rack. It had been ninety-eight dollars, then it was forty-eight, and then twenty-four. It's a Ralph Lauren, and I got it for two dollars, *plus* my discount, *plus* my VIP. Came to a dollar-twelve."

I pat her on the back. "That's great, Mom. It's a great jacket," and, as jackets go, it is great, especially for a buck, give or take a few cents.

But my heart is still aching. Her body is still crooked, and her eyes are still hazed with cataracts and wild with desire. What I want to do is pull to the side of the road or get back on the plane and sit in a room with her by the ocean and listen, for hours on end, to her real stories, to the stories she would tell if both her eyebrows could talk, not only the innocent brow, but the one that is arched sharply, the one that does not understand the world, the one that sees something unjust but cannot name it. But my mother, like all mothers, is a one-sided creature. You either get the kind of mom who sugar-coats everything for you or you get the kind who criticizes the air you breathe. In your little role as the offspring, you do not get the luxury of watching your parents become their own, oddly whole human beings with quirks and jaggedly adorable perfections. As soon as you no longer depend on them, you blame them, and as soon as you learn that blaming them for who you are or whatever pain you feel is ridiculous because you are just fine the way you are and pain accompanies every ecstasy of life anyway, just at that moment, you wake up and see that your parents have entered into a whole new territory called old age. You cannot go there. You cannot meet them. You cannot enter.

I look at my mom. Her gray hair beneath her cap is a little wild this morning. She can barely reach the gas pedal. Her face, beautiful to me, is also somehow foreign. When did she become old? At what point did the laugh lines around her eyes turn to effort? At what point did her every tomorrow fill itself with question rather than with promise?

Suddenly, and as if lunacy is a common experience for me, I say, "Mom, I have to take you to see the avocets."

She says, "Do they carry avocets? I've never seen avocets in the store."

"No," I say. "You've got to turn around. They're not here, they're in a marsh."

"Marsh? I don't know where there's any marsh," she says.

Eventually, I convince her. I say, "We can come back to the store right after we see them. I promise."

She says, "Well, OK. But they have some really good buys in there, and this is the last sale where I will get my discount."

I take over the driver's seat. I drive away from the shopping mall, down the boulevard of strip malls, and onto some back roads that lead to an open space. The marsh is a mile walk on flat terrain, a distance of which I know my mother is capable.

I park the car and get out. My mother remains seated, her eyes creased with worry.

"Is it OK to be here?" she says.

"Yes, it's OK. Why wouldn't it be OK?"

"It's so empty. Is this somebody's land? We're not trespassing, are we?"

"No, we're not trespassing," I assure her. "Let's go."

Cautiously, looking in all directions, she gets out of the car. We enter the trail as if it is foreign terrain, an illicit journey into what has always been possible. In moments we are surrounded with trees, sway-ing cottonwoods that give voice to the wind. In a window of sky between the green, the bent figure of a great blue heron passes, his movements deliberate, graceful. My mother knows these birds; they hunted on the small pond behind her used-to-be-home, now my home. She says, "There's Big Blue." And I nod. "That was Big Blue, wasn't it? I didn't know he was still here."

"He's still here," I say, and we continue walking. Though the earth is loose and uneven, my mother's gait is fairly steady, her posture almost upright. Meadowlarks sit on mullein stalks and sing as we pass. These, too, she had forgotten were so abundant in our neck of the woods. And we see, as well, the patterned flight of hundreds of swallows, the labored flight of several magpies, the signs of coyotes and foxes, the flash of bright yellow and red of the western tanager. She says, "I've never seen that bird before. It looks tropical. I didn't know we had those birds here."

When the trees open up to a small lake, we round the bend and walk toward the marshlands. The land is less verdant here, more cracked and arid. She says, "This should be taken care of. This is not very pretty. Don't you want to go back to the prettier lake and see Big Blue?"

I stop on the dry land, and I point. The marsh is golden, the morning sun still angled on the horizon. "Look," I say.

My mother looks toward the mucky water. Her eyes light on nothing. Worry creases her brow. "I liked it better back there," she says.

I remain standing in one spot. I don't point again; I just watch the six or seven avocets standing steady on their too-tall legs, their golden heads and white bodies reflected perfectly in the shallow water that moves like mercury. My mother's body shakes backward and forward at the waist. I had not seen this before in her, but it is there now, and it can be expected to stay. She looks from the water to me, and looks back toward the prettier lake. She is clearly put out, but repressing it. Whatever it was about these avocets I wanted her to see was a miscalculation on my part. I watch them for a second, then start to turn back.

But my mother's body has suddenly stopped shaking. Her brown eyes are somehow clear again, and she is, for the first time in a long time, silent, not because there is nothing to say, but because there is too much. She says, "They're beautiful, aren't they?"

I nod.

She says, "Did we have to pay to get in here?"

I say, "Mom, you were with me. You remember. Did we have to pay?"

"No," she says. "But I don't know why not."

I take off my jacket and lay it on the ground. Then I sit down. She looks at me, and I think she is going to remind me the ground is dirty and full of fleas; but she takes off her jacket, her Ralph Lauren, and covers the ground with it. She sits next to me. I put my arm on her shoulder.

As if delivered on a screen from a slide show, the words to a poem appear in my head. I say the words aloud:

if I lay down tonight in
this wet field of light

would I feel the flesh
of this terrain folding over me—
a seed planted of

understanding. would I
feel the losses shrink away
before the hope of

what will already
never return haunts me.

My mother says, "Are you praying?"
I don't look at her. I say, "Yes."

When we get back home, she seems to have forgotten about her discount and the last sale at her department store. My father is at my house—he came to visit the dogs, as he often does—and my mother starts telling a story, one she has not told him before, about our recent trip to Sea Ranch.

"We went to the lighthouse in Point Arena," she tells him. "It's one of the tallest lighthouses in America, one hundred and forty-five stairs to the top, and I climbed them all."

She remembers this event accurately down to the last detail. She says, "We climbed to the lens, to the part of the tower that sends light out to sea, but to get there, we had to climb these very narrow stairs. They were completely vertical."

I agree with her, confirming that her description is not an exaggeration.

My father says, "Did you climb them?"

She says, "Of course I climbed them."

And I say, "Tell him the rest of the story, Mom."

She cocks her head, not knowing what else of significance happened. She made it to the top, that's all that matters to her, and so I say, "She made it to the top," and my father smiles and nods.

But what happened after that matters worlds to me. With all the signs at the entrance of the lighthouse that warned about the difficulty of the climb, we never considered that the descent would also be difficult. My mom, who collects lighthouses, whose favorite book is *To the Lighthouse*, who falls asleep with a miniature lighthouse glowing in her window, was so excited about making it to the top of the lighthouse, she neglected to consider coming down. But as we turned away from the circle of unending ocean that surrounded us at the top of the light, she was faced with a narrow channel with no arm rails and two-inch-wide iron steps that were placed one below the other in a spiral. As she turned and saw the challenge ahead, I could see the fear in her eyes. But she had no choice. She had to balance; she had to descend.

"I'll spot you, Mom," I said, but there was really no way to do that. "You'll have to turn around and climb down backwards."

My mother's eyes froze. She said, "I can't do that," but then she turned around backward, placed her quivering foot on the first rung, and praying for balance in her every breath, she placed one foot behind the other, concentrated, and without looking, she descended.

What she didn't know was that a group of tourists were crowded in the landing, waiting to ascend to the lens. The twenty or so of them watched breathlessly as my mother's tennis-shoe-clad feet dangled and then blindly found their way to the next step, one after the other, carefully, confidently, to the bottom, with no hand rail, no light. I was so focused in on her, I didn't notice the crowd either. But as my mother's two feet finally landed on deck, the crowd broke into cheers. Several people patted her on the back; others called out, "Good job," and they meant it. Like her, they were caught in the moment; they could feel the tension and fear she overcame with every step. And at the end of it all, they released their breathless doubts about her ability to make it or not, and they cheered.

My mother smiled and lifted her face toward the sky like a victorious athlete.

"You did it," I said.

"Yes," she said. "I did."

Taking Care of Charlie

CATHLEEN CALBERT

$\mathcal{A}$n ugly brute, mop-headed, with blank, black eyes, he had dead-fish breath when he arrived. My put-upon husband and I took him to the vet and had his teeth cleaned; to our dismay, seventeen of them promptly were extracted. Now he no longer stinks, but he only eats expensive canned food, which he can't always stomach. When ill, he prefers vomiting in the crevices between cushions on our ivory-colored couch. And, of course, since he is at heart a bad dog, he urinates on things: rugs, the wastepaper basket in the bathroom, my husband's underpants. The scent he leaves is strong and spicy (he still bears his testicles proudly), almost as bad as a cat's.

Charlie is my mother's dog. That is, he was (it's still hard to believe that he is in any way *mine*). He is the last creature that my mother loved. Living alone in her Berkeley apartment, she kept a dirty, red Christmas sweater on him through all four seasons and held him close to her chest as she paced her two rooms. She fed him Pupperoni Sticks and Fancy Feast cat food even when she had no money to buy more than bagels and apples for herself. When she walked him up College

Avenue, he continually leapt up at her side, performing a terrier/poodle spring that seemed to defy gravity. Too quickly, he was once again in her arms, where he softened like a sleeping child, obviously deeply relieved that he would be carried, assured that he would not be parted from her on the street. I have never seen such neurotic devotion in a dog. I had seen it before in my mother.

In my childhood, she was, I thought, the perfect mother. I did not understand, or approve of, other mothers, like Betsy Twills or Janet Ferguson, who walked around their front lawns in bikinis, enjoyed highballs in the evening and painted their nails bright pink or red. My mother did none of these things. She was too good, too pure. When I was very young, I suffered some confusion regarding my mother and Catholicism. I knew that we worshipped Hail Mary Full of Grace, that she was the mother of God, the Queen of Heaven, and I knew that my mother, also named Mary, was worthy of such worship. At four, I half-believed that we were praying to her, that we were asking my mother to intercede on our behalf. *Blessed art thou among women, and blessed is the fruit-of-thy-womb-Jesus.* I realize that my misapprehension implies that I saw myself as baby Jesus, but I'm sure that wasn't the case.

A little older, I still saw my mother as a martyr and myself as her protector. I shadowed her, thus staving off car accidents, making sure that she always found her way home again. I envisioned growing up to be a writer, eventually penning her biography so that the whole world would know what a wonderful person my mother was and I could offer up to her a permanent memorial, make of her the icon that I felt she deserved to be. I believe that I wanted to call it *A Sad Life,* and I even pictured a photograph on the cover of this best-selling tome: my mother, with a pained face and a scarf tied under her chin, trudging up a hill through the rain. I don't know where I got such a picture. Certainly, my mother never struck such a pose. Perhaps I was inspired by movies about World War II refugees. I know that I imagined including in the book detailed accounts of my mother's selfless goodness to her four children—her unfailing attention, unconditional love—balanced by tales of my father's cruel indifference.

It took me until my thirties to admit—under the pressure of an earnest therapist—that my mother may have had a hand in the souring of my parents' marriage, although I still regarded, still regard, her as largely an innocent and injured party. Why? Perhaps because she always was sweet with me, even if not always in the healthiest, most "empowering" way. She never encouraged me to believe that I could ever do anything involving physical grace, and she continually encouraged me to be afraid, as she was afraid, for my safety in this dark and treacherous world.

In my thirties, I wrote a love poem to my mother, celebrating, I thought, the comfortable nights when I slept in her bed as a child. Those are some of the dearest moments of my childhood: that dreaming closeness between the two of us. She let me crawl into her bed—my father and my mother had taken to sleeping separately—and sighed herself into sleep while I curled against her back and fingered the curls of her hair. As I fell asleep, sometimes I imagined the bed floating away into space, out there among the blackness and the stars, the two of us circling. I tried to capture some of this in the poem: wanting to stay forever in her weightless bed. I included my having confused her with the Virgin Mother, too, and a line about my being none too clean as a child, bathed but once a week as part of our working-class Saturday night ritual of ablutions. I sent the poem to her before it appeared in my first book. I didn't know—I didn't admit to myself—that she was sick then, but I felt that I should send it to her, that I shouldn't wait. The line about my lack of cleanliness, of course, was the one that she fixated on. "I bathed you more than once a week," she scolded. "I'm sure of it." She was mortified that I would present her to the world as a mother who didn't bathe her children daily. Still, I like to think that she felt some of the tribute that I intended. I dedicated the book to her, but I have never brought her a copy. She can no longer read. Half the time, she can no longer even register what she is seeing.

Our birthdays are just four days apart—"We're both Gemini," my mother informed the nurses in her convalescent home. We always were close, even through a number of incarnations: when she was a stay-at-home mother, apple-cheeked and pleasantly lumpy, and I her small devotee; when she became an alarmingly red-haired secretary at the local fire station, a divorcée who was dating various and, my brothers felt sure, inappropriate men, as I was thrashing my way into my own emerging sexuality; then as she settled into her middle-aged resignation of loneliness and poverty and I into my younger, academic resignation of loneliness and poverty.

Throughout it all, my mother always had been forgetful, "spacy," as she said, having adopted our slang in the early seventies and retaining it: "Bummer," "Hang-up," "Mellow out." Then there was the falling, the forgotten keys, her belief that someone else must have entered her place and moved all of her things. Frightened, I teased her about the lapses of memory. My mother told me that she was sure she didn't have Alzheimer's but that she might be suffering from wisenheimer's disease. Since she could make a joke like that, I figured she must be OK.

But she wasn't OK. When my siblings and I finally admitted that something was wrong, something more than the eccentricity born of too much time alone and too few resources, both inner and outer, in short order came the half-forced departure from the apartment building where she had lived for twenty years and a devastating move in with my sister. My sister meant well, and something had to be done. My mother had begun throwing money away (literally) and had smoked herself out of her apartment by lighting a fire without having opened the flue. But, like many people who detect some inner failing, my mother had taken a number of precautions to appear better off than she was. There were pink and yellow Post-its stuck up throughout the apartment—*Turn off stove, Make sure you have your key*—and she'd taken to cutting our phone conversations short as though she feared the inevitable circularity of her questions, her inability to process answers. Around her apartment there also were notes: *Cathy coming in April? Mike back from Thailand.* The move in with my sister both revealed and deepened my mother's increasing dementia. "Mom, please don't be crazy," my sister pleaded, caught between her ideal of daughterhood and the reality of living with my mother in a state of unreality.

In a sense, the untenable situation at my sister's resolved itself when my mother broke her hip and ended up, after surgery, in a convalescent home. I could almost feel my heart breaking, a distinct heaviness in my chest, when I picked up the small spiral notebook by her bedside. After pages of earlier lists—*Pupperoni, bananas, aspirin*—in a strangely shaking handwriting, she had written 223, 223, 223: the number of her room. She was trying to hold on to what she knew. She pleaded desperately with us to deliver her from that place where the beds were jail cells and she was tied into her wheelchair so she wouldn't fall. Finally, frustrated that I would not untie her, put the rails down, get her out of there, my mother blinked up at me and said, "If you don't do right by me, I will haunt you when I'm dead." I bowed my head, letting the curse fall upon it.

Then there was the move into another convalescent home near my brothers, then a broken femur. Now she is bedridden. "Non–weight bearing," as the staff says. After the last surgery, a psychiatrist prescribed an antidepressant to ease her despair. On my mother's chart, he wrote his five-minute diagnosis: "Depression, as evidenced by an expressed desire to die"—as if wanting to die were an inappropriate response to her plight, to losing her power of movement, to losing her mind.

Now I visit her every six months or so, put in time at her bedside, respond as patiently as I can to the questions that are asked one hundred, two hundred times. *Is this where I sleep? Will someone help me? Do you hear something?* There are a few good moments too, those for which I travel three thousand miles, although they are fewer each time. And every visit, her blue eyes look a little paler. She laughs at jokes that are incomprehensible to me. Sometimes she asks if I am having the same dream. Sometimes, after babbling over the invisible writing that she reads on the curtain drawn around her bed, she seems to take me in and says, with a rumble of pleasure in her throat, "Oh my baby, my baby, my best friend." Once she raised her eyes to heaven. "Jesus Christ," she said, "take care of my little girl." Once, after I had spent every morning and afternoon for a week in the madhouse din of the convalescent home, trying to reach her, trying to comfort her, trying to give her something, she looked up at me surprised and said, "Cathleen?"

"Yeah, Mom," I answered her.

"Cathleen Mary?"

"Yeah, Mom," I said. "It's me."

"Fantastic!" she said, as if she had just been invited to a splendid tea.

The last afternoon I spent with her, she could not process any of my words: *Are you OK? Are you comfortable? Do you need anything?* Then she turned toward me, staring—her pale blue eyes are strangely wide open these days—and said, "I'm sorry that you lack tranquility because of me."

She was right; I do lack tranquility. I find it hard to accept the truth that I can do nothing to stop the horror that has taken over my mother's life, nothing to halt the progression of this disease, the erasure of memory, and along with that, understanding, interest, love. "I miss my mom," I have sobbed into my pillow as my husband stood over me, his hand uncertain but tender on my back.

Each time that I go back to California my mother has further receded. She is less there. She is less mine. I was glad to meet her current nurse's aide, Amanda, because she seems genuinely to care for my mother. She likes braiding my mother's long white hair and tying it up with fancy hairbands. She has more tenderness, more courage, than I could ever have, turning my mother on her side to "clean her up," then the talcum, the rose-scented lotion. I also noticed that it was hard for Amanda to give my mother over to me for a week, to allow me the opportunity to spoon into my mother's indifferent mouth carrots and peas, to cut up her Salisbury steak. All the other weeks, my mother is one of Amanda's aging babies. I see my mother once every six months. I just want it to be the two of us when I am there in the hope of that moment when I can give her something that no one else can, that moment when she might give me something that I can hold on to until I see her again—or if I never see her again.

Hoping to have a meaningful goodbye with her at the end of my last visit, I waited until the aides had tucked her into bed and she was comforted at being prone and covered up into gratitude, which is immense, despite her nightly despair at having her slippers removed. I think she is afraid that without her shoes she will not be able to walk, that she will not be able to leave when the right time comes. "Goodbye, I love you," I said, and she said it back to me: "Goodbye, I love you. My darling."

I tried to tiptoe out, not wanting to corrupt that parting—it could always be the last goodbye—when I clanged into another patient's wheelchair. She had rolled herself into the wrong room and was trouble; that much I knew. Soon she'd be screeching as the residents did in their confusion, sounding like wounded peacocks. Or she'd rummage through the chocolates I had left for my mother, clip a sock, a sweatshirt. This skeletally thin woman seated in the chair reached for my hand, which I gave her, although I am reluctant to get too close to the residents for fear that their insanity will be turned on me, which it sometimes is. One woman swears constantly in a deep, guttural Spanish and claws the arms of anyone who passes too near; I make sure to stay clear of her reach. A one-hundred-year-old man will turn from empty pleasantries to condemnations of what a shameless slut I am. More likely the fever-dreams that are their lives mean that they want to gaze endlessly into my eyes, to show me something in the air beside us, something that isn't there, to have me help them do something: get into bed, go to the bathroom, escape, run away. And, to speak plainly, they smell bad; bad things often are coming out of their orifices. Of course, the same is true of my mother. Sometimes the combination of rose lotion and stale urine that rises from her makes the back of my throat close, but she is my mother, so I do not hesitate to bend close and kiss her.

The woman, dark and hollow-eyed, pressed my hand to her lips. "I love you so much," she murmured with great passion. "I love you so much." Then she looked up at me. "Don't you care at all?"

"I do," I said to appease her, glancing back at my mother who, thankfully, had descended into sleep. "I care very much." I was surprised by how much I seemed to mean what I said.

She whispered gratefully into my hand, then let me wheel her into the hall, where we offered our tender goodbyes. She had shared a moment of love with her daughter, and I had parted from my mother in another guise. For, of course, they are all our mothers; we are all their daughters.

My mother's slow dissolution has left me alone to ponder the decisions I have made in my own life thus far, how far away I have traveled. Have I made the right decisions with my life? I am a tenured professor living on the other side of the country from my family. Should I be there for her? Yet I could not move "home" again unless I were willing to rearrange my existence radically. So my mother, much beloved—*protect us now and at the hour of death*—slips from me, long-distance. I even have stopped calling her. She cannot understand the phone, my voice, any of it. I can barely reach her. Soon I will not be able to reach her at all.

Instead, I have her dog. My brothers and sister were adamant: They didn't want him. One brother said that he'd take care of Charlie quickly and simply: euthanasia. The other pointed out that our mother would never know the difference. My sister came up with the novel idea that Charlie was, miraculously, an affenpinscher, and therefore desirable to someone in the world (he's not; he's got mongrel written all over him). My siblings were united in only one thing: They wondered what the hell I was doing. *Why?*

I don't know why. Perhaps flying Charlie back to Providence, tucked away in the belly of the plane as I knocked back Bloody Marys, was a mistake. Certainly, I wouldn't say that he's been a welcome addition to our household. But he was my mother's mistake first, her last, and I would argue, most horrible baby. Thus, he is something of a canine brother to me, raised by the same woman, with the same adoration, ineptitude, irresponsibility.

So I bathe Charlie. I believe this is the first time in his life that he is without fleas. I take him for shots. I take him for long walks with my own dog. When he lets out a lonely bark while dreaming, I stoop to shake him, occasionally stroking his ropes of fur. Sometimes there is little one can do. I can take care of Charlie. He is the black pearl of my penance. For what? I don't know. Nothing. Everything. All I know is that he eases my pain; he allows me to sleep.

Good Morning, Dear

SANDRA BUTLER

$\mathcal{M}$y mother calls me on the telephone when she awakens. Her's are the first words I hear, the sound of her voice our morning ritual. She reports how she slept and what her plans are for the day, how her health is and whatever else expresses the domestic connection she longs for and has only with me. It's three hours later on the East Coast where she lives, so approaching my desk each morning, I find the reassuring and welcoming blink of the machine containing her voice.

"Good morning, dear," she always begins.

I relax then, knowing I have my mother for another day.

My father never imagined she would stay in their home after his death. "After I'm gone," he instructed her, "the best thing would be to use Tim Hines to sell the house. He'll do the best by you. No need for you to rattle around in so many rooms by yourself."

It was a phrase she was to hear many times in the next eleven years. From her grandchildren, her friends, her niece. "What are you doing rattling around in such a big place? What do you need it for?"

But she stayed, the routines of her life comforting and reassuring. Friday, the garbage was put out. Tuesday, the gardeners came to rake or shovel, plant or sweep. Summer mornings, she had her coffee on the porch, looking out at the garden that still held so many memories. She was only seventy-three when he died and wasn't ready to leave her life in their home behind.

My mother didn't cry when my father died. During the first months, she drove to the cemetery several times a week. In the trunk of her car was a rubber mat, a small brush and some stones. On the occasional times I accompanied her—"going to see Daddy," it was called—she knelt on the carefully positioned mat, swept off the stone and placed a rock upon it. When she began to move her lips, I discreetly moved away to stand beside the birch tree at the edge of the Temple Ohabai Shalom section of the cemetery. She was talking to Daddy about her life without him.

"I want him to know what I am doing now. I don't really believe that anything happens after you're gone, but I know he hears me. I need to believe that he does," she whispered to me as she walked across the grass studded with names engraved in stone. Then her eyes filled with tears she hastily brushed away before they threatened to spill over and lubricate the dry skin of her cheeks.

After the shiva period, I returned to my life three thousand miles away, calling every several days to check up on her. But within just a few months, my mother began to take bridge lessons and started playing twice a day. She left her now-empty house at ten a.m. and often didn't return until midnight. She threw herself into this new world with the frenzy of grief and the relief, I imagine now, of being finally alone. It was an unfamiliar environment for her, one of women, of intrigues, of jealousies, of competition, of new friendships, of unfamiliar skills. She entered this world with a passion I had never seen in her before.

Now, my mother forgets to go to the cemetery for months at a time. Now, her life is filled with herself. Now, at the end of her life, she has the turn her life had never before allowed. When she was finally ready to leave their home eleven years later, my mother had become an old woman and didn't want to rattle around in so many rooms.

She began to look at condominiums, accompanied by eager friends delighted at the possibility that she would move into their building and become a part of the daily social worlds they created: worlds of care and attention masked as bridge, grocery shopping, walks. She called me to ask for help in the moving, assuring me that the movers were already hired and would pack everything. There was really very little to be done, she promised, but she would feel more comfortable if I were there. She didn't want to intrude in my life. . . . Of course I went. Of course.

My mother peered out the front window smiling eagerly at the sight of me as I climbed the stone steps. We embraced, but as I drew back and looked around the expanse of living and dining room, I saw that nothing had been done. Nothing. The movers were coming in the morning and everything was precisely the way it had been for the past thirty-six years.

"Ma," I said. "How come nothing is prepared for the move?"

"Don't worry, sweetheart. They're going to pack everything." She smiled nervously as though caught in a mistake.

"But Ma, the toilet articles. The papers. What about the food? The furniture you won't need in the new place?"

Her face fell and she began to look frightened and confused.

My voice was shrill. "And what about the clothes and the collection of straw hats. The checkbooks? The goddamn garden equipment you won't need anymore?"

My mother started to cry. "I guess I didn't think about it. When the movers said they would pack everything up, I felt relieved and just put it out of my mind."

I put my arms around her, apologetic and overwhelmed with the task she had left me. Closing the home she had shared with my father for twenty-five years and lived in alone for another eleven was left for me. Imploring and ashamed, she looked at me, and I patted her back, murmuring something reassuring, straightened up and went into the kitchen to begin the first of hundreds of lists, engaged in the task of gathering up the artifacts of her life.

Each vase, every necklace, all the paintings had a story. Each anecdote had to be told as the item was being packed: where she and Daddy were when they bought it; why the artist was singular, how they spotted his potential years before anyone else; why this piece of amber or that bolt of silk captured precisely the essence of their adventure. It wasn't the packing my mother was waiting to do; it was telling me the stories.

I gathered up each object and she told me their histories throughout the night and the next morning until the movers came. She supervised them as they went about their work and I hastily completed the sorting and packing. As we drove away from the house, she didn't look back, not even once. She sat quietly beside me as I drove her car to the new apartment. I was unwilling to interrupt her thoughts, and we remained silent together in the car until the moving van pulled up in front of her new awninged entrance.

Returning home five days later, I called my mother, pressing the volume button on high in order to be able to hear her thin voice in the cacophonous sterile corridors of the airport.

"Hi, Ma. I'm at the airport. Just wanted to say goodbye once more."

"I know you're at the airport. I just went into your room looking for you. There was something I forgot to say but you weren't there," was her poignant reply. I can see her wobbling across the living room, wearing house clothes, her "going out" clothes neatly folded and returned to their sachet-lined drawers the moment she returns home. She is wearing no-skid sneakers, cotton drawstring pants and a cotton tee. Braless, she cannot bear anything pressing against her body, nothing containing or binding her. Finally, she has loosened all the constraints that shaped her body and her life. My mother's skin is filled with purple bruises, a new one blossoming each day. Thin skin, she diagnoses.

"I bump into something and before you know it, I'm black and blue."

The same thing happens to me now. I look down at my body during my morning shower and see new bruises I don't remember getting. My mother and I are thin-skinned women.

Now my mother calls me from the small, very modern kitchen in her new home, the telephone wires our point of contact. "Good morning, dear. I listened to an interview with a reverend at Harvard. He spoke so beautifully he reminded me of Abba Eban. Remember how he spoke? This reverend—he is black—sounded just like him. He also spoke very highly of the Jews. It was very interesting. Sometimes I think you are the only one in my life that I learn anything from. The women at the bridge club talk about television and clothes. I get so bored I have to leave. But when I watch a good interview on channel two, I want to discuss it with you. Also, Carl Sagan died today. He's the man who did everything in the cosmos. They replayed an interview with him and he talked about the cosmos like a loving child."

I call my mother every two or three days, being sure to focus on the Harvard reverend, the death of Sagan. We have lengthy conversations where she "learns" something. Often she sends clippings about current events that she hopes I will find interesting. I save them by the phone so we can refer to them when we speak. But, increasingly now, she forgets words, frequently returning to the start of the sentence and beginning again quickly, hoping, perhaps, to rush up to the missing word before she loses it again. She becomes embarrassed, frustrated, impatient with herself, and I try to find the word that is lost, offer it to her, like lobbing a ball into an empty net.

"Good morning, dear. First of all, I'll give you the weather report. It's too slippery to go out. I'm just afraid of falling. I get up, make the bed, have my breakfast and clean up the kitchen, then I have to rest. The whole day goes that way. I'm just slowing down. Yesterday I didn't even make the bed. I had palpitations and felt funny. I feel out of breath. I'm going to call the woman who checks my pacemaker and tell her that. Last night I had a dream that a young girl came to me and said here's your mail. Can you imagine such a thing? What would make me dream something like that? I don't even know a female mailman. Furthermore, I had another dream where a pretty reddish-brown dog was in my bedroom. He came very close to me and was smiling. The door to the rest of the apartment was closed, but I knew there was a young man and woman outside the door wanting me to feed the dog. 'I can't keep a dog here,' I called out to them. 'They don't allow dogs in here.' I got up out of bed and walked around the house, imagining they were feeding him in my kitchen."

I try to explain the idea of dreams to my mother, try to help her understand the unconscious, manifest content, free associations. But she becomes bewildered and literal. For her, the dream is about what she is reporting. Nothing else makes sense to her. I stop trying to explain and begin instead to simply listen carefully to her dreams.

My mother's message is halting this morning. I call her as the water drips through the paper cone, through the coffee grounds of my other necessary morning ritual.

"What's the matter, Ma?"

"Nothing. I just get low once in a while. Then it passes."

"What are you feeling low about?"

"My life," she whispers. "My life. I think and think about everything. I go over and over it in my mind. What did I do? Exactly what did I do? I ran a house, took care of my husband. Took care of my children. And it all seems so plain. Such a plain life. I never did anything."

Unable to think of what to say, I remain silent and wait.

"When I was a young woman, I used to go downtown after you and your brother were in school. I signed up for speech lessons so I wouldn't make any mistakes when I talked. I used to go to the department stores and walk around the housewares department and the furniture department to see how they arranged rooms, set tables and made centerpieces. I wanted so much to learn how to do things the right way. And look what happened. You know I lie in bed and can't stop myself from funny thoughts. Now that it's winter, it gets dark early. I get into bed earlier than usual and I have a lot of time to think, just lying there."

"What do you think about, Ma?"

"All the funny twists and turns in a life. The time you made one decision and not another. And how you never know how it will change things."

My mother's younger dreams are gone—as are most of mine. I thought the world would change before I had grandchildren, was certain that the political organizing, activist demonstrations, feminist psychology would begin to bridge the chasms between peoples. But the world hasn't changed and I have no grandchildren.

"Good morning, dear. I slept a little later this morning than usual. I just feel slow today so I'll stay in and catch up on my reading. You know how I enjoy being home. It doesn't bother me, not being able to go out, it really doesn't. I like to sit in the den and read. You know my friend Bev who lives downstairs. She's a real run-around. Of course she has a daughter who comes to take her. But she is always going. I'm not restless that way. I enjoy my own company. Bev is always inviting me to go places with her, but I guess I'm just cynical because I'm just not interested in all those revivals and movies with the "F" word in them. I'd rather stay home and read. Besides, my legs aren't working so well, and I don't want to have to take my walking stick. Nobody needs to see that I use one."

Today my mother had a driving accident and calls to demand my allegiance about the injustice of it.

"All those cops are crooks. I'm telling you, they all stick together and you can't do a thing."

"What do you mean, Ma?"

"First of all, he was driving a dented, rusted shitcan. I don't even know why he was so upset. It wasn't even my fault."

"Did you hit a car, Ma?"

"You couldn't even call it a hit. Like a little bump, that's all."

"Are you OK?"

"Of course I'm OK. I told you it was only a little bump. It was the cop that was so unpleasant."

"The cop? Did you hit a cop, Ma?"

"Not the cop. His car."

There is a long silence that I don't attempt to fill. She and I both know what this will mean.

"I may even sue," she finishes in a small, defeated voice.

The expected letter arrives within the week, informing her officially that her driving days are over. I am grateful that she won't eventually cause an accident, hurting either herself or someone else. I also know that this is a terrifying loss of autonomy and freedom for her. She describes wandering around the apartment and weeping all that week, emptying out the trunk of the car with the mat, the brush, the stones no longer needed. Her rainhat, gloves and Kleenex thrown in the trash.

Each day her messages are filled with frustrated proclamations.

"If I can't drive, I'm selling my house and going someplace. I just can't be without my car. Bev drives and she banged right into the garage door. Alma can't even see in front of her and she still drives, although her daughter is trying to convince her to stop. And my driving is better than both of them put together. I'm so upset I'm beside myself."

But by the end of the week she reports, "I've been doing a lot of thinking. Even though the cop is a big liar, it is true that I'm not good at backing up when there are a lot of cars around. They said I needed a note from my doctor saying he felt I could drive. Then I could come downtown and take a test. I could never pass a test and I know it. So, I'll just have to do without a car. After all, it's not the end of the world. You know, sweetheart, I've been doing a lot of soul-searching. When I evaluate myself I'm really nobody special. I know I can't do what I used to do anymore. I get up in the morning and I'm grateful I can move my legs and see through my eyes. There are so many things I can do. So I'm ready now to give up the car. And I will say it only to you, I'm almost relieved. There were two other altercations I didn't tell you about. Twice when I was at the market, cars parked too close to me, and I had to wait for the drivers to come out and drive off before I could get out of my parking space. So it's a blessing to stop worrying about all of it. I used to go out very early in the morning when everything wasn't so crowded. To hell with all of them. I don't have to run every day. I even used to make up things to do so I would have a reason to go out."

After the car is sold, she calls to tell me.

"Good morning, dear. I think I'm going to stop using that salve on my eyes because they get red and I look like I'm crying. Well, I guess maybe I am crying a little bit. It's hard to tell myself I can't drive anymore. But maybe it's a good thing in disguise. I know I shouldn't have been driving, but it's still a sad, sad day when I can't even get out of the house under my own steam. But on the other hand, yesterday I took a walk around the building and the geese started to follow me and they were talking to each other. They seemed so sweet and friendly to one another."

I encourage her to find out if there is a bus that takes seniors on errands.

"Don't call me a senior," she replies scornfully. "I am an elderly and I'm not going on that thing with the old ladies. And that's final."

"Good morning, dear. Call me when you get a minute. I want to talk something over."

It has only been a few weeks since the car has been sold, since she can no longer take a drive or get out under her own steam. I make coffee and call her.

"What, Ma?"

"You know I have a lot of time now that I am not driving. So I've been thinking things over. First of all, I don't want a pine coffin. I know that's what you picked for your brother, but I don't want it. I want a dark wood and a liner so the ants don't get to me too fast. And furthermore, I don't want anyone throwing sand on me. I'm just not ready to go. There are so many things that I'll miss. I know I'm different from other women. You don't have to tell me. I've always been different. I'm just an oddball and I can't help it. And to tell you the truth, I don't want to help it. I like myself just the way I am. Of course, I'm lonely sometimes and wish I could talk to other women the way you do. To tell my feelings and so on. But it's not my way. I'm a very private person and at this age, I'm not going to change."

Now that she has said the words, we are able to talk about plans for her funeral. There is something surreal about sitting at my desk on a sunny California morning, holding the phone to my ear, chipmunks racing across the branches outside my window, while my mother tells me how her funeral is to be conducted. She wants to have a graveside service, I am instructed. No flowery speeches, no fake rabbi who never even met the deceased, she commands. My mother will be the deceased, I remember, and lower my head to the computer screen to feel its comforting, steadying coolness.

"Whoever wants to come will just have to drive out to the cemetery and stand there while the appropriate prayers are read." Do I understand what she is telling me?

Yes, I say. I understand. I am left to imagine inhabiting a world without my mother in it, without the sound of her voice. It is unbearable, but I will have to manage to bear it. It is in the natural order of things for daughters to grieve their mothers. One day, if death remains orderly, my daughters will have to do the same.

"Good morning, dear. Here it is the first day of another year. I want to wish you a happy new year for this year and all the rest of the years whether I'm here or not. You know I'll be watching and listening from wherever I am to be sure you're all right."

Then I hear the schedule of dinners and bridge. The one who can drive determines how the outing is planned. Some of the younger ones (women in their late seventies and early eighties) still drive at night. Others are more confident in the daytime, although the dented fenders on their cars suggest the folly of such assurance.

"Good morning, dear. I went with Bev to see *Shine*, and it was so exciting with the music and everything that I had to take a Tylenol when I got home. It's about how a father ruined his son's life in the name of love. It was wonderful."

We talk about the love of parents for their children, the ambitions of mothers for their daughters more pointedly, and the conversation ends with the importance of letting children find their own way—something she learned only recently. It was not easy for my mother to accept that my hungers were not an extension of her own. They were not for success and acceptability but more akin to those of her working-class socialist father.

My mother comes to visit me to celebrate her eighty-eighth birthday. I give her my bedroom so she can lie in bed and watch her two favorites, *Jeopardy* and *MacNeil/Lehrer*. I sleep on the sofa bed in the living room, restlessly listening to her padding in and out of the bathroom every few hours. She usually awakens at five-thirty but has been instructed that she needs to lie in bed and listen to National Public Radio until seven o'clock when she can come and get me. So each morning at exactly seven she stands beside my sofa bed, teasingly making "ahem-ahem" sounds. I rise, filled with the pleasure of seeing her face, and we feast on coffee, cottage cheese, rye bread and prune juice.

I bathe my mother's body when she visits. My bathtub is small and it is difficult for her to get in and out. She sits on a chair in the tub, her body spindly, nipples unexpectedly pink, body as hairless as a child. Ten years ago I had a partner who died of breast cancer. One of the side effects of her chemotherapy was that her pudenda became hairless like my mother's is now. My mother's skin is falling off her bones and her pudenda is that of a child's. I remember the vulnerable bodies of my own babies, the years spent washing them, rocking them through fevers and bandaging open wounds and broken bones. After my mother leaves to return to her own home, I brush my teeth with her toothbrush.

Once, after a tense phone call where we disagreed about a decision my youngest daughter was making (neither of us was asked to assist her), she called back after only a few minutes. "Sandy, it's me again. I made a mistake, I think. I said you're crazy. It's not so. I'm talking about myself. Sometimes I think, Sandy, that you're my mother. Isn't that funny? I must have said the wrong thing. You're not crazy at all. You're very smart. I'm sorry."

Last week, my mother had bad dreams. Shadow figures were wandering through the rooms calling her name.

"From now on, I am going to sleep on the other side of the bed. Anyhow, I think it will be better for the mattress. Don't you think so? In addition, I want to tell you that I bought a Saul Bellow book but it was disappointing. It was only a novelli, not even a complete book. That's probably why I couldn't get into it."

Often I suggest books I imagine she will enjoy. I am always wrong. Her attention span is abbreviated now and she needs a very plot-driven book, thrillers mostly. She doesn't know the books I read now, nor do I know hers. We shift to the news, avoiding the Middle East because she identifies herself as a hawk and me as a dove. So we stick to social programs in the United States about which we agree. Agreement has always been important. It keeps us feeling close and connected to one another.

"Good morning, dear. Today I'm not going to the reservoir to try to walk around it. Yesterday I had to go slowly. But I think it's all right if I don't go so fast. I still get the exercise, don't I? I'm going to start with the weather report. I'm not going to walk today, because I heard on the radio that they advise the elderly not to go out. I think that means me. But yesterday I had palpitations."

I sink into my chair, afraid of what comes next. I'm nearly always afraid of what comes next.

"But I called the doctor and I'm fine. It's a pulled muscle or something. I'm just telling you because I don't want you to worry."

My mother is increasingly frail, and I open a tentative conversation about the possibility of her moving to an apartment where there are social services, nursing care and transportation on the grounds. But she digs in her paper-thin heels and in response sends determinedly cheerful morning messages in her attempt to reassure me and herself.

"Good morning, dear. I feel terrific this morning. I went for a walk outside the building and only had to sit on the bench twice. Gloria and Eve called to see how I was feeling, and Alma brought a kosher chicken from the good place on Harvard street. I'll make soup later. It's important that you understand that I have so many friends here who care about me. Not that you don't care about me. I don't mean that. It's just that I don't think you understand what it's like to live someplace for more than sixty years and have people know you when you go someplace. If I left here, I would be an 'also.' I would only be your mother. The phone would never ring. I just can't do it. I know you worry about me and I'm grateful. I really am. But this is my home. And I'm staying here. I'm going to go sooner or later and I want to be where I have lived my entire life."

I am increasingly frightened, not sure my mother is eating properly, having enough exercise, taking her medication regularly. Carefully I suggest this time that she move across the country to be near me, perhaps in an assisted living facility.

"I'm not going into a nursing home. You promised that you would never put me in one of those places. I'm surprised at you for even saying such a thing."

"Ma, it's not a nursing home. Things have changed. This is a place where you have your own apartment, your own kitchen, but there are additional services available to you if you need them."

"Services? What do you mean services? Like what?"

"You know, things like a van to take you to the doctor's, linen service once a week . . . "

"It sounds like some hotel for old people. I don't want to be with old people."

"Ma, you are an old person."

"I don't care. I'm not going to a place like that. I'm staying in my own place where I belong."

"Ma, God forbid, if you fall, the rest of your life will be terrible."

"I won't fall. I promise you. I walk very carefully and I use the walking stick, even in the apartment when I'm wobbly. You'll see. Everything will be fine."

I hear my tone of voice, anxious and parental, and hers, that of a placating child. Yet nothing has really changed. I am the sixty-year-old child, she is the eighty-eight-year-old mother, the one who must decide about her own life. At least as long as she can. It's almost a shift in roles, but not quite. We have made the legal agreement that if there is an emergency, I have both medical and legal power of attorney. But I don't want it to be that way. I want us to talk it over and for her to agree that she will either move into assisted living where she is or move to a facility near me. But I don't think that will ever happen, and I am left three thousand miles away to reach for the phone when I awaken, relieved again to hear the robotic electronic voice say, "You have one new message. To retrieve, please press the pound key."

Then I can relax, knowing I still have my mother for another day.

The Minyan Connection

SHEILA GOLBURGH JOHNSON

"That's why she died."

"Daddy . . . "

"I never should have sold the house. She never felt well after that."

"For years she complained the house was too much for her. Thank God you sold the house."

"I never should have let her go into the hospital. 'Once you go in, you never come out.' That's what the old folks say."

"She was deathly ill. The wonder is that she lived a normal life so long. Ruth Sternlieb said Mother was playing bridge at her house just two days before she went in. And who are the old folks?"

"I still say I shouldn't have sold the house. She never got used to the new place."

"Maybe you're right. But you did what you could at the time. The apartment is smaller, it was easier for her to get around. Now you'll have it for yourself. It will be easy for you, too."

"Easy I don't need. I need your mother."

Daddy and I strolled through the streets of Boston day after day beneath the full August foliage of a New England summer, trying to walk away our grief. My mother had died of cancer only two weeks before.

"How did she go so fast?" my father asked. "Why didn't they try to save her?"

"Daddy, she was very fragile. Treatment would have been worse than the illness. She had a good, long life. A healthy life. We have to be thankful for that."

"Thankful I don't have to be."

Our rabbi had visited while we spent seven days "sitting shiva," a period of intense mourning when we simply let ourselves be comforted by visitors. At first I didn't recognize Rabbi Broderman, whom I hadn't seen for many years. As I watched him place a sandwich between pink lips that glistened between the wiry hairs covering his cheeks, I shuddered.

I was a girl again, studying for my bat mitzvah with a much younger Rabbi Broderman. I was dressed in my favorite short, pleated skirt and knee socks, chilly, as a cold December dusk crept into his office. I looked up from the siddur.

"It's too dark, I can't read."

"Come, darling, come sit on my lap for a moment," he coaxed, holding out his arms. He was clean-shaven then, and I remember he wore a satin yarmulke clipped to his hair with a bobby pin.

I crossed the room and climbed onto his lap, hoping for a bear hug like one my father would have given. He put one arm around my shoulders and the other around my legs, patting one bare thigh. I welcomed the heat of his body and was comforted for a moment. He slid his hand up under my skirt and started to stroke the cotton crotch of my panties. The sensitive flesh beneath started to tingle.

Daddy coughed suddenly, a piece of sandwich caught in his throat. His face was contorted with grief, his eyes hidden in puffy flesh. He is going to need a lot of care, I thought.

I left my father in Boston. He didn't want to move, and I wasn't sure he should. My mother and father were born in Boston and had spent their lives in the suburbs with friends they had known since childhood. I was one of the loose nuts that slid to California when someone tipped the continent. That's what my friends always said about Californians, and it's true everyone seems to be a little crazy, but we don't arrive this way. It's the desert, that great empty bowl behind the string of coastal mountains that creates an interior landscape, a schism. At certain times of year, hot desert winds blow down the passes with a ferocity that takes our breath away, and we know that at any moment California might explode in flames. We live on more than one edge.

I moved to California with Carl and our children when we were a young family. We had reasons to come, we thought. Thirty years later, I know there was another reason we came, one we never talked about; I wanted to get as far from our families as possible. I had grown up in a suburban Jewish ghetto surrounded by an army of relatives, each trying to be more pious than the next. I can't remember my mother and father ever inviting to our home a guest who wasn't Jewish. Outside of the family, our lives revolved around Temple Beth Zion on Beacon Street in Boston. My mother was active in the Temple Sisterhood, and I studied with Rabbi Broderman. Daddy went to brotherhood breakfasts every Sunday. When I left home for college, I felt like Miranda in *The Tempest*, who lives on an island with only her father and various creatures of the spirit world. When other mortals arrive on the island, she is astonished and delighted with the beauty and variety of the real world.

A year after my mother died, my father decided he wanted to come to California. He had never cooked for himself and ate a bagel and coffee for every meal. I had visions of him collapsing from malnourishment. He had fallen on the subway platform one afternoon, and when Daddy fell he couldn't get up by himself. He lay there while the afternoon rush surged around him, until finally one man helped him up and brushed him off. I found a place for him in Friendship Manor, an apartment complex for the elderly that had once been a dormitory for the University of California a few blocks away. It was an easy twelve miles from my home in Santa Barbara.

For a year or so, Daddy and I kept busy setting up his rooms and shopping. He had eye tests and ordered new eyeglasses; I found a good internist and he had a checkup. We went out to eat, we went to movies, we walked. His balance wasn't good enough to walk on the beach, but we strolled along the boardwalk and spoke of my mother. It was some comfort to both of us. I signed him up with Jewish Family Services and he attended parties and meetings for senior citizens. Sometimes I went to these parties with him and felt like a visitor from another planet.

I took him to the businesses I used, where he chatted with the tellers, the postal clerks, the cleaner and the cobbler. He inquired about their families and asked how they liked their jobs. He admired pretty women out loud, and they were not offended; they were charmed. I had been doing business with these people for twenty years, an anonymous face in their crowded days, but now I had status. I was known around town as "Mathew Golburgh's daughter."

Once, when a waitress told him how dapper he looked in his bow tie, he stood up and kissed her. I cringed, expecting a lecture on sexual harassment.

"You're an old sweetie," she said, and hugged him.

We were in Starbuck's one day and I was about to hand over six dollars for our two lattes. He turned to the man at the next table. "So much money! I come from Boston, you know, a wonderful city. You can still get a cup of coffee there for a nickel."

"Oh, Daddy, I don't think so. Maybe fifty years ago . . . "

"I'm sure it's still a nickel," the man interrupted, nodding at Daddy. Why didn't anyone ever argue with him except me?

One day he found a dead mouse in his wastebasket. He insisted it had walked in the door when he was entering or leaving the apartment. For weeks after, every time I arrived to pick him up, he would open the door a crack. "Take that! And that!" he scolded the imaginary mice, thrashing around the entrance with his cane. I knew it was absurd, but I couldn't help falling into the game and stamped at the mice myself once in a while.

Daddy made friends of his own at Friendship Manor, but I had a lot to learn about growing old. As the years passed, his new friends, most of whom were younger than he, died. Each loss was a reminder of my mother's death, and he became depressed and lonely. I put more energy into my writing, and I had less time to spend with him. He would call me at home the moment I arrived after I had spent the day with him.

"Sheila, you should come see me more often."

I let the answering machine take these calls sometimes, and later in the evening I would wallow in remorse. I promised myself to be more patient.

One year my work won a fellowship at a writer's colony on Whidbey Island, a tranquil, wooded place off the coast of Washington. The fellowship offered a cottage in the woods for three months, a perfect place to finish a manuscript without interruptions. I went.

My husband and daughter visited Daddy and took him out, but whenever I called him from the island a thousand miles away he reminded me, "You don't come visit often enough." My father was ninety-one years old, in such excellent health he took no medication. His heart and lungs were strong, his blood pressure low. I knew we would have more good years together, but I dreamed of him now, and in these dreams something horrible was always happening: He was caught in a vortex or his arm was resting on a tree limb that was being severed by a chain saw. I started to scream to warn him, but I always woke up with the sound in my mind.

When I came home, I saw him more often. We celebrated the Jewish holidays at Temple B'nai B'rith, where I didn't know anyone, and we had merry family gatherings. On his ninety-third birthday one of my cousins sent a box of party hats and whistles. We took them to a restaurant, sang, got a bit tipsy and sent the other guests into gusts of laughter. The entire room joined our "Happy Birthday" chorus.

Daddy became more and more dependent. When I was with him he would no longer talk to people, but insisted I do all the talking. He could no longer take walks around Friendship Manor alone; even with the cane he didn't like, his balance was so poor he stumbled. When we did errands together, I held on to him, and I often had to jerk back in a lunatic dance to keep him from the pavement when he fell forward. It was a struggle to help him in and out of the car. Once, when I was rolling up his window I didn't notice his fingers were still on it. He yelled. I reversed the window and grabbed the poor hand. A deep red line crossed his fingers where they had been jammed.

"Move it! Move it!" I shouted. "Is it broken?"

He wiggled his fingers for a moment, then burst out laughing.

"You make such a fuss about nothing," he said. "Look, the pink is already fading."

I almost cried. What if I had injured my father's hand? At the same time, I felt like slapping him.

We bumbled along together, Daddy and I.

One Sunday at my house, he told me a young man from University Hillel had come to his apartment to ask if he would like to attend the Saturday morning minyan when they held Shabbat services. It was two blocks from Friendship Manor at the University Religious Center.

"And . . . ?"

"And I went."

"How did you get there?"

"This guy, I think his name is Zev, walked me there. I met his wife and little girl. They're expecting another baby in a month."

"Did you enjoy it?"

"Oh yes. I met the rabbi and the rebbetzen, they're wonderful. You should see their little girl, Rachel, she's so smart! She knows more than I do. And their little boy isn't even talking yet."

"That's great. Maybe you'll go again."

Daddy went again, and again, every Shabbat for over two years. It was a new life, a new set of young friends and their children without me to interpret or speak for him. Sundays, which he had spent at my house for years, were now livelier. I no longer had to grope for conversation; he was full of stories about his friends and their families.

Zev told me he's worried. His wife's been due for two weeks now and nothing has happened.

Marion, the rabbi's wife, came to pick me up on Shabbat. I told her it was an honor. 'The honor is all mine,' she said. Isn't that something?

You should come with me and hear Judy sing, she's the cantor. She sings like an angel. You'd enjoy it.

We have a doctor in the minyan, a woman doctor. Isn't that amazing? I never knew a woman doctor before. Women can do anything these days.

Zev's wife had the baby. Another girl! She brought her to the minyan today and you should see her—she's the cutest little thing! Why don't you come to see the baby?

I never went. I was so pleased that Daddy had found something—the only thing—that he could do without me, I thought I would let it be his special Saturday morning adventure. Or was that an excuse?

My parents had ensured I had a good Jewish education when I was young, but it takes more than education. I struggled for years to believe in God, but I could never make the leap of faith. Perhaps it was Rabbi Broderman who undermined the faith I knew my parents had in him. I could never believe in him, although I was so young I hardly understood what he did to me. Yes, he had put his hand between my legs, but it was the 1950s, after all. The only talk my mother ever had with me about protecting myself was the admonition not to let strangers touch me "down there," with a vague gesture. He was hardly a stranger, and it is not easy for an innocent to recognize evil. And yet . . . I think I was uncomfortable with him before that. I had trouble learning from him. I did well with my Hebrew school teacher whose classes I attended four days a week after school, but when it came time to study my portion with the rabbi, I could never remember it. I even stumbled at my bat mitzvah, a humiliation that haunted me for years.

Daddy's rabbi at the minyan, Steve Cohen, called me one afternoon. "We have a doctor who comes to Shabbat services every week," he said. "She doesn't like the way Mathew looks. His skin is yellow. I don't mean to interfere, but we thought you'd want to know."

"Daddy has an appointment for a checkup in a week," I said. "Do you think I should insist his doctor see him earlier?"

"I don't know. Shall I have our doctor call you?"

Every person has a certain measure of time to live out a life, even my beloved father. It turned out to be pancreatic cancer, which took him in a mercifully short time. He was in the hospital only two full days before he died. The morning after I checked him in, I was dressing with heavy limbs to go to the hospital. The phone rang and it was Daddy's friend, Zev, already at his bedside. When I got to my father's room, I was not alone. Zev was holding Daddy's hand and talking to him about the new baby. Drugged for pain, Daddy was barely conscious, but I knew he heard us. Zev and I stood for hours on either side of the bed and chatted over my father, rubbing his hands, stroking his head, pausing to address him directly from time to time.

"Everyone turned to Mathew when they needed a word of encouragement," Zev said. "When I was worried about Edna having the new baby, I told him. He said there was nothing to worry about and everything would be fine. It's silly, but I felt a whole lot better."

I reached for Zev's hand. "I know you, and I know your wife and lovely baby. I know your older daughter, too. Daddy has been telling me about you and the children and everyone else in the minyan for years. It was a very special part of his life."

"Don't forget he gave us a lot. He was our patriarch."

Rabbi Steve Cohen called, and I met with him. He was younger than I had expected; my image of a rabbi had been formed by the huge, heavyset Rabbi Broderman with his humid hands. Steve has the face of a Chagall angel. He asked me a few questions about my father's life in Boston, but I somehow got off the track. I started to explain, with an overwhelming sense of guilt, why I had never attended the minyan with Daddy. I ended this performance by bursting into tears when I finally heard what I was saying. I was talking about how lonely I had always been in California and about all the rich tradition I had missed sharing with Daddy by making up endless excuses, and it was too late now. Steve assumed I was crying for the loss of my father. I also cried for myself and the child I was who was able to recognize a hypocrite but didn't even have a word for it yet. Steve simply let me cry, gazing at me sympathetically with dark eyes. I was grateful he didn't speak, and I never told him of my ugly experience with a rabbi. It was enough that I could finally cry for that little girl.

Together, Steve and I planned a memorial gathering, and the next Saturday after Shabbat services the University Religious Center was crowded with friends. My son flew in from college, my husband and daughter and even my first husband came, and everyone, even the small children of the minyan, told stories of the wonderful things my father had said and done. Judy, the cantor my father had loved, sang a traditional song a cappella, her pure soprano rising and falling over the mourners like balm. Finally, we stood and chanted the Kaddish, the ancient Hebrew prayer for the dead. For a few moments I was not a middle-aged orphan, naked and helpless without a parent to protect me. I was a young girl standing between my mother and father in synagogue, praised for chanting the Kaddish before I even knew what death was.

The peace of that Shabbat memorial service did not stay with me. My father had wanted his remains buried in the Mishkin T'filla Jewish cemetery in Boston, beside my mother. Would the rabbi at Mishkin T'filla allow me to bury ashes in our family plot? Cremation is against Jewish law, but it was all I could manage at the time. I would have to wait for a meeting of the board to find out. I had to make arrangements with Stanetzky's Funeral Parlor, and then call all my relatives in Boston to find a rabbi who would perform a traditional burial service for ashes. I plodded on through the maze of red tape, consulting Steve from time to time. Finally, six months after my father's death, his remains were buried next to my mother's, during one of the worst rainstorms in Massachusetts history. I dropped my torn umbrella and let the torrent strike me as I bent to dig the first shovelful for Daddy's casket, grateful for the screaming wind that muffled the sound of mud when it hit bottom.

Since Daddy's death, I had attended the minyan every week to chant the Kaddish for him. The Kaddish doesn't mention death; it is a doxology, a chant of praise that signifies the mourners' faith in God even in the face of death. The Hebrew words have a meaning of their own even if the mourner doesn't understand them: *Yitgadel v'yitkadash shmei raba.* . . . The sounds, cadence and the flames of Hebrew letters on the page carry the meaning. Comfort comes from the syllables that reverberate in the collective Jewish memory and forward through the ages.

When I returned from my father's funeral in Boston, I continued to attend the minyan and chant the Kaddish for the remaining six months required. When I stood for the last time and chanted as a mourner, members of the congregation again spoke of my father, of his goodness and piety, of how he loved the children. In that year, I had somehow become a member of the minyan. Daddy's friends were my friends; I prayed before his altar.

Another year has passed. I continue to pray and study Torah with the minyan on Shabbat, to break bread with them after the service, and celebrate life with them on occasion. It would be good if I could write that I found faith. I found something else: a kind of peace, and a solace for loneliness. I take comfort from what Rabbi Steve said when two of our members fell to quarreling.

"You don't have to argue whether man or God wrote the Torah. It doesn't matter."

A Bridge of Sparrows

MAIJA RHEE DEVINE

$\mathcal{A}$ small bowl sits in my cupboard. It succeeds in catching my eye as I try to avoid it. I could have gotten rid of this last reminder of Mother after her funeral three years ago. But I keep it and let it perch where I must look at it several times a day. Each time, recalling one particular dead-winter day Mother filled it with honey, I torment myself.

The size of a coaster, the chinaware sits about half an inch high. The blue faraway mountain range on the inside has faded, making the peaks look as though they are floating. In the foreground, a stream swirls around rocks. A willow branch droops from the rim. Unlike the vivid memory the bowl evokes, the gold on the lip has been rubbed off over time. Mother, from Korea, loved using the china she brought to America. Small, low bowls like this were used for dipping sauces of soy and red bean paste, and side dishes such as fried beans or *maeruchi*, salt-water minnows.

The day I most clearly remember Mother using the bowl, she didn't have sauce or *maeruchi* but honey in it. She stooped over the

101

kitchen counter and mumbled in Korean to the bowl, "This honey, I put it on my gums all night, and it took away some of the pain." She opened her mouth and ran her finger over the ache, fixing her gaze out the window. This was how she talked to me. She muttered to a bowl, to the air, to the refrigerator, to the sky, to the yard. Always away from me. I had trained her to do it. I had told her never to mention pain to me, which meant I robbed her of nearly all conversation.

"If you need to see a doctor, tell me and I will take you there," I told her in Korean, "but please don't tell me about your daily aches! How your head hurts, how your stomach bloats, how your back snaps, how your teeth throb, how your joints groan, how your nerves jitter, how your toes swell and how little you slept! I've heard all about these every day ever since I was five, ever since Father's mistress came. I can't stand it anymore. I can't deal with it anymore. I can't. . . . " She had looked at me, stunned. That was twenty years before she died, and the last time she made eye contact with me.

I said this knowing that she lived with my family in the United States, fifteen thousand miles away from her family and friends in this foreign country where she knew so few other Koreans. I said this knowing that she longed to phone her sister in Korea at least once a month, maybe even every other month, but she didn't, because I let her know that I couldn't afford international calls more than perhaps once or twice a year. I said this knowing that my American husband, our children and I spoke English to one another, and Mother might as well have been deaf and dumb. Despite myself, I sometimes wondered what it felt like to have words hail on her and understand nothing. Yet my Korean to her was terse. "Get ready to go to the doctor." "Here's your medicine." "Have you seen Brian's shoes?" "I'm going to work. I'll be back by three." I spat them at the wall, at the kitchen table, at the sink.

So she communicated her pain nonverbally. When she was sure that I was watching, she limped, placed a hand on her temple and squeezed her eyes shut and dropped the corners of her mouth. I combated her gestures with a fierce frown or a determined show of nonchalance.

But the more I steeled myself against her manipulation, the more clearly I heard in my head the words she imprisoned in her mouth.

This morning, as usual, I see out of the corner of my eye the bowl when I open the cupboard to reach for a tea mug.

"How come we haven't gone to Grandma's grave for so long? We haven't done it for three years, Mom. Not even on her birthday," Lisa said a few days ago when she came across a photo of Mother and me in the hallway drawer while looking for her own school pictures. Taking after her tall Caucasian dad, at fifteen she's five foot seven, but she has my large brown Korean eyes. Mother was forty-nine in that picture, younger than I am now. I was a college student at the time. In the photo, she had managed to let her disappointments in life and love recede into a dark place behind her half-smiling eyes.

It was already the end of September. Winter could set in any time. I craned my neck and saw out the window the gauze of first frost on the lawn.

"We missed March thirteenth, the anniversary of her death, Mom." I remained silent.

"You talked about going there when Grandma's favorite begonias bloomed, but look at them. The frost got them all brown and yucky. Are we going to go this year?"

I fidgeted with my cup, tilted it and looked inside as if I were looking for a clue.

"Mom?"

"Yeah?"

"Did you hear what I said?"

"Uh huh. We should have gone. Let's do it on a sunny day with no wind." I said this knowing that in Wyoming waiting for a windless day could take a while. Lisa found her photo, waved goodbye and walked out the door.

The most emotional of our five children, she was Mother's pal from the time she was a toddler. Afraid of Lisa catching Mother's frequent colds, I forbade Mother to kiss her on the mouth. But more than once I saw my girl bouncing into Mother's lap like a rainbow-colored beach ball and giving her a jelly-smeared kiss on the lips.

While brewing garden sage tea, I think of my relationship with our children, three boys and two girls, ages thirteen through twenty-three. I'm glad that I found out several years ago that, contrary to what some American women seemed to think, teenagers still like being hugged and kissed daily, sometimes even in public. So I kiss them every day, although I slowed down on it for a while, thinking they'd be embarrassed. Every kiss represents an act of desperation on my part: that my relationship with Mother not affect me and my children.

As I strain the tea into my mug, I think of what Lisa said one day not long after Mother died. "So many of my friends' parents are stupid, you know," Lisa blurted while turning lettuce over to coat it evenly with dressing during our lunch.

"What do you mean, 'stupid'?"

"You know, they won't let their kids do anything or go anywhere. They ground them for every little thing. I think you guys are doing the parenting thing just right. Not too strict, not too lenient."

Thank God.

I plunk down my tea on the kitchen table instead of on my writing desk. It is one of those mornings when writing is going to be particularly hard to begin. Thoughts of Mother whirl in my head. I think for the millionth time, *Poor Mother*. I think I even understand her pain. If I lost my husband to a mistress because I couldn't produce a boy and had to live with them in the same house, I would have thrown myself into a well or taken a gulp of lye soap. If I had no nerve to do that and had to drag myself through life, hearing through thin rice-papered doors the groans of my husband as he made love to his mistress, I'd feel pain in every cell of my body every day, too. I remember, as a five-year-old, hearing Father's snores booming from the mistress's room a few feet beyond the rice-papered window of Mother's bedroom where she and I slept. I had no capacity then to fathom how Mother must have felt as a woman. But as a wife myself, I've attained that ability.

When I placed myself inside her skin and imagined my husband's snores rattling from the next room with his mistress tucked in his arms, I felt faint. So I should have understood Mother's pain and tried to ease it, but I didn't, couldn't. Perhaps Koreans are right about a *sahl*, death of a relationship, between people of certain astrological signs. Mother was a snake; I'm a lamb. That made me a lamb bitten by a viper. The lamb needed to rid itself of the poison, but didn't know how.

I think I even understand Mother's liaison with Lee—if my suspicion has been correct. Had I been in her shoes, I probably would have taken a dozen lovers. Lee. Father's best friend's eighteen-year-old son. Son-hungry, Mother called him *ahdeul*, son. I called him *oppah*, older brother. A brother from heaven in a navy uniform—the whitest white borders on dark blue sailor collars, the whitest white hat cocked just so over shiny black brows, the whitest white teeth grinning at me, me. A peach seed forms in the middle of my chest when I think of him. Even now, as I stir my tea. She was a lonely, deserted thirty-four-year-old wife. But my empathy for Mother is all in my brain. How do I get it to travel down to my heart? A black night sky stretches between my head and my heart.

I sip my tea. A Korean calendar that came from my relatives in Seoul hangs on the kitchen wall across from me. It shows lovers from a fable—Geon-woo, a cow herder, and Jeek-nyo, a beautiful weaver maiden. I remember the story from my childhood. Long ago, Geon-woo left his cows unattended in a remote mountain valley, because he fell in love with Jeek-nyo and followed her. Wroth, the God of Heaven, banished them to the opposite sides of the Milky Way. When they wept and begged for mercy, the God of Heaven granted them the privilege of meeting once a year on July seventh. That day, the God of Heaven gathered hundreds of sparrows and bade them to form a bridge by locking wings. The lovers walked on the birds' heads and fell into each other's arms. At night, they parted, shedding many tears. That's why it always rains on the seventh of July, and why sparrows briefly show bald spots.

I need such a bridge, so that I may walk across from my head to my heart—a distance that seems as far as the length of the Milky Way.

I saw Mother last night in a dream. I was going upstairs to bed. She appeared at the top of the stairs. Her hair was straight and long, down to her hips. Standing there facing me, she opened her mouth wide and yellow fluid gushed out. It ran down the steps and into the living room. I shrieked, "Oh my God," and with a dishrag began mopping up the mess, which spread like a river.

Before the second frost, I must go see Mother. The tea no longer warms my fingers wrapped around the mug.

One winter night before we moved from Illinois to Wyoming, when Lisa was still in grade school, Mother used the honey on her gums from the blue bowl after she took the medicine, two Tylenols that my husband Michael gave her. Banned from mentioning pain to me, she developed the habit of going to him, not for medicine—she knew where it was—but for what I was not willing to give her.

"Yogi, aahyaahyaah, here, it hurts," she'd say to him, looking up at his white American face, curly hair and blue eyes. She pointed to the joints in her shoulders, arms, legs.

"Oh, I'm sorry about your aahyaahyaah," he said to her. A sensitive man with Peace Corps training in Korea, he walked over to the medicine cabinet, took Tylenols and offered them to her with a glass of water, his voice softly falling on her wrinkled eyelids and tightened mouth.

Mother's pains began when I was five with the arrival of Father's mistress. She came, adults said, to bear Father a baby boy, a baby with a kochu, a pepper, or penis. Such an offspring was needed to carry on his family name and support him in old age. Mother had only me, a girl, who, grownups said, was not good for anything. "She eats the food a boy should be eating," they said. "She uses up fabric that should be hand sewn for a boy. She drains the good luck that gods reserve for boys."

That night after Father and his mistress went to sleep in the mistress's room a few feet away from where Mother and I slept, Mother fell ill. She made chattering noises with her teeth. Her body shook against mine. My cry woke Father. He rushed in and turned the lights on. He put his ear on her heart, then massaged her arms and legs, and kept whimpering and muttering, "Come on, come on. Breathe, please." After a while, he listened to her heart again. He then let out a relaxed sigh, but continued to massage her arms. The mistress stood at the doorway, her hands tightly clasped over her chest.

The next day, the herbal doctor came and held Mother's wrist, placing his right ear on her chest, prying her eyes open and poking her head all over, like someone trying to find lice.

"She's in shock," he said to Father. "Brew this all day over a low fire and feed it to her six times a day. I'll be back in three days." Mother lay in her cotton-filled *yo* on the floor. Her skin looked yellowish and her lips were the same color as her face. Except for the moans that gurgled out of her throat and nose, she looked like what I imagined a dead person to be.

Relatives, friends and neighbors streamed into our house. They whispered every time they came, "If only Maija had been a boy, her mother would not be dying like this." On one of those days, I heard Soon-ja, my best friend at the end of our block, shout for me from beyond our stone-studded wall. "Maija, Maaaiiijjjaaa! Come out and play!" I didn't move. I sat in a corner of the room where Mother let out "Uuuhhh uuuhhh" every few minutes.

"Maija! Come play *kong-ki!*" That was Chol-soo's voice from across the street. He was my favorite partner at the five-pebble tossing game. But I kept sitting in the dark room breathing in the bitter smell of herbal medicine and thinking of the penis with which I should have

Maija Rhee Devine   107

been born. Mother's illness went on for a year. She eventually rose from her "deathbed," but every so often she collapsed and remained bedridden for a few days at a time, even throughout my teenage years. Every time that happened, although no one was there to say I was the root of her ailments—and Mother never said it—I knew my being a girl caused Father to be taken away from her. I lay next to her and imagined the parts of me that made me a girl turning into snowflakes and melting. I tossed words: Someday I will live where I won't hear of Mother's aches.

It's dinner time. Three days have gone by since Lisa asked me to go to Mother's grave. Our children bombard me with questions. "Mom, did you see my school supply list? I need to see it again!" "Where is the hole puncher?" "Scissors?" "Mom! Brian's not helping set the table!" "Mom, I set it all by myself last night when Lisa wasn't home!" I have all four burners going. Corn on the cob boiling. Taco meat simmering. A grilled cheese for Brian—he won't eat tacos—must be watched closely. A vegetable beef soup on another burner. "Mom, phone." I tuck the receiver between my left shoulder and neck, and talk while chopping lettuce, onion and black olives. I need something to put the olives in. Without looking, I reach for a bowl. I dump the olives in it: It's Mother's bowl with the faded blue mountain peaks. I consider emptying it and using another container, but the silliness of doing so turns in my belly like a small marble. OK, I'll use it this time. All through dinner, the bowl bothers me. I think again of the frowns and decades-long silent treatment I gave Mother and the perpetual bad mood I struggled to peel off so that I could flash happy smiles to my children.

I was nine. Father's mistress had been living with us for four years. Lee began to visit. When we went for walks, his buttocks motored up and down under his tightly stretched Navy pants to the *tap tap tap* of his shiny black shoes. When he stayed overnight, he slept in Mother's and my room. In the morning Mother always got up first, rolled her *yo* up off the floor, pushed me into his bedding, gathered my *yo* too and stacked them on top of the mother-of-pearl lacquerware chest by the wall. "Here, sleepy heads, sleep some more," she said. Then I would hear the wooden cutting board from the kitchen. *Ttok, ttak, ttok, ttak.* The sunlight filtered through the rice-papered window and played on his sculpted lips breathing on my eyes. His breath smelled of dry hay with a hint of shaving lotion. His thighs butted against mine.

One night after I fell asleep between Lee and Mother on our separate *yos* and *eebles*, comforters, I had a nightmare.

In it, a mountain is high; I can't see the sky. Large, round rocks pile up on top of one another. One minute, they look soft like pillows. Next, a rock moves, and the whole pyramid rumbles down on me. I awake in terror. I rush into Mother's bedding on my right. I touch her. Her arms, waist and back all feel slippery like a fish, except her skin is hot and sweat runs down. Her body jerks, and my fingertips touch a leg—did I feel hair on it?—sliding off hers as she moves her hips and buttocks in a way that seems strange to me. Mother's naked arm pushes me out of her bed.

Back on my own mat, I play dead. Slowly, I stretch my left arm and grope over to Lee's *yo*. He isn't there. *I am having a bad dream,* I think to myself. *This must be a part of the nightmare I woke from.* In a few minutes, Mother proves it otherwise.

"You uncaring child. You slept right through all my moaning and pain. Your brother helped me while you slept away," she says.

Lee is mother's son. Lee is my brother. We are a family.

Her pain. She says Lee is with her to help her with it. Where is she hurting?

After that I never touched her again. Nodding or shaking my head became my standard mode of communication with her. I began calling her *omai,* instead of *ommah,* mommy. *Omai* is a dialect word that resembles *ohmuhni,* mother, from as far south as Korea stretches. *Omai* was a samurai sword I held out to her: *Yes, I am an uncaring child. Don't come near me. The moment I touched your slippery body, I stepped out of love, as out of a hopscotch square. I looked back to hop in, but it disappeared.*

"My daughter-in-law is a saint," Grandmother said of Mother, because Mother taught the mistress how to cook.

"What a magnanimous person she is. She has the heart of Buddha," my neighbors said of Mother. Father looked at Mother adoringly and gratefully. "What a wonderful wife, self-sacrificing and as chaste as snow," he bragged to Mr. Han, our closest neighbor.

Mother's face showed one of the rare moments of happiness. It said, "Yes, I am good. My heart is big. I am pure and saintly."

No soul suspected. I kept my secret, telling myself it was only a suspicion. I dared not do anything else, lest people spit at Mother. They'd say to her, where was your *changdo,* the loyalty knife? I knew about *changdos*—the knives that originated from three thousand maidens of Pakche Kingdom. We children read about them in our grade school textbooks. Maidens stabbed themselves with their *changdos* to keep their bodies pure rather than risk being caught and made dirty by invading foreign soldiers. People say we women carry our *changdos,* because faithfulness is our life; we save our womanhood, we save our purity for one husband, dead or alive, even if his penis rots with diseases from womanizing. They'd say to Mother, *You slut.* They'd say to me, *You slut's daughter.* And I said, *Yes, what I saw and touched was my imagination.* Every day I resisted the itch to share the secret with my best friend. I curled up into a ball on my mattress and wondered why it had to be with Lee. My *oppah.* The picture of her and him moving under one cover filled me from the top of my head to the bottom of my feet with yellow fluid. I walked and the liquid swished. I lay down, and it adjusted its form to fit my shape.

"Why do I have to come home by eleven? Why not midnight?" Lisa asks me. It's Saturday night. A week has passed since I told her I'd visit Mother's grave.

"Because you are fifteen and that's the time you need to be home. On weekdays, it's nine-thirty."

"Why should I be home by eleven? It's not like I'm going to hang out with you and Dad."

"What do you mean, 'hang out'? At eleven or midnight, we go to sleep."

"Well, we never hang out other times either. My friends hang out with their moms all the time. There's nothing wrong with our family, but we're not close."

"Not close?"

"Yes, like Codi. She loves to play tennis with her mom. She loves to watch movies with her. That's like her favorite thing to do. Her mom's like her best friend. We are not that close. We just haven't been brought up that way."

Not brought up that way? I kiss her at least once a day. What about what she herself told me about our doing the parenting thing "just right"? What about the ceramic pottery we've done together? Every Christmas, our tree gets loaded with homemade ornaments accumulated over two decades: ceramic bells with each child's name handwritten across the middle, clay angels, clowns, lion's faces, all signed and dated on the back by each of us. What about the times we pressed Play-Doh through a strainer to make hair strands for angels? What about all those sprays of water that hid their faces as they squinted and struggled to hold on to ski ropes behind our speedboat?

I float among images: My leaving the kitchen when Mother enters it. Moving out of the living room when she comes into it. Never sitting down to eat meals with her unless other family members are also there. Only doing my obligation as an only child to support her.

Seventeen years of duty. Now Lisa's words seem to show that what the children didn't understand was still felt every day. Suddenly, I feel as though I've lost all my children. My kisses and hugs aren't enough.

Pink begonias bloom into my memory. We were living in Ohio and had just had our third child. I was on a maternity leave. Mother, two of my children and I shopped at Gold Circle, where I bought a dozen begonia bedding plants. Mother assigned herself the duty of planting them in our yard and was struggling to pull them apart. She finally asked me, "How do you separate them?" I snatched the clay pot from her, tore the roots loose and threw them at her feet, screaming, "There! Don't you know anything?" She looked up at me with her usual silent hurt. I turned around and stepped into the kitchen. Just then Chris, then three years old, ran into me, wrapped his arms around my legs and buried his face between my knees, half giggling and half crying about his brother chasing after him. I instantly transformed the frown I wore toward Mother into smiles, kisses and hugs. Did our children notice the difference between the two faces of me? No, they were too young, I comforted myself. After I put the children down for an afternoon nap, I charged out to the yard where Mother still knelt.

"I need to talk to you. Do you know why I hate you? Why I've hated you for twenty years? Why the sight of your face disgusts me? Do you?" I formed my fingers into claws and thrust them toward her.

Mother scrambled to her feet and stood, her back hunched.

"I've been hating you since I was nine. Since that night when I woke up and went into your bed, and, and . . . " I slowed down to catch my breath. It didn't even occur to me then that it was a good thing I was screaming in Korean and our neighbors wouldn't understand my words. "You slept with Lee. I touched you. You had no clothes. Do you remember that? At all? Do you?"

Mother tilted her head as if doing so would help her understand me. Her eyes, which used to be large for a Korean, had become thin slits pressed by drooping eyelids.

I looked down on the concrete step, astonished at how I had flown over the wall of the secret-packed heart I couldn't jump over for three decades. *I'm cracking up*, I kept thinking. Now my suspicion would become either a truth or a lie. All those years I could have confronted her but didn't, because as long as I didn't hear what I was afraid to hear confirmed straight from her mouth, there existed even a millet-grain chance of her innocence. I still wanted my suspicion to be a mistake, a child's silly nightmare.

I looked at Mother's face.

Her words fell on me. "I can't believe something like *that* has caused this much hate all these years."

I crouched on a step, searching for an interpretation. Was she saying she did? She didn't? Or, was she saying that as an adult I shouldn't care, should understand?

I lowered my face onto folded arms and rocked my body until I felt a hand squeeze my shoulder. Michael's voice.

"Do you want to come in and lie down a while?" Then to Mother, "*Halmoni, duro gasaeyo*, Grandma, please go inside."

I ran away without asking Mother to clarify what she meant. Like a snail afraid to keep its head out long for fear of it being snapped off by its predators, I shrank back into the security of not knowing the truth about Lee and Mother—into a trap where no true resolution could occur.

That night in bed, Michael said what he had expressed before. "I know that terrible things happened to you in your childhood. I think I understand how horrible beyond words you must have felt, but that was years and years ago. People who experience traumas do overcome them in time. Isn't it about time you began to put these things behind? Couldn't you at least try to be civil to your mother?"

"You don't understand. And I don't expect you to. How could you? The worst thing that ever happened to you were skinned shins from sliding into third base. I do want to be civil to Mother. I do! I do! But I can't!"

I pulled away from him. I mentally beat my chest; it responded with as much feeling as that of an iceberg. He sighed and held me, his thighs against mine. A memory of the warmth of Lee's thighs awakened a sensation down my legs. I began my nightly prayer to Buddha. *Have mercy on me. Forgive my sins, my cruelty to Mother and my inability to face truth and begin to love and respect her again. Send me sparrows of the heart, so that they can build a bridge between what I want to do and what I am not able to do.*

Lisa and I stand in Greenlawn Cemetery, two weeks after our conversation about visiting Mother's grave. The pine tree at the head of the plot has grown a foot since I saw it last, a few days after the funeral when the tombstone was set. The Indian summer sun feels warm on my face. As I sit at the foot of the grave, the wheat-colored grass pokes my bare ankles. "Vandals steal flowers. Some flowers get blown away," the cemetery keeper told me the day I chose Mother's plot. So, I sealed pink plastic begonias with duct tape into the stoneware vases, one on each side of the headstone. The color of the flowers has faded to bone. The name engraved on the headstone is Korean. *Pak Kap-soon.* The handwriting, transposed to stone, is mine. It was my one gift to her: her name in her own language on a piece of Wyoming granite.

Lisa takes the old flowers out and places the new ones she brought. During Mother's open-casket viewing, an urge to hold her hand seized me for the first time since I was nine. If I didn't touch her then as she lay in her casket, her face tinted pink from the reflection of the silk lining of the coffin, I would lose the chance forever. Not wishing to admit even to myself the desire to make contact with Mother, I used the pretense of threading her Buddhist rosary between her thumb and index fingers and felt her skin. Her hand was rigid, like frozen rice cake, and the memory of the day my parents and I visited Changgyong Palace came to me. On the way there, they held my hands and pulled me up by the arms over puddles on the mud road. I flew over the holes with feet tucked under my bottom, her hands soft and warm like sun-heated tomatoes. Standing by her casket, I allowed my hand to linger on her icicle fingers.

I wait for a revelation, some kind of communication from Mother's spirit to me. But nothing. The Snowy Range Mountains flow in folds of purples, indigo blue, and farther away, in unwilling blue—like the color of Mother's bowl, which I keep but do not use. I look up at the sky. She called it "my blue blanket." She said that, of course, to our children, not to me.

Lisa finishes fussing with the flowers and sits next to me, her fingers twirling her silver rings, our thighs touching. We sit wrapped by the silence of the day. It is one of those rare days in Wyoming. Sunny, no wind. As I think on the massiveness of the mountains on the horizon and the way Koreans have been singing their steadfastness in poems and paintings for three thousand years, an ancient folk saying comes to mind: *Shipnyon i-myon gangsang-do byonhon-da.* Ten years are long enough for even rivers to change courses and mountains to move. I am struck by the realization that even if my heart had calcified as hard as a mountain toward Mother, sufficient time has lapsed for me to soften four times over. As I sit by Mother's grave, what I should have said and wanted to say to her long ago sweeps down inside me, soars, then dips back down like a hawk surveying a valley: *Forgive me.* If I had said that, Mother would have responded with, "A bad karma from our lives has done it to us." I would have shown a weak-tea-colored smile, for I would not have wanted to shift the blame on anything outside myself. But I would, nonetheless, have been touched by her love to cover even the worst of my sins.

She's Fine

SANDELL MORSE

*T*hursday. Late morning. Boynton Beach Mall. Boynton Beach, Florida. Barneys' Coffee and Tea Company. A raisin scone. Double espresso. No hint of the world outside where the temperature climbs into the high nineties. Humidity is somewhere above ninety-five percent. In her hospital room ten miles from this mall, my mother has turned her air conditioning off. She is cold. Last night, she slept with two blankets. But she is doing better—much better, after Monday's stroke. She is talking; she is walking. Earlier this morning, she stood at a sink and held on to the rim while I pumped lotion soap from a dispenser onto a thin, rough, hospital washcloth, then swirled the cloth on her back, moving it lightly over her dowager's hump, over her loosened flesh, over spots that have darkened with age. Her hospital johnny was untied, swinging open, revealing her flat behind, the side of a sagging breast, the deep purple bruises from her blood-thinning drugs.

This is my mother's third stroke in less than three years. But, as strokes go, she is lucky. Hers are "mild." She loses speech, loses function

116

in her left side. Over time, she gets them back, but not completely. Her vocal cords have been damaged; her strength is diminished; she loses balance. Tomorrow, though, she will go home.

Home is Palm Village, a continuing care retirement center, run by a large corporate hotel chain. It is a complex of buildings consisting of one main residence, villas that are freestanding double bungalows and a health center called the Patio. Most residents live in the main building, choosing a one, two or three bedroom apartment. Entering the building last night, I stepped into a large lobby furnished with over-stuffed couches, upholstered side chairs and, on the walls, large botanical drawings of birds and flowers. There were low tables and large vases filled with showy arrangements of artificial flowers. The lights were dim. A power failure. "We're on auxiliary power," a receptionist said. She sat behind a high desk, then stood as I approached. "You must be Mr. Kaplan's daughter. How's your mother doing?"

In the lobby, my father was happy to see me. He smiled that old smile, charming, engaging. Moments earlier, the woman at the desk had told me my parents were adorable. A lovely couple. Who were these adorable people? This lovely couple. Here my father was a kind, considerate man, yet I remembered years of tension, anger and rage, my father ranting through my childhood, my adolescence and into my marriage—*Don't ever come here. We don't want to see you. Don't call. You're not my daughter.* What did I do? Select the wrong card for his birthday? Forget to call at a prescribed hour? Incidents didn't matter. They served as triggers, opening deep rifts.

In the lobby, my father pecked my cheek. He introduced me to some of his friends. His affectation is affability. The lights came on. Full power. "It happens all the time. On. Off. It's the heat," my father said. "How are you? How's everybody?"

"Fine. We're all fine," I said. We crossed the lobby, passing a room lined with bookshelves and old donated books, mostly paperbacks. This was the library. Across from the library, the card room was filled with players, men and women shuffling, dealing. I followed my father down a narrow hallway where doors led to an indoor heated swimming pool, an exercise room, a beauty parlor. When the corridor opened up, we stepped into an entertainment area with a stage and a snack bar. Near the elevator, I saw the billiard room with a heavy, dark wooden bar.

Next to the billiard room, the dining room had emptied out. The tables, though, were set for lunch with pale pink cloths, water goblets, five pieces of flatware, bread and butter plates. Turquoise napkins folded into triangular hats sat in the center of each flower-rimmed service plate. This was my father's dream, to spend his old age living in luxury. He wanted service. A hotel where attendants greeted him, opened doors. When I was a child, he filled me with tales of rich relatives I never met who lived in apartments on Fifth Avenue, the upper East Side, then moved to hotels overlooking Central Park.

But Palm Village is not a hotel, and my parents have paid a hundred and fifty thousand dollars for the privilege of living here. In an apartment they don't even own. Entrance fees at Palm Village range from a hundred to two hundred and sixty thousand dollars. In addition, each person pays a monthly fee. My parents have chosen a standard service for which they pay two thousand dollars each month. This includes one meal a day, weekly housekeeping (forty-five minutes), all utilities except phone, scheduled van trips to shopping centers, doctors' appointments and churches. No scheduled trips to a synagogue. But on Jewish holidays, the dining room provides special meals. Also included are activities: ballroom dancing, line dancing, billiards, bingo, movies and entertainment on Saturday night. One Saturday night when I visited, I watched three blindfolded men sitting in chairs on a stage, each trying to put on a pair of pantyhose. It was a race. I've also listened to singers who sang badly, to comedians who weren't funny.

At Palm Village, my father is an important man. He's on the council. People look up to him. Growing up, I remember my father leaving the house, night after night, going to meetings of the Chamber of

Commerce, of the Kiwanis. My father was a Boy Scout Commissioner. He taught a photography course in an adult education program at the local high school. Once he ran a candidate's successful mayoral campaign. We lived in a small town in New Jersey where my father owned a camera store. He and my mother worked side by side, but it was my father who went out for lunch with "the men" while my mother ate cottage cheese out of a carton in back of the store. Sometimes she ran across the street, sat on a stool at the counter and ate a tuna fish sandwich at the luncheonette.

In his apartment, my father tells me he drove my mother to the hospital, and I'm shocked. "You didn't call 911?"

"I called the doctor."

I feel as if time has collapsed. It's three years earlier. He didn't call an ambulance then, and he was full of similar statements. *I didn't know it was a stroke. If I'd a thought she needed oxygen, I would've called. You think I'm not a good enough driver?*

"Besides," my father says. "We didn't want to cause a commotion in the lobby."

Image and control: These have been and still are my father's concerns. I am staying in a guest room down the hall, not in this apartment with my father. This has been my request. I need privacy. I need space. Finally, I've asserted this. I'm fifty-nine years old, and I'm clutching the handle of my suitcase, holding on so that I don't flee.

Late Thursday afternoon. We have returned from the hospital. In his apartment, my father and I plan for my mother's return the next day. We talk about dinner, and we argue. I want to have dinner sent up. He doesn't. He wants my mother to go, not only to dinner, but to the Friday group, a gathering of friends, six couples who meet in the bar Friday nights to share hors d'oeuvres, bottles of wine and conversation before they all sit down at a long table in the dining room that has been reserved for them.

Not only is my mother recovering from a stroke, she is deaf, wears two hearing aids and strains and struggles to follow conversation. "Dad," I say, "she can't go to a cocktail party."

"It's not a cocktail party. These are our friends."

"I know, Dad, but still, it's a strain."

"She'll go for a few minutes."

"She's not ready for all those people."

"She'll have to face them sometime."

On a shelf inside the large bay window, my mother's plants look dry. Leaves yellow and wither. I'll water them later. "Dad," I say, "why doesn't she choose? Cocktails or dinner?"

"No," my father says.

I water the plants, then leave. Exit signs line the hallway. I'm drawn to them. Opening a door, I race down two flights of stairs. Outside the heat is still brutal. Lizards scurry. What I want is one more visit with my mother before she comes home. A visit when we'll be alone. Alone, she tells me stories about Selma, her friend who used to drive her parents' laundry truck; about the Irish boy who worked in the store next to my grandfather's store. This talk bores my father. Tomorrow, at home, we'll be three.

My mother sits up in her hospital bed. Her dinner tray is pushed aside. This is a moment that comes to me whole, all of it—my mother's trembling body, her bulging eyeballs, her tears, the darkened skin under her eyes; the young nurse, a furtive look on her face, right hand holding a cell phone to her ear, left hand taking my mother's pulse.

I rush to my mother's side, her left side, the side of her body that has gone limp. I see her flipper-like hand, the droop in her cheek. I touch her face, then bend to kiss her hair. She cries and mumbles. In halted speech she tells me she loves me. "I love you, too," I say as I climb up into her bed and curl my body around hers. Her head leans into mine. In slow, jumbled speech, she asks me why. "Why is this happening to me?"

My heart searches, then finds words that I can speak. "It's not happening to you, Mom. It's life. And it's hard. So hard."

"I have to f-f-f-fight."

The word itself is a struggle. I hold her close. I tell her I love her. I whisper, "Rest, Mama. Rest. Sometimes we fight best by resting."

She nods and tells me her head aches. She can't move her left leg, her left hand. I kiss her cheek. Smooth her hair. She takes a long, slow breath.

Dr. Ginsberg is here in the hospital. He orders a CAT scan, then resumption of the heparin, the ICU for the night. But there is no bed in ICU. An attendant wheels my mother to a room where the nurse on duty monitors fewer patients. My mother's bed is next to the windows. To get there we pass an old woman who twists in her bed, mumbles, pulls her sheet. She rips off her diapers. A nurse closes the curtain.

My father arrives. He seems disoriented. At eighty-three, he has had two major heart attacks. He's forgetful. He walks slowly, nearly shuffles. He stands at the foot of my mother's bed, talking to her, talking to me. "Janice drove me. I didn't even have to call a cab. She took me right away." My father's car is in the shop. Janice works in the main office. There was no scheduled trip for the van and my father has been singled out for special treatment. He gloats. "I'm telling you, it's a terrific place. Just terrific."

I concentrate on the nurses, two of them hooking up IVs. Oxygen.

When we leave at eleven, my mother is resting. She has recovered some of her speech, some use in her left side. But she is tired, so tired.

❧

The next morning, after an early visit with my mother, I get in my rental car, blast the air conditioning, and I drive. It's still unbearably hot, too hot to walk, too hot to stand and look at the ocean. Still, I head in that direction, crossing over the interstate, driving west to east. My parents sold an ocean-front condominium in Boca Raton to move to Palm Village. There, even in summer, they felt an ocean breeze. There they lived among people who were younger. They had an outdoor swimming pool, a beach where children who visited used to play.

I'll never understand why housing for the elderly is not designed to include a mix of ages, a mix of races. Why there is no town center. Why there are no parks, no walkways.

In Palm Village, residents range in age from late seventies to over a hundred. In the main building, where my parents live, and in the villas, all are ambulatory. They may use canes or walkers, even a wheel-chair in the halls, but to enter the dining room, a resident must leave her wheelchair at the entrance, then walk to her table. If she can't walk, she moves to the Patio. At the Patio residents receive assisted living care, Alzheimer's care or skilled nursing care. The level of care is preselected in the original package. In the standard package that my parents bought, they are entitled to three hundred and sixty days at the Patio. Together. Not each. They may, if they choose, apply the refundable portion of their entrance fee to care at the Patio. How much of their original fee will be returned? "Not less than half," my father told me, then added, "unless we need more care."

My father has shown me every public room in the main building of Palm Village. He has walked me to the lake to see the villas and the outdoor pavilion. He has shown me the party boat, the small raised gardens where residents, including my mother, grow tomatoes and beans. Marigolds and daisies. He has never shown me the Patio, where residents have their own lounges and activity areas, their own beauty shop. Their own dining room.

This is what my parents want. Life care. A guarantee.

I'm looking for a coffee shop that I remember finding when I visited last January, but when I locate it, I see an out-of-business sign tacked to the front door. This entire area near the beach looks deserted, nearly boarded up. Clearly, I'm out of season. I pull a U-ey and head for the mall.

I like the turquoise and peach tiled floor, the blond wood chairs, the peach formica table tops. I like the small raisin scone, the dark espresso, both strangely familiar now. Sitting alone at this table, drinking espresso, eating a scone, I think, again, about Palm Village. When my parents are well, they are both busy, so busy, with meetings and committees. My father, of course, is on the council. My mother is on the welcome committee, the birthday committee, the decorating committee. On Mother's Day, she brought photographs of me and my husband, of our three sons, our daughters-in-law, our granddaughter for a display in the dining room. On Halloween the residents dressed up. My mother was a cat. She wore leggings, a long black sweater, a half mask. She fashioned a tail. She drew whiskers on her face. My father dressed as a Chinese farmer. He wore overalls, a rubber mask. No one knew him, he told me proudly.

When I'm old, old, I want a place that's my own. I want dignity. I want to think. I want to write. I want to see films, go to plays, listen to concerts. I want to celebrate with my family or with my old, good friends. If I end up in a place like Palm Village, I'm sure I will have gotten there kicking and screaming.

Friends tell me I'm lucky. *Your parents are taken care of. You don't have to worry.*

In the mall, I buy batteries for my mother's hearing aids, magazines, a bran muffin. She likes bran muffins. Back at the hospital, I sit beside my mother's bed and watch her rest. I hand her a tissue. I read my book. My father is not with us. There is a meeting he must attend. He is the chairman.

Saturday morning. My mother sits up. She eats the bran muffin I brought her yesterday. Tomorrow, she's scheduled to go home. Tomorrow, I'm scheduled to fly to Boston, then drive to Maine where I live. Of course, my mother thinks I should go. "You've left your husband. That's enough." She sees uncertainty in my face. "You don't have to worry. This time, I mean it. I'm taking care. Your father understands. We'll have dinner sent upstairs. He'll go down to the snack bar and bring up lunch."

I don't believe her. It's not that she doesn't mean what she says. It's that my father hasn't decided what is best. Not yet.

Sunday morning. I feel as if I've been given a gift. Dr. Ginsberg recommends an interim facility. Rehab. Days before, at my request, we stepped into the hall. I was concerned that at home, my mother would perform social obligations, obligations my father perceived. Now, Dr. Ginsberg tells my mother her condition is stable, but she needs rest. A place to recuperate between hospital and home. She also needs therapy. Hand therapy, walking therapy, speech therapy. When he leaves, my mother holds my hand. "Your father's not going to like this."

He surprises us both. "If that's what the doctor says, that's what you'll do."

I fly home, then telephone every day. In rehab, my mother learns to find her balance when she walks. "Do you know how I do it?" she says to me. "I remembered when you took dancing and you used to spot. I do that. I find a spot on the wall, and I walk toward it. I told the therapist. She said it was a good idea."

After a week, my mother comes home. For two days, she and my father ask to have dinner sent to their apartment. On the third night, my mother goes to the dining room. We're talking on the speaker phone. That's the way it is, a three-way conversation. Always. My father speaks, and I hear that old pride in his voice. "They all clapped when she walked in. It was something. Really something."

"Yes," my mother says, then changes the subject with hardly a pause. She speaks rapidly. All of this is new. A result of the stroke? She is telling me that today she went and had her blood checked. "Would you believe it, when I left the hospital it was too thin? First it's too thick, now it's too thin. He—Dr. Ginsberg—wants me to walk with a cane. But I walk fine without it."

Historically, my father turns away from loss and pain, from physical deformity. He fully supports the rule excluding wheelchairs from the dining room. People who can't walk to their tables disappear to the Patio. Is this what my mother fears? Disappearing? "Mom, use the cane. It'll help your balance."

My father interjects. "That's what the doctor said."

"I'm doing great," my mother says.

"She must've gotten about a hundred cards. And phone calls. The phone won't stop ringing. And people. They all want to visit. I've never seen anything like it," my father says.

"Mom, are you tired?"

"I'm exhausted."

"She's fine," my father says.

Two months pass. My mother has had the flu. An arthritis attack. Terrible headaches, for which Dr. Ginsberg prescribes Darvocet over the phone. He has not seen her since the stroke. I speak to them late one Sunday afternoon. They've been visiting a friend. Earlier they went to brunch. "It's new," my father says. "And it's wonderful. Everything you can imagine. Smoked salmon, as much as you want." I take a breath. My father continues, "Bagels, cake, muffins. Roast beef sliced from a round." I don't speak. My father fills the silence. "I'm knocked out."

"What about Mom? How're you doing?" I ask my mother.

"I may as well tell you. She won't tell you," my father says.

"I was going to tell her."

"No, you weren't."

"I was."

I interrupt. "Will somebody please tell me?"

Saturday was a bad day. My mother's head ached so badly she couldn't hold it up. She couldn't get out of bed. She asked my father to drive her to the hospital. Instead, my father called Dr. Ginsberg who once again prescribed painkillers over the phone. "That was what she needed," my father says.

They went to dinner and after dinner they stayed to see the evening entertainment. My mother tells me she was tired; she left early. This is her version of taking care of herself. Then, with my father still on the line, she says that Kate, the social director, followed her and held her elbow as she walked up the stairs to the elevator.

"Three stairs," my father says.

I'm twelve hundred miles away, and I'm tuned into every nuance in my father's voice. He's uneasy, tense.

My mother continues. "She told me if I ever want to go to the hospital and your father won't take me, I should call her. She'll take me."

I can't believe what I'm hearing. Not only has someone else seen what I've seen, but my mother is saying this with my father on the line. I jump into the space my mother has cleared for me. "She's right, Dad. If someone wants to go to the hospital, you should take them."

We argue. He tells me I think I know more than the doctor. He knows what it's like in emergency, you sit and wait for six hours. He rants. "You're always asking about the pills. They're pills. They help."

My mother retracts. "Don't blame him, Sandy. Please, dear. You know when you're in pain, sometimes you say things you don't mean."

The phrase echoes. *He doesn't mean it. He gets upset, that's all.* I say goodbye and hang up. It is summer. Still light. On the other side of my screens the ocean is cast in pink. It stretches farther than I can see.

In it, lobster buoys mark pots. They bob white, illuminated now by the setting sun. I think of my mother. Now, my father is right. She didn't want to go to the hospital, didn't want him to call 911. He has closed the space around her, and she is as gated as the community in which they have chosen to live.

Before her stroke, my mother, along with members of her committee, decorated the lake-side pavilion for Memorial Day. They hung streamers. They arranged flowers. There was a picnic. A cookout. On the phone, my mother told me what she ate, half a hamburger, what my father ate, a piece of chicken. Only the white meat. There was potato salad, cold slaw, watermelon, cookies. "But when they got to us, the cookies were gone. I went to Don. You remember Don." (I did.) "I told him, 'When you got to us, you ran out. We didn't get any cookies.' He went to the kitchen and came back with eclairs." Her voice was buoyant, clearly triumphant, yet I felt as if I were listening to a child. Cookies. Eclairs.

I thought of Don. He was a man trained and paid to keep the residents of Palm Village satisfied and happy. That was his job. I'd seen staff members patronize and smile falsely as if they were real estate agents or counselors at summer camp.

Am I judging too harshly? I'm not eighty-one. And I'm not married to a man who slowly and surely destroyed whatever it was I might have become. There in Palm Village, my mother is probably as happy as she's ever been. She takes pleasure in an eclair, in decorating a pavilion. When she's well, she plants tomatoes in her small raised garden. Here in Maine, I plant a larger garden, digging down into the earth and loving her from far away.

The Decisive Match

MARTHA HENRY

$\mathcal{T}$ he only person I play tennis with these days is my mother. If not for her, I'd have given up the game years ago, but she always reminds me to bring a racket on my summer visits to Maine. My parents built a house on a lake and moved into it after I graduated from high school. It has never felt like home.

"Ready for tennis?" my mother asks on the first sunny day since my arrival.

I'm feeling particularly guilty about all my parents have done for me. "Ready when you are," I say.

We get into my mother's blue Toyota with our rackets, a bottle of water and a broom in the back seat. She drives us to the courts at the Catholic college a mile up the road. My mother has a pass that allows us to play on the courts, but she never bothers to bring it. She's that type of person—confident and slightly oblivious.

She waves to the guard at the gatehouse and drives by without stopping. She parks in front of the two asphalt courts. Luckily, no one else is playing yet, no one a lot better than us to make us look like fools, and no one a lot worse to annoy us. The college kids are on summer break, and except for a few strolling nuns, the campus is deserted. One of the courts has a huge puddle from last night's thunderstorm, so we choose the court with the grassy crack instead. I get the broom from the car and sweep the gravel near the base line to the edge of the chain-link fence.

We warm up. Neither one of us has played since we played together last fall. Sometimes we hit the ball dead on and it makes that pleasant *thwacking* sound. Sometimes we miss the ball completely. More often we hit it into the net or over the high fence into the bushes. A couple of balls land in the puddle on the other court; we bounce them hard to shake off the water. It's a hazy day with no clouds and the sun is getting hot.

"Ready to play?" I ask.

"Ready to beat you," she answers.

My mother taught me to play tennis, and that is, in part, why I continue to play with her. I consider these hours payback for the hours she spent patiently tossing the ball to me as I was learning to hit it. At summer camp, where tennis lessons were mandatory, I learned how to serve and keep score. I didn't like the game then, and given the choice, I would have preferred to be swimming or out in a boat. Anything would have been better than being baked and embarrassed on those long, steamy afternoons. Even now, I can't wait to finish playing and go for a swim.

My mother wins the toss for the serve, then takes all the balls and stands just behind the service line. She's wearing a flowered bathing suit with no pockets, and she stuffs the two extra tennis balls in the front of her suit so they look like additional breasts. When I was younger, this would have horrified me, but today I'm only amused.

A white bonnet keeps the sun off her face. A few months earlier she had a growth removed from her nose—malignant melanoma. The doctor told her that continued exposure to the sun would increase her chances of a recurrence. My mother has always loved the sun. Usually the only piece of jewelry she wears is a gold sun pendant my father gave her one Christmas. Each summer when I arrive home, I find her sitting by the lake in a lawn chair working a crossword puzzle, her face turned toward the sun. "Hello," she'll holler. We'll talk for a while, then she'll hand me the puzzle to fill in the remaining blank spaces.

Since her small operation, she has *not* avoided the sun whenever possible, though she has made concessions. She wears sun block when she's outdoors, and if she's out for a long time she wears the new white bonnet. Though I know there's a danger to her being in the sun, I'm relieved she doesn't avoid it completely. She wouldn't be my mother if she did.

I win the first game, breaking her serve. Then I win the next game and the game after. It's getting hotter and we're both sweating. I open the bottle of water and offer it to my mother. She takes a short drink and hands the bottle back to me. I take a long drink and offer it to her again, but she shakes her head. My shirt is so damp with sweat I take it off and play in my flowered sports bra. If I had a young daughter, I wonder, would my playing in a bra embarrass her?

I serve and win the fourth game. My mother's drop shots aren't making it over the net. It's a boring match so far, we can't seem to keep a volley going. Serving the fifth game, my mother double-faults twice. I break her serve for the third time. The score in games is now 5-0.

"Maybe you should have your racket restrung," I say, only half-joking.

The Prince graphite, a gift to her from the court bailiffs when she retired as a judge in 1990, is better than mine. During her seventeen years on the bench, she never took a sick day except when she broke her hip and had to be hospitalized. If she was ill with a cold or the flu, she worked anyway. Though I was never as healthy as my mother, I had a perfect attendance record in junior high school. If I didn't feel well, I still had to go to school. There was no one to stay home with me.

One week during the late seventies, my mother probably should have called in sick. We were playing tennis at a park and she slipped on loose gravel and hurt her back. The doctor prescribed Valium to ease the pain. She was completely zonked out on pills, but still went to work. She still heard cases, still freed the innocent and sentenced the guilty, though I'm not sure how she could tell the difference in her Valium stupor. At night she'd get home and collapse on the bed until morning. She was somebody else that week. Rather than being helpful, I ignored her as much as possible. She got better and stopped taking pills, but I never wanted to play tennis with her again. I was afraid she'd hurt herself permanently.

The next summer she insisted I play with her. And I finally did give in, though I insisted we take a broom to the courts to sweep off any gravel. And we continued to play a couple of times each year. And by the end of each summer, we'd be as good as we were the summer before.

I win the first set 6-0. We're both surprised. I don't remember ever shutting my mother out of a set. I wish I felt like gloating, but I don't. On the other side of the court I see an old woman. This is and is not the woman who always had more stamina than I had, especially in the hot sun. My mother's greater stamina always made me feel inadequate. I felt I should be able to match it, and I couldn't.

She serves the first game of the second set and loses. The temperature must be close to ninety. My face is flushed with the heat, but my mother's face is pale and strained. She hands me the balls at the net as we switch sides for the second game.

"It's getting hot," I say. "I'm hot. Do you want to stop?"

"I'm just getting warmed up," she says.

I win the second game easily. We are not having long volleys. She is not, as they say, returning the ball well.

Sometimes she and I get into a perfect groove playing tennis— playing very well for two very bad players. Each point becomes its own engrossing competition, as we stretch for the perfect slide at the net or run back fast enough to miraculously hit the high lob. We surprise ourselves, knowing our best shots owe more to luck than skill. On perfect-groove days we can play for hours. "This is fun," we'll say to each other. "Good shot. Great point. Excellent volley."

Today is not one of those days. My mother loses every point in the third game. I offer her more water. She says she's not thirsty.

By the fourth game, I'm feeling guilty about winning so easily. I try more difficult shots, thinking I'll miss a lot of points and my mother will win a game and this sense of unease growing between us will lessen. If I purposely lose points, she'll know and never forgive me.

My strategy doesn't work. I win the fourth game, even after making a questionable line call in her favor. Now I'm afraid if I win the match with two 6-0 sets, my mother will insist on playing a second match. She's unusually quiet on the other side of the court. She doesn't yell or swear when she misses a point. Maybe I should just hurry up and win and get us both out of the sun.

"More water?" I ask her.

"Let's just play," she says, taking off her white bonnet and throwing it to the sidelines.

"Shouldn't you keep that on?" I say.

"It was blocking my visibility."

"What about your nose?"

"Let's just play."

It was at my grandmother's memorial service that I realized my mother's own brush with cancer had changed her life. The whole family had gathered in Ashland, Kentucky, where my grandmother lived most of her life and where my mother and her brothers and sisters were born. My grandmother had died three months earlier in Florida at the age of ninety-six. We were all gathered for a family reunion and to bury her ashes in the family plot.

My grandmother lived for almost a century and died an ordinary death. I'd had a chance to say goodbye to her; in fact, I'd been saying goodbye to her for years. This reunion was more of a party than a funeral. For me, it was a chance to see aunts, uncles and cousins I hadn't seen for years. Some of my cousins had young children, and this was their introduction into the bigger family. My mother's younger brother, Uncle Louis, had died a year earlier of lung cancer. If there was a sorrow to the occasion, it was the memory of his sudden death, rather than my grandmother's expected one.

The afternoon at the cemetery was humid and sunny. My cousin Donald, who had just been ordained as a minister, placed the metal box with Grandmother's ashes into the hole.

"Can I hold it for a moment?" I asked.

"Of course," he said.

I knelt down on the damp grass, getting my skirt wet and thinking if Grandmother were here she'd chastise me for not wearing a slip. I lifted the box out of the hole, which was shallow and didn't seem at all like a grave, but more like a hole for a fence post. The box itself was gold colored and looked like a gift box of good Scotch. Grandmother, who loved Scotch and drank it most every evening of her life, would have been pleased. Engraved on one side of the gold metal box was *Hannah Russell Putnam 1896–1993*.

I passed the box to my mother, who also wanted to hold it. Then it was passed around to various relatives, then back to me. I placed the box back in the hole.

After the service, my mother and I went to Wal-Mart to buy film for our cameras. When we had made our purchases and were waiting for other relatives, I suggested to my mother that we sit outside. As I started toward a bench in the sun, my mother said, "You go ahead," and walked into the shade. I stood where I was and watched her. And for the first time that day, I wanted to cry.

I win the fifth game and by now it's clear I'm going to win the set and the match. My mother isn't going to make a comeback today. I try to stop worrying about her reaction. She's trying hard to win just one game, trying not to get old, and failing. I win the second set 6-0.

"I'm embarrassed," she says. She takes a long drink of water and passes me the bottle. "Here, finish it."

"You're seventy," I say.

"You're not that good," she answers back.

Her remark doesn't sting me. Beating her in tennis used to make me feel triumphant. Today it only makes me sad. With my overdue victory comes the unavoidable recognition that she will be defeated— that she will die. Probably not suddenly or accidentally, but with a sure, unsteady slowness. I've always feared her death, but abstractly, hypothetically, in nightmares and the late-night ring of the telephone. Now I fear her dying.

I'm sure she can see these emotions on my face, hear them in my voice when I mention her age. I'm sure she finds my sadness annoying, intolerable, in need of reproach.

"You're not that good," she repeats.

"Do you want to go for a swim?" I ask.

"Yes, I could use some exercise."

❧

She swims her usual twelve laps between the stone piers, swimming with her head held out of the water and her awkward flutter kick. I swim out past the piers and the moored boats, heading for the small island in the middle of the lake. My mother doesn't like it when I do this. It always makes her nervous. She's afraid I'll be run over by a speedboat whose driver doesn't see me. She yells at me to be careful. "I will, I promise," I yell back. I've been swimming out here for years. Somehow this old dynamic, her worrying about me rather than the other way around, is comforting.

After we swim she sits in the sun in her usual lawn chair. She puts on her white bonnet again and rubs SPF 30 sun block on her face and neck and arms. I sit in the chair next to her, my bathing suit dripping wet.

"We'll play again tomorrow," she says.

I don't say anything because I don't want to play again tomorrow. The weather forecast is for rain anyway. We talk about what we'll have for dinner, what needs to be picked from the garden, when we'll go to the grocery store.

She finishes rubbing the sun block into her skin and hands me the bottle. I've never used sun block before, but for the first time in my life, I put it on.

Cookie and Me

PATRICIA A. GOZEMBA

$\mathcal{T}$ he Beak, my mother, had to die before Cookie and I could have a relationship again. I was eleven years old and he was forty-one when it ended, just after we moved fifteen miles from our two-family house in Somerville, Massachusetts, to the seven-room ranch in the Glen Meadow East development in Waltham. A paradise with trees, a working-class dream come true, this was the closest I was ever going to get to living in a house like the ones that Dick and Jane and Nancy Drew had. We were moving up. We even got a better car, a baby blue and white Chevy Bel Air.

Before all of that, Cookie, my father, had been a buddy. He taught me how to swim when I was five; how to throw a ball, swing a bat and play shortstop so that I outshone all the boys; how to ride a bicycle; how to read the sports section in the newspaper and, best of all, how to use some of his tools. I really thought that he knew everything worth knowing.

The move to Waltham triggered big changes. The Beak began an affair with a priest, based in part on their mutual interest in gambling.

She spent her two hours after work on the phone with Father Sweeney and then the bookie, betting on horses at California racetracks. At around five-thirty, she'd throw some frozen or canned vegetables in a pot, slap some meat in a frying pan, flip the burners to HI and get in a few last-minute bets. Cookie earned his nickname for rushing in after work and salvaging supper by turning down the burners to LO. Soon he started working a second job in the pressroom at the *Boston Herald* and putting in extra overtime at his regular job at Boston Linotype Print. He was drinking more. I found myself embarrassed, coming home with friends on the weekends and seeing him slouched on the couch asleep with a beer bottle in his hand.

The Beak's new part-time job as a full-charge bookkeeper and the glamour of going to the track gave her the status she thrived on. Around the house she seemed larger than life, leaving the rest of us to live in her shadow. We made our lives elsewhere.

My father turned into a workaholic and an alcoholic. We had a better house, a better car, but Cookie was not part of my life—not even to talk to. He didn't seem to talk with anyone. The Beak talked to and at everyone. I spoke mainly in self-defense.

Cookie and I began talking, really talking again forty-one years later on the day of my mother's funeral. Finally, the Beak, who had beaked her way into every piece of business on her radar screen, could no longer interrupt, shut us up or belittle us. Never sick a day in her eighty-two years, the Beak's wish about dying in her sleep came true on New Year's Eve, 1993. That night, as her soul took off from a condo overlooking Cape Canaveral in Florida, I watched fireworks over a volcano in Hawaii. All of us would rendezvous on Cape Cod in Falmouth for her full-on Irish Catholic wake and funeral.

Cookie and Beak had moved to Falmouth, supposedly in shame. After I gave an interview to the *Boston Herald* about my life as a thirty-eight-year-old lesbian professor at Salem State College, the Beak reminded me ad nauseam that they had to move. "What will the neighbors think?" Falmouth seemed far enough away for no one to know that the once-married Pat Gozemba was the daughter of John and Mary Curran. They slapped a bumper sticker with the town slogan, "Isn't Falmouth Nice?" on every car they owned.

Cookie cried at the wake and funeral. I think he really missed her. I cried once, mostly in relief, grieving about the lost parts of my life. To be fair, the tears came when I spoke about her and mentioned how it was too bad that she wasn't born later when women had so many opportunities to have careers and live independent lives. She used to say, "Well, if feminists are liberated and do what they want to do, I must have invented it. What's the big deal?"

"Yeah, yeah," I'd heave, just to acknowledge that I had heard her. What was the point of trying to explain that feminism didn't mean getting what you wanted at the expense of everyone else?

On January 8, 1993, we buried the Beak in St. Anthony's Cemetery in Falmouth and toasted her at the Willow Field Tavern. When people said, "I'm sorry about your mother," I didn't yet think or say, "You should be really happy for Cookie and me." But later I would.

The ceremonies over, we went back to Cookie's house to figure out life without the Beak. My sister Peggy would fly home to Kansas in two days. Johnny, my brother, would go back that night to his house in Stoughton, forty-five minutes away. I didn't start classes for another week, and my partner Karen was still in Hawaii. "What next?" nagged at us.

When the four of us gathered around the dining room table to try and figure out if Cookie could manage, there were certain fortunate givens. He could cook for himself; he'd been doing that for years. And by edict of the Beak, his chores included cleaning the house and doing the wash in addition to outside maintenance. He still drove, so he was mobile. Since he had never phoned us, we weren't sure that he knew how to make a long-distance call. We wrote our numbers on loose-leaf paper, reminded him to dial "1" and had him practice on my answering machine. My sister showed him how to write a check, and he paid his first bill that way.

Since secrecy and lying were key operating behaviors of my mother, none of us, Cookie included, ever knew how much money there was. He had no idea how much the household expenses were each month or the amount he got from Social Security and the retirement fund of the International Brotherhood of Printers.

Fortunately, when the Beak died, she and Cookie were in Florida for the winter, and she had all of their important financial papers in one place. My father brought out the army-green steel strong box and my mother's purse. "The key's probably in there," he said. She had been dead a week and he still hadn't opened her purse; he was well trained. Peggy ferreted through it and came up with a little blue envelope that held the right key. She and my brother sorted through the papers, three bank books and stock certificates. I searched the house for old bills and examined the checkbook to figure out monthly expenses.

It took about an hour to determine that Cookie had a working-class family fortune of thirty thousand dollars—what remained of my mother's big insurance settlement from falling on the broken brick step at her friend Louie's house on the way in to a poker game. My brother held ten thousand dollars of the fortune in his name for safe-keeping for Cookie. In eight years, when he would be ninety, Cookie's house would be paid for. All the secrecy for all those years about having or not having money and whose name it was in seemed absurd.

Watching Cookie sit at the head of the table, looking dwarfed by the strong box, I could see that he was overwhelmed. He got up to pour himself a Four Roses highball. My sister and I followed his lead, had some wine and took a break from the financial excavation.

Back at the table, I looked straight at my father. "You know, Cookie," I said, "the Beak and I never had a good relationship, because she was so mad about my being a lesbian. I want you to feel that you can call me any time if you feel scared or unsafe or lonely or . . . "

Interrupting me with a sweep of his arm, his eyes fixed on the ceiling, he intoned in his nasal alcoholic twang, "You know, I never felt the same as she did about you being that way. That was just her."

Speechless, I turned to my sister. She just shook her head. "I'm serious," he said, keeping his gaze away from us.

I remembered what a family taboo I broke every time I spoke and had eye contact with any of the family. "Cookie . . . thanks. That means a lot to me. . . . "

With the papers in his hands, Johnny chose that moment to interrupt. "We've got to get this insurance stuff straightened out."

Angry, I muttered, "I just don't believe it," and retreated to the kitchen for another glass of wine.

Peggy followed. "He is a jerk," she whispered in solidarity.

When we returned, Cookie was belting back his highball and Johnny was spouting insurance jargon. Still stunned by my father's passive declaration of support, I didn't know what to say. I felt vindicated, stupid, infantile and relieved.

Johnny spoke up. "What's the monthly expenses?"

I slumped in my seat. Cookie picked up the newspaper to tune out. I passed my tally of the mortgage, cable, phone, electric, gas, newspaper and taxes to Peggy. She read it aloud and announced, "The good news is that you have money for food, Cookie." He chuckled and returned to the paper.

Since Peggy was leaving town, and I wanted no part of going to the stockbroker and straightening out my father's fortune, Johnny volunteered and then promptly left.

My sister and I worried aloud with Cookie about whether he could handle things. He agreed to let us take him shopping the next day. Peggy suggested he come out to Kansas for a few months—"It'll be lonely for you here"—but he refused and went to bed.

My sister and I anguished some more that night about leaving him on his own. I wanted to discuss how stupid I felt for not pursuing the conversation with Cookie after his revelation that he didn't "feel the same way" about me as the Beak did. I shifted the blame to Johnny's insensitivity, but that wasn't fair. Eventually I would realize that it was my own shock that had confounded me. At just that moment, when I had finally achieved some modicum of acceptance from my father, the man who had been silent with me about anything of consequence for over forty years, I choked.

Two days later, it was just Cookie and me at the house, a pattern that would become familiar. We made a plan to leave Cookie at my brother's house while Johnny and I went to New York to pick up the Dodge Shadow, which had just been shipped back from Florida.

The forty-five-minute drive marked the first time that my father and I had been alone in a car in a very long time. He actually talked to me. At first, it was the weather and his car and how long it took to get to Johnny's. Then he said, "You know, your mother always blamed me because you were a lesbian."

When I heard the word "lesbian," I nearly drove off the road.

"What do you mean, 'blamed you'?"

"She said that it was in my family genes. Lumpy Hirshberg, that cousin of mine—she was sure he was gay."

I couldn't believe that "gay" had come out of his mouth.

"Why did she think Lumpy was gay?"

"Who knows? You know how she got things in her head. She said my uncle was gay, too." He looked straight ahead at the road.

"Is any of it true?"

"Who knows? Why argue?" He shrugged.

"What about her Uncle Matt who never got married and lived in San Francisco? Was he gay?"

"Ah, who knows? Who cares? Mirback told her it wasn't passed down in families."

"Why was Mirback, your heart doctor, discussing that with the Beak?"

"According to her, that was the cause of my heart trouble. All that worrying about passing on homosexuality from my family."

It was hard to believe this conversation was actually happening. "You're kidding," I said. "What did you say?"

"I told her to shut up and keep my family out of it."

"In front of the doctor?"

"Yeah."

Lesbian, gay, homosexuality—all words I'd never heard him speak. Now was the time to ask him. "Cookie, is it a problem for you that I'm a lesbian?"

"Naw. Karen's nice. When's she coming back?"

When the Beak was alive, I went to Falmouth about twice a year, usually when my sister and her family visited. More often, I got to see her and Cookie in other neutral spaces like my siblings' houses, restaurants and racetracks like Wonderland or Suffolk Downs. Although I extended invitations, they rarely came to my house in the Witch City. With the Beak dead, I began making the drive from Salem to Falmouth four times a month for an overnight visit. Books on tape saved my sanity. I listened to every non–right wing and non-Christian book at the Salem Public Library.

For the first year, we went out to dinner, usually at fast food restaurants, and then to a movie. At Papa Gino's, his favorite, the kids greeted him with a "Hi, Jack" whenever we came in. He was a regular, and since I was with him, I got the senior citizen discount. We were given the Silver Menu at Friendly's Ice Cream and Sandwich Shoppe, where he had a toasted BLT, fries, a Diet Coke or a coffee, and a Happy Ending Sundae every time.

He saw more movies than he had seen in his whole life. The teenage ticket sellers at the Falmouth Mall Cinema, like their Friendly's counterparts, automatically pumped out the senior discount tickets. The day one of them said, "Oh ma'am, your husband dropped his hat," I grimaced but recovered soon enough to preserve my senior status. That I could be mistaken—even in this way—for my mother made my skin crawl.

We did make quite a pair. Although he insisted that he was still five foot eight, he had shrunk to about my height of five-two. With white hair and blue eyes, we looked like matching bookends. He outweighed me by only fifteen pounds, so I felt secure in catching him when he stumbled. And stumble he did.

As the months wore on after the Beak's departure, Cookie became more taciturn, and it seemed as if he had decided that freedom of speech was overrated. His favorite retreat was into the newspaper. My brother and sister both complained about how hard it was talking to him on the phone. Tell him about your lives, I suggested, since I knew that neither one of them would talk about politics with him or what was in the *Boston Globe* that day, both my old standbys. I also shared what was going on with Karen and me, and he was interested. That was big, and I appreciated it. Since she was a newspaper editor, he felt a bond with her; even a feminist paper like *Sojourner* counted. He even read it occasionally, and I wondered what he thought about the lesbian stuff. Sometimes I played Twenty Questions with him. The effort was hardly worth it. I wondered if he was seriously depressed. His father, also an alcoholic, stuck his head in the oven and committed suicide when Cookie was sixteen. I told myself not to worry: His was an electric oven.

My father became master of the monosyllabic answer as his hearing deteriorated. Only a hot political issue could get him going: Dole versus Clinton, Clinton's health care plan, gays in the military, the 1993 lesbian and gay march on Washington, Newt Gingrich and the Contract with America and on and on. He talked more reasonably about lesbian and gay issues than I ever imagined.

As I had to raise my voice more, our conversations began to lack subtlety. The phone helped—he could turn up the volume. But in a booth at Friendly's, there wasn't much hope. Finally, I could take it no longer and suggested a hearing aid. I made an appointment for him the next week in Boston. Passive as usual, he didn't object.

Not long after that, I brought my eighty-year-old gardening mentor, Mary, to meet Cookie and go out to brunch. We had just discovered that the two of them had both worked for the Wilburs at Tudor Press in the 1930s. When Mary and I walked in the house and I hollered, "Hi, Cookie," he didn't hear me. In the living room, I realized he didn't have the hearing aids in. But when I introduced him to Mary, he stood up and shook her hand, and a big smile broke across his face. He showed genuine interest in meeting her. I don't know if he noticed that she wore two hearing aids. When she sat across the living room and talked in a normal tone of voice, he couldn't hear a thing.

I beaked in. "Why don't you try your hearing aids? Mary's wearing hers. It'll help you out." He didn't resist when I helped him get them in.

At brunch, he spoke with real enthusiasm about printing for the first time since I was a kid. Seeing Cookie enjoy himself was wonderful. My rehab program was working.

My father entered a new era of freedom. He wrote checks, paid bills, went out to eat, bought all the Four Roses he wanted, hung out at the Falmouth Mall people-watching, drove to Chappaquoit Beach every day and watched the wind surfers, selected what he wanted to eat at Star Market and carried about a hundred dollars in his wallet all the time—freedoms never allowed in the Beak Age. He also decided not to wear the hearing aids. They hurt and they whistled, he said. The hearing aids went into permanent retirement. Two thousand dollars down the drain. I refused to nag him and regretted being so pushy about making him get them in the first place. Eventually, I went back to shouting, and he settled into selective hearing. Undoubtedly, it was his best defense with the Beak and now with me.

❧

In June of 1996, Cookie's two and a half years of freedom came to a screeching halt when fluid built up around his heart and one day he could barely breathe. After surgery to install a pacemaker, he looked great and had a good appetite, but his heartbeat remained irregular. The doctors gave him what Cookie called "one of those big electrical blasts," but it didn't take. His movements grew more labored, but when he went home, he managed. Careening from the couch to the bathroom, or the car to Friendly's, he defied gravity and left people shaking their heads in amazement. More than once I caught him by his jacket as he headed down for the count.

Two months later, he got pneumonia. Things looked bad, but he made it through. Two weeks in a rehab hospital introduced Cookie to a new gravitational device—a walker. I wanted to kiss the physical therapist who got him to use it. Canes have the "old person" stigma, she explained to me. Aluminum walkers are much more appealing to octogenarians. Cookie claimed that it was even better for walking than leaning on a shopping cart at Star Market. Relieved, I threw out the cane that had been catching dust in the living room for two years. No more whirling dervish moves on the way into Friendly's.

The heart surgery, which Cookie, now two years later, still calls his bypass surgery, ended his driving, his shopping, his housecleaning and his cooking, and started an endless stream of home health aides. In the whole confusing mess, the saving grace was Francine, the neighbor we hired to be my father's cook and guardian from noon to bed- time. She was our eyes and ears and made it possible for him to stay in his own home, which I can't help wishing was still in the development in Waltham. Every time I pass the Waltham exit on Route 128, after driving forty-five minutes from Salem, I remember the Beak worrying about what the neighbors would think. Then I drive on to Falmouth for another hundred and five minutes—if there's no traffic.

⟡

Considering all the problems that could have come up, Cookie has been pretty lucky, and so have we. For a year, life was stable, and in the 1997–98 academic year I took a ten-month teaching exchange position in Hawaii. Johnny became Cookie's main family support, shopping for him every week and visiting. Peggy stayed with Cookie for a week at Thanksgiving, and I came home for two weeks over the Christmas holidays.

His current challenge was making it to the bathroom in time to pee. This meant helping him get off his wet chinos and boxer shorts and getting him into clean, dry ones before we could go out for a ride in the freezing New England temperatures. I worried about Christmas at someone else's house and went to the CVS Pharmacy to see what they had for incontinence protection for men.

Incontinence is big business—a whole men's and then women's section. I was overwhelmed. Some diapers shaped like little bikini bathing suits in S, M, L or XL appealed to me right off—not too bulky. Then there were some that looked like briefs and those with overnight super absorbency. For $12.98, Wear-Even special superduper models caught my eye. I hadn't had such a meditation on penises or penis pouches in a long time. I could help Cookie get off his wet clothes, and with the camouflage of his long flannel shirts and my deftly averted eyes, avoid looking at his penis. But why me shopping for male incontinence protection with a family full of experts? After a half hour studying all the products—nothing in my work in women's studies had prepared me for this—I selected Depends Briefs. When I looked closely at them, with their low-cut contour and their stylish elastic legs and their slick three glue tabs on each side, I wondered again, "Why me?"

As soon as I got home, I bit the bullet with Cookie. Sitting down on the couch beside him, I began. "I want to help you with your peeing problem."

"What d-ya mean?"

"Well, you know, when you can't make it to the bathroom, you pee yourself, and then unless someone helps you get off the clothes, you sit around here wet."

"It dries all right."

"But what about when you go out in cold weather or go to a restaurant or like when we go to the Hiltons' tomorrow? You can't just ignore it with other people around, and you can't just pee on their furniture."

A pause. No answer. He turned on the TV.

I persisted over the blast of the Spanish channel, which, of course, he couldn't understand, but he clearly liked the bodacious woman, Carmen, bouncing and flouncing around the stage with her breasts in pretty clear view. I lowered the volume and opened the package of Depends. "Cookie, you could wear these and keep yourself dry."

He shot a glance at them and then at the ceiling. "No way."

"Why?"

No answer.

I glanced at the instructions. "Look. Here's how they go on." I modeled a pair over my jeans, showing how they fit with the little glue tabs. "They're easy and not too bulky."

"Forget it. Wear them yourself if you think they're so great."

I had to laugh as I sank back into the couch, defeated in my Depends. Carmen finished her dance and Cookie channel-surfed with dizzying speed.

"Well, would you be willing to wear jockey shorts so you won't just spray all over your pants?"

"I don't like them."

I stuck the Depends in the closet.

June 7, 1998. I was back from Hawaii. Cookie and I were in Friendly's eating our favorite meal for about the two hundredth time.

"I can always tell when you're feeling well," I said.

"How?"

"You wolf down everything put in front of you."

"I'll have to remember that."

"Why?"

"To put up a good front."

The statement didn't click until the next day. That night, he stayed up three hours past his bedtime, and we watched the final game of the NBA championships, which Michael Jordan saved for the Bulls. In the morning, when Candy, one of Cookie's favorite home health aides, woke him up, he was disoriented and weak. He couldn't get his legs to move right. He must have been feeling sick the day before. Dehydration, his solution to the peeing problem, did him in. Between the hospital and rehab, five roller-coaster weeks followed, with pneumonia always threatening. Everyone told me that he felt safe to be sick because I was home. Oh great, I thought. Not the homecoming I longed for.

Once again, rehab made another big difference in Cookie's life. His physical therapist, Luann, explained more about why he couldn't walk very well. Like other printers, she said, he had inhaled carbon tetrachloride, kerosene and ink fumes every day in his fifty-two years at work. And that, along with his heavy drinking, had shot the muscles and nerves in his legs. Luann worked miracles for Cookie in getting a brace for his weak right leg. On his walker, he could do four hundred feet in under ten minutes—a record. He left rehab in Depends.

His solution of not drinking any fluids so he wouldn't have to pee had precipitated the whole scenario. Now Depends were an answer. On his first day out of rehab, after a late lunch at Friendly's and a ride to the beaches, we went home. After Cookie announced he wanted to go to bed, I helped him get off his shoes, his brace and his chinos. When I spotted the Depends, I said I would help him change it.

"Nah," he said. "The diaper's clean."

"Come on, Cook. It's been about five hours."

"Forget it. Get my pajama top and give it to me."

Was he embarrassed? Relief flooded over me. Was I doing the right thing? The next morning, Lori, the know-it-all, guilt-tripping home health aide, confronted me at the dining room table with wet sheets, a wet blanket and a wet Depends. All before my first cup of coffee.

That night I knew what I had to do, but I really didn't know how. "Cookie, we've got to change your Depends."

"Naw."

"It's got to happen."

"I think I took a dump in the diapers."

"That's OK. I'll help you."

With that, he flopped back on the bed like a worn-out rag doll, and from that prone position he put his arms behind his head and looked up at me. Briefly, I caught his eye.

"I'll bet that you did this lots of times for me, Cookie."

He nodded, staring at the ceiling. We were both pretending not to be there. When I pulled off the diaper, I was shocked seeing his penis, small, drooping and almost white looking, with a sparse down of white pubic hair. I got him cleaned up and in a new diaper and kissed him good night.

In the kitchen, I poured myself a Grand Marnier on the rocks.

The last time I had seen his penis was forty years ago.

As a teenager, I used to get angry and embarrassed by Cookie's drinking. He'd start on a Saturday morning and be really loaded by noon. In 1958, when I was eighteen and a sophomore in college, Father Sweeney, still my mother's paramour and racetrack buddy, gave her a job ironing priests' vestments and altar linens for a Jesuit seminary. The Beak farmed the job out to me and took a twenty-five percent cut. Good pay, still, and I could do it at home. Hush money for not talking about Father Sweeney. Weekends, I was at the ironing board in the dining room, watching old movies, wrestling or whatever TV had to offer, as I sweated over the sacrosanct cloths and vestments.

When the Beak wanted to bag out with Father Sweeney to the racetrack on Saturdays, she'd yell at Cookie about doing something besides drinking, like doing the starching in the cellar and hanging the stuff up, or keeping an eye on the dryer which left its telltale rust if stuff sat in it. I felt bad for him, but I profited too from her nagging.

The cellar was where he drank his Haffenreffer Beer, and he turned a trash barrel down there into his toilet, because he didn't want to walk upstairs to pee and run the risk of being hollered at by my mother. By noon, with the Beak on the lam, he usually had a good buzz on and would frequently emerge to the kitchen, where he stood propped up against a counter drinking or slumped in a chair at the table. When I verbally sparred with him about his drinking, he often would come right over and get himself as close to me as possible and ask what the problem was.

"Quit that fronting up or I'll really let you have it," I'd scream and push him away. I always won when it came to shoving matches. Sobriety gave me an edge.

One day when he didn't fold right away, he challenged me. "Fronting up, huh. Fronting up. I'll show you what fronting up is." With that, he unzipped his fly.

At eighteen and still a good Irish Catholic virgin, I got to see my first adult penis. Yuck. I ran out of the kitchen, and he, in his drunken stupor, chased me around our seven-room ranch with his flopping penis hanging out. Disgust, not fear, rose up in me. I knew that drunk, he was no physical match. I got to the dining room on the second time around and threw the altar cloth I was working on down on the floor in front of him, grabbed the hot iron, yanking the plug out of the wall, and dared him.

"Step on that altar cloth and you'll have Father Sweeney and the Beak to answer to." That was mean, to remind him of the lovebirds, something I had never done before. It stopped him in his tracks.

"You fruitcake," he blurted out. "I'm going to teach you a lesson."

"Put that thing back in your pants."

"Up your bucket," he shot back pathetically.

"Up yours, too," I fired, walking out of the room with the iron in hand. I left it in the kitchen, went to my room, grabbed my book bag and headed for the Waltham Public Library to read Milton's *Paradise Lost* for Monday.

Being drunk. That's a great strategy for avoiding responsibility for what you do. Passivity. That's another good strategy. Cookie's a grand master of both ploys. Now he relies on passivity.

When the home health aide, Kathie, suggested that instead of wearing Depends, Cookie could get himself on a schedule of going to the bathroom every hour, he listened. Of course. She wasn't one of us. She was convinced that rehab hospitals steal people's will to independence with diapers, stool softeners and rules about not getting out of your chair.

"So Cookie, what do you think?" I asked.

"Wellllll, the diapers are easier."

I thought of the barrel in the cellar in Waltham.

"But your rear end and scrotum are becoming red and raw from sitting in the wet diapers," said Kathie. "Doesn't it hurt?"

He shrugged his shoulders and looked to the ceiling. "OK," he said. Agreement from the Grand Master of Passivity.

True daughter of Beak, an hour later I reminded him to go to the bathroom. Later, he didn't want to go. But I nagged and he did. I kept track of his trips back and forth, so much so that before dinner, he snapped at me.

After he put away a huge meal, his usual thing was bed, but not on this night. He went to the couch and sat down. Abruptly, he got up, heading too late for the bathroom. When he decided to go to bed, I didn't mention the accident as I took off his shoes and brace, slipped off the wet chinos and boxer shorts and put on the Overnight Depends that Kathie suggested, because, thanks to Lasix, he soaked the bed every night.

This was only day one in boxer shorts.

Who knows about all of this? It's a world that I never prepared myself for. Somehow I always imagined that Cookie would die first, because he had heart trouble, and then it would be hell on earth with the Beak. Probably, if she had gotten to Cookie's broken-down state, I'd have had little problem finding a nice nursing home for her, the way she did for her mother.

But everything changed for Cookie and me on the day of her funeral. What if he had died first? I never would have known that one of my parents thought I was OK. I never would have known that he didn't harbor grudges or feel ashamed, the way the Beak said he did. But can I really admire him for all of those years of silence and passivity? Was it just his instinct for self-preservation that stopped him from defending me to the Beak, or even telling me that he thought it was OK that I was a lesbian? Did he fear that if he sided with me, the Beak would have made his life miserable?

In so many ways, we're still in her shadow. The large psychological and philosophical questions about our family relationships remain—a therapist's dream.

The more immediate issue of how long Cookie can stay slouched on his own couch, even with the support of home health aides, Francine and me, is more day-to-day and time consuming. Through it all, Cookie remains passive. He buries his nose in the newspaper or TV, while I drive two hours to see him. He wants to check out the Patriots game, while I want him to chuck out the Depends he's been wearing for five hours. He wishes Joe Kennedy would run for governor, while I wish for enough money to keep paying for home health aides. He knows the latest plan for Iraq, while I worry if he has enough Lasix. He's discovered the secret to a long life. My strategies are still emerging. He may still know everything worth knowing.

The Promise

DIANE REED

$\mathcal{I}$ was sitting at the computer in my home office, deeply involved in work, when my mother walked in with a piece of paper in her hand. I hated interruptions.

"Here. I want you to keep this," she said, with an urgency in her voice. "I want you to talk to the doctor about it."

Sighing, the programming code fading from my mind, I looked at the paper. Once again, she was giving me the death potion "recipe." She did not want to continue living.

"I am old," she said. "No one needs me anymore and I feel useless."

My mother had been living with me for five years, since the death of my only sibling. She was a petite woman of eighty-eight years, with snow-white hair worn in a youthful cut swept back from her face. Her unlined skin denied her age, and her limber steps were the result of daily two-mile walks. Dignity and independence were her hallmarks. It was important to her to feel useful, and she claimed the laundry and cooking as her domains. I indulged her and did not mention it when the care of my clothes was not to my satisfaction or when meals were not prepared well. I wanted to help her feel needed and competent.

Even so, she still talked often of dying, asking me to promise that I would not let her suffer or linger. Her doctor, a mature woman herself, assured my mother that if the quality of her life were to be compromised in a permanent manner she would "help her out." She wanted the right to decide when she would die.

In the summer of her eighty-sixth year, my mother was knocked to the street by two large dogs as she walked our puppy. The resulting concussion caused bleeding into her brain.

"I have lost a part of myself. I can't find it. It is just gone," she told me the day after the fall.

My mother began to lose physical vigor and she fell frequently. The change in her personality was agonizing. Worrying irrationally about finances, she secretly called friends and family members to tell them that we had no money. She had a series of stroke-like "events" and barely recognized me. I was terribly afraid of losing her. The doctor stopped all her medications and told me privately that the end was very near. "Be prepared to lose her," she said. I knew from all our discussions that this would be my mama's desire.

But instead of worsening, my mother's health improved without her course of medications. Her physical functioning returned to its normal state, although she tired easily and her memory was still badly affected.

"I don't want to live beyond my usefulness," she began again one morning, asking me to talk with the doctor about it. "I want you to give me some pills and just end it. I am ready now."

But in the treatment room with her doctor, things were different. When I explained why we had come, my mother soberly looked at me and said she didn't know why I had "dragged" her in there. The doctor said that because my mother's current mental condition was "far from normal," she could not justify assisting her death.

This was to become a frequent pattern. My mother decided it was time to end her life; she talked about dying; she pleaded for it. We had close, long talks well into the night. She begged for my help in convincing the doctor she was ready. The next morning, she would tell me to forget what she said the previous night, and spend the day watching television.

I felt afraid, exhausted and very unsure of the correct thing to do for my mother as she deteriorated quickly into dementia. Alone and isolated, I could not leave the house to work, so I sought work-at-home contracts. My entire life became one of caring for my mother. She turned into what she feared most in the world: She became useless and incompetent. Her brain trauma condemned her to stay alive because she did not meet the criteria for making an informed choice about her life.

She remained in that condition for a year. I worked at contracts when I could find them; I had very little social life. My mother could not accept having a daily caregiver while I went out to work, and I was not able, after the first year, to find work to do at home. She was drinking wine steadily, almost a bottle a day. In the shower one morning, I began sobbing out of control. I sobbed through the shower and shampoo and while I dressed. I sobbed until I phoned a therapist friend who helped me calm myself. Clearly, my resources were running out.

I found a job and a retirement community close enough that I could run in to see her, take her things and frequently eat meals with her. With my support she got along well. My life took on new dimensions. I had a job I enjoyed and worked with some friendly, social people. I met a very supportive man, Phil, who willingly helped me with my mother's care. Eventually, he moved into my house with me.

After several months, she was diagnosed with pneumonia. When the doctor did not want to hospitalize her and her condition did not improve, I brought her home. The room I fixed for her was a living room of sorts, but near a bathroom and the fireplace, with a view of the ocean and the afternoon sunshine.

The next morning, a Friday, I called her doctor to say that my mother was no better. Pneumonia, she told me, is "the old man's friend." The condition was irreversible. My main job was to make her as comfortable as possible. The doctor would not be available over the weekend, but the on-call doctor would be updated about my mother's case.

"Am I going to die?" my mother asked me that night.

"I don't know for sure," I said, "but pneumonia is difficult to overcome. You also have chronic lymphocytic leukemia, which keeps your body from fighting it."

She looked out the window for a while, and then said, "Could you get me those pills now and just end it all?"

I told her I would try.

On Saturday morning, when her breathing was labored, I put in a telephone call to the doctor on duty. He pulled up her record on his computer. Without my asking, he told me he would prescribe a "very large bottle" of something that would end her life and make her comfortable at the same time. "This is what I would want for myself," he said, adding that there was no need for her to suffer. This doctor had met neither me nor my mother.

I went to the pharmacy in the back of a large drugstore and paid for the prescription. Walking out, carrying the brown paper bag that contained a death sentence, I felt like a murderer and imagined that people looking at me knew what I was going home to do.

My mother's eyes locked with mine as I took the large bottle of purple fluid out of the bag. I held a spoon in my hand next to it, waiting for her to speak.

"Is that it?" she said. And when I nodded, she said she was ready to get on with it.

"Are you sure?" I said.

"As ready as I'll ever be." She looked for a long time out the window, and then, turning back, she asked for the medication.

I gave her the dosage written on the label, and she swallowed it.

"Am I going to hell, do you think?" she asked.

"No. Definitely not," I answered.

I sat with her, rubbing her back, stroking her hair. She seemed restless and did not fall asleep.

"Would you like to get bundled into the car and go see the ocean?" I asked.

"Not unless you are going to put me in it," she said.

She drifted off for a couple of hours and woke up as Phil and I were having bowls of hot soup and hot bread and wine prepared by my next-door neighbor. "My," she said, "that smells good. Is there enough for me?"

I got her up, amazed that she could be hungry, and helped her to a chair in front of the television where we were having our supper. She ate a bowl of soup and some bread, conversed and watched Lawrence Welk. The medicine had not done its intended work. Instead of ending her life, it made her feel better. I was confused but heartened. Perhaps she was improving after all. Had I somehow misunderstood what the on-call doctor had said? I was sure I had not.

After a time she asked for help getting back to her bed. She sat on the edge of it while I lit a fire. As she reminisced about a trip she had taken to England eighteen years before, she was lucid. She was my mother again. The firelight played over the skin on her face and legs, bathing it in a glow. Sitting with her legs together and turned to one side, one arm laid gracefully across her lap, the other supporting her lightly, she was beautiful. For those minutes it was hard to believe she was ill. We tucked her in and went to bed, confident that she would recover.

The next day, Easter Sunday, I was excited that my son Eric and his family would find "Grandma" so much improved when they visited. When they arrived she was taciturn and withdrawn and almost rude. We left her alone and watched from a distance. When Eric said goodbye, a loving smile of recognition suddenly lit her face. I was relieved she remembered him.

Shortly afterwards, my mother descended into some kind of hell, shouting in terror and twisting on her bed, throwing her body back and forth, back and forth. I rushed to her side and touched her shoulder. Startled, she looked up to see who I was, her eyes filled with fear. She came back from wherever she had gone and recognized me, but then began shouting again. I talked quietly with her, and she finally was able to tell me there had been a plane crash. I asked if she had seen it or been in it, and her response was a loud and vengeful, "Wouldn't you like to know!"

I gave her another dose of the medicine and then another. Then another. After two hours, there was no response to the medication. She kept on with her fear and her twisting and her agony. Her agitation was consuming. I gave her one more dose and sat with her for a long time, touching her and saying that I loved her; that it was OK for her to let go; that I'd be OK; that she had been a good mother and deserved to be at rest. She twisted and shouted. How could I make this agitation stop? I felt unequal to the demands of my mother's distress. My poor little mother—always peaceful and dignified, now she was suffering so badly. I wanted it all to end for her.

I called my next-door neighbor, a hospice nurse, who willingly stepped in to help us in our torment. No longer alone, I finally had a professional I could count on. She advised me to ask the doctor for a "Do Not Resuscitate" form so that when my mother died, the paramedics would not try to keep her alive. Before she went to work and after as well, she came in to help make my mother comfortable with the things only nurses seem to know. Amazed at my mother's agitation, she said she had never seen a patient suffer in this way. Nor a daughter.

I will always think of the next day, Monday, as the Day of the Medicines. I was beginning to accept that my mother would not recover. When she could no longer communicate with me, I kept thinking about her requests to me and her pleas to her doctor that she never wanted to live beyond her usefulness. Early that morning, I put in a call to her regular doctor, who was back from her weekend off.

When she returned the call, I told the doctor that it was time to talk about my mother's death, that it seemed clear she was not going to recover. I told her what the on-call doctor had prescribed. I told her about the agitation and how exhausted my mother was from it, and how it continued night and day. I asked why the weekend prescription had not been effective. "Not strong enough," was the short reply. I told her how distressed I was, knowing that my mother was suffering so much and I was unable to help her. I reminded her of my mother's many requests to be allowed to die. I wanted morphine for her, I said.

The doctor prescribed a large bottle of it, as well as Nembutal suppositories and a major tranquilizer, Mellaril. In my kitchen, I rolled the Mellaril pills between sheets of waxed paper to reduce them to powder and then dissolved them in honey and water to make it more palatable. Never still, my mother kept writhing and calling out. The shouting was so difficult to hear, and my agony as I watched her twisting, throwing her arms and kicking off her covers, left me with feelings of utter helplessness. She was only conscious enough to continue her agitation. I filled an eyedropper with the liquefied Mellaril, slowly dropped it into my mother's mouth, and let it roll down her throat.

I had never been with a dying person before. My experience included only books and television and movies where nobody shouted or was so agitated. The person lay peacefully, stretched out their hands to place on a loved one's bowed head and drew one last breath. Neatly. None of this suffering, sweating or turbulence.

A few minutes passed. She calmed down. In half an hour she fell asleep, deeply asleep. She did not move. I was exhausted. My mother slept for seventeen hours without moving. Her peace was marvelous, even though it was drug induced.

When my neighbor came by the next morning, and we turned my mother over, the horror of her appearance was shocking. Her face had swollen tight, the skin pulled taut over the flesh. Her eyes pulled up at the corners. Her fingers were elephantine. She looked nothing like my mother. Pus from the pneumonia ran from her mouth as she could no longer swallow. Her cheek, arm, nightgown and sheets were saturated with the yellow ooze. The disease that was overwhelming her life force was now visible.

Why did she not die? Why was she hanging on just to suffer? Eighty-eight years old, stricken with pneumonia and leukemia, her heart beat on and her breathing, while compromised, was regular. She had wanted to die, had asked to die. Her strength was astounding. Never, the hospice nurse said, had she seen anything like it.

We bathed her, changed the bed, turned her over and put a towel under her cheek. We rearranged her arms and legs. I began to feel as though I were trapped in some particular form of hell from which I would never escape and that she would continue suffering for longer than I could stand it. The nurse went off to work, and my mother lay there unconscious, her breathing sounding much like a percolator resounding throughout the house.

Alone, I sat and watched and listened. My mother and I had always been close. When I wanted to go to college and my father thought it was a waste for a woman to get educated, she went to work to pay my way. When I decided to go for a master's degree, she helped again. Even after she had dementia, she still listened and talked with me and was interested in my life. On the last day she could speak, she said she wanted to stay and "protect me." We had a rich, respectful relationship, and now it was drawing to an end. What would I do without her?

I was alone. The doctor had given tacit approval to end my mother's suffering with the arsenal of medicines now at hand. Did I have the courage to do it? I paced the floor. I listened to her rattling breaths. I remembered the many times she told me what she wanted, and how that desire persisted even after her brain was injured. She resumed her restless, agitated movements.

I went to the kitchen and removed a Nembutal suppository from its package. I cut it in half and put it in place. In her unconscious state, my mother batted at my hand to avoid the discomfort. I sat and waited. Nothing changed. Could I do this? I still didn't know. Two hours later, I inserted a whole Nembutal; again she batted at my hand. I waited an hour and repeated the procedure.

I felt so alone. Ending the life of a loved one—even if she is suffering, even if she has begged you to do it—is a difficult thing to do. Sometimes, before this final illness, when the responsibility of her care was overwhelming, I used to daydream about going to her in the night and holding a pillow over her face. I could never have done it in actuality.

Early in the afternoon, I knew I had to carry out her wishes. I gave her half a dropper of morphine. She was still agitated, so I prepared some Mellaril and gave her a quarter of a whole pill. I gave her more morphine. Waiting for a time, I inserted another Nembutal. Her breathing continued, noisy but regular. Morphine should have depressed her respiration. I gave her more Mellaril. No change. She stopped shouting but was twisting and restless and not at peace.

I began to believe that she would never die. The nurse came home from work and checked in with me. When I told her my decision to medicate my mother until her life stopped, she said, "OK." That was it. No questions. Just support. She gave me the courage I needed to carry out my conviction that this was what my mother wanted all along. Now it was time to keep my promise. I wanted it to be quick and I wanted her suffering to end.

We turned my mother onto her back, bathed her, gave her clean sheets and tipped her head back to help with her airway. She started having small convulsions affecting only her upper body. Her face was now fully exposed to me for the first time since her illness began. Her beloved, beautiful face twitched spastically in small areas. I prepared another full dropper of morphine. I prepared another dropper full of Mellaril. Gathering up all the drugs, I went to my mother's bedside. I inserted the remaining five Nembutal suppositories. I put endless droppers of morphine into her mouth, more Mellaril. The nurse held my hand. We watched my mother. Her breathing continued. What a strong woman she was!

In a while, my neighbor went home, leaving me sitting on the floor by the bed. I held my mother's hand and told her I loved her. There was, amazingly, a vocal response from her. She was "talking" back to me! When I said, "I love you," she vocalized something of about the same length back to me. We "talked" back and forth for a number of minutes. I was going to be fine, I told her. I would miss her terribly, but it was OK for her to slip away, that it was time. I said all the things I needed in order to say goodbye. She vocalized back. I want to believe that she heard me and was answering.

If she were still alive in the morning, I promised myself, I would call an ambulance to come and take her to the hospital. I had the Do Not Resuscitate form, and as it was part of her medical record, the hospital would likely not accept her. She would be shipped to a care facility to vegetate until she died. I would lose control of the ability to help with her comfort, and I would not be able to fulfill her wish to die in her own home and in her own time. Nevertheless, I could not keep on with what I was doing much longer.

I gave her one more dropper of morphine and went to lie down on my own bed. Although I couldn't sleep, I tried very hard not to listen for the breaths. They had changed to deep, bass, shuddering noises with long moments between them. How would I live through this? I wanted to call her back, to tell her not to go, that I wasn't ready to lose her. I lay still. In an hour, I got up to check on her. She was in the same position. Her skin was cold. I returned to bed.

Soon Phil went to her room. When he came back, he held me in his arms. "Your mother has passed away," he said.

I went to her and touched her skin. She was still cold. We talked about whether to call the paramedics right away or wait until morning. Deciding to complete what had ended, I called at three in the morning, told the paramedics about the Do Not Resuscitate form and asked them not to use their sirens. When they and the police arrived, they quietly and professionally went to work. My nurse came in with tears streaming down her face. She sat with Phil and me, holding my other hand as we watched the tasks of death take place. They examined my mother, filled out their forms and pronounced her dead, covering her beloved face with a blanket.

I called the Neptune Society and asked them to come and pick up the body. They said they would be there in two hours. Phil went back to bed. The nurse went home.

Alone with my mother, I pulled the blanket back from her dear face. I stroked her hair and held her hands. I rubbed her feet. I talked to her. I cried over her. She was beautiful. She was at peace. In her stillness, I grew to know her in a totally new way. When the Neptune Society arrived, they placed her body gently into a shroud and carried her out of my house. I would never see her again.

Dutiful daughters take care of their aging mothers. I had no other moral choice. Sometimes I was very angry; often I was very tired.

Sometimes I felt quite sorry for myself. Now that it is done, and she is gone forever, I miss her. I even miss the burden of her. She was my mother. As I helped her die, I felt only love and the conviction that I gave her the best gift possible. I was dutiful to the end. And I kept my promise.

Somebody

JANET MASON

"**F**or Chrissake, will you stop calling me 'your wife.' They know who I am, believe me. I'm somebody in that office. I'm important. Even if I have to die to get that way."

My mother's voice is a cold razor slicing down the length of my spine. Somebody. My mother defines the concept according to the commentators on the news hour, *Viewpoint,* that she watches on public television each week: "They are all women, black women, white women, young and middle-aged, journalists, editors, TV personalities. They are all *somebody*. They have position, title, influence." My mother's definition of the opposite of somebody: *nobody, invisible, non-existent, unimportant, herself.*

My mother, who has suddenly become everything to me, thinks she is nobody.

My father's hand trembles as he holds the phone to his ear.

She glares at him from the dining room table.

"You're still mine," he says when the receptionist at the doctor's office puts him on hold.

"Your what? Your garbage can? Your car? I'm not an object. I'm not a thing called Your Wife."

"You're still mine," he repeats, his attempts at a smile swallowed by the graveness of his features. A year, a month, a week ago this would have been a spirited banter between the two of them. But no one is laughing now.

Everything has changed.

"I saw it on her face," my mother tells me after my father has cleared the table, done the dishes and gone out for his walk. "After the doctor helped me sit up on the examining table, she looked at me, and I could see it on her face. When she gave me the results of the first MRI, I told her I wasn't surprised. But I just said that. It was a way of protecting myself. Of course I was surprised. How could I have known?"

The next three days go by in a blur. I am staying at my parents' house, my ankles hanging over the end of my old bed, the mattress so narrow I am afraid to roll over. I look at my old bureau and desk: tiny pink flowers painted around the shiny white knobs. Through my pre-teen years the walls were hung with *Tiger Beat* centerfolds, Davy Jones, the Partridge Family, replaced in my teen years with spike-haired lightning bolt David Bowie and black-eyed Alice Cooper *Welcome to My Nightmare* posters, along with the silkscreens I made in high school, Robin Trower, my oversized marijuana leaf, the Statue of Liberty sinking in a sea of bubbling pollution, in place of the torch her outstretched middle finger making its final statement. The posters gradually came down in my college years, the walls checkered with blank spots, and when I moved out, ripped down forever, the thumbtack holes and tape marks covered with a fresh coat of primer and an outer coat of ivory paint. My mother moved her things upstairs into my old room: her bookshelves, sewing table, a few framed prints on the wall, one with three horned owls sitting on a log. "That's us," my mother used to say, before the stairs got too hard for her to navigate and she left her prints and books upstairs and moved back downstairs into the smaller bedroom. "Those three owls sitting like bumps on a log. That's you, me and your father."

At the doctor's office, I feel like I am swimming underwater through the wavy sea green wallpaper of the small waiting room into the even smaller examining room. The pale yellow walls are shafts of light filtering down to the depths. The waters part momentarily when the doctor enters the room: Her deep-set eyes are compassionate, deeply caring, reflective of our fear and grief. This is the new internist my mother has turned to out of frustration with the old one. Surely she has some hopeful news, a weighted rope ladder she can toss down from her lifeboat for us to grasp. I sit on one side of my mother, my father on the other, our backs to the yellow wall. Shafts of light illuminate the doctor's words. "I wish you had been my patient sooner"— she looks gravely at my mother—"before things got this far." Light bounces from the pale yellow walls onto the crisp clean paper stretched across the examining table, back to the walls, reflecting off an anatomy poster, each muscle, organ and bone precisely outlined and colored accordingly: ruddy pink, purplish blue, bone white.

As the doctor talks, I brace myself by holding tight to the metal arms of my chair. My white knuckles are the only thing between me and the sea that threatens to submerge me in an underwater canyon. The doctor's words—*cancer fourth stage terminal metastasized oncologist*— are pushing me under. *Terminal.* My heart is the leaden weight that will drag me to the bottom. I try in vain to hold back the tears that threaten to pour out the ocean that is inside of me. My body that is mostly water cannot absorb any more.

Nothing has prepared me for this.

I am lost in a maze. In a shopping mall nightmare, I am treading long loops, off and on ramps that go nowhere but where you already are, the hard glittering sense of doom that you are lost, lost, lost deep in the center of somewhere you have never always been. My parents and I are across the parking lot from the shopping mall. The bituminous surface of the asphalt soaks up the heat of a cool autumn day. We are searching for the entrance to the oncologist's office in a maze of brick and glass. Finally, we find a chrome door handle. I push it and it does not open. There is no sign pointing the way. We walk to the other side of the building. My mother's feather-light body leans on her cane. My father and I are on either side of her. We place our helpless hands under her elbows. "You're only making it worse," she says. "Let me walk by myself." She takes one slow step after another past what seems like miles of red brick and silver chrome. Finally, on the other side of the building, a glass-windowed door that opens.

Inside, six receptionists sit in a black rectangle in the middle of other rectangles, separate waiting rooms that interconnect. One receptionist takes my mother's name, her insurance information, and directs us to the waiting room on the far left side of the building. We pass a wall of fish tanks on the way. Large carp with ruffled fins hover in blackness. A few swim to and fro in spacious confinement. They are slow-moving blobs of iridescent light, unnaturally bright. The waiting room is full of silent people. We find three seats together. With my father's help, my mother eases herself into the center chair. We sit down on either side of her, our backs resting uneasily against black vinyl. A wide glass and chrome coffee table in front of us holds one of every magazine there is about health and wellness, positive living and positive dying. I pick one up and fan through the oversized glossy pages. I let one page fall open on my lap, then another. A large quote divides the page between columns of text: *Death is the final destination. We are, all of us, each day, moving one step closer. . . .* My eyes blur. The columns turn into rivers. I sense the silence around me, the absence of any outwardly expressed emotions, no grief, no rage, no stifled sobs. I will the tears back into the ocean that is my body.

"Look." My mother turns her head to me, then to my father.

The magazine on her lap is open to a glossy photo spread of people on a beach standing in a circle. They are wearing colorful but muted winter clothes, one with a maroon and white striped scarf, another with the side flaps of a dusty pink South American knitted cap pulled down over her ears. Inside the circle they have formed with outstretched arms and clasped hands lies a loose garland of flowers. Hibiscus, it looks like, something dark, vibrant, tropical, a sacrifice dropped at their feet. Their faces, unguarded in their vulnerability, are as familiar to me as their clasped hands, reminding me of the other students in a tai chi class I once took, a Wicca circle where I joined the others in calling the directions, North, South, East, West, the circles of my childhood: *Ring around the Rosie, a pocket full of posies, one, two, three, we all fall down.*

Another photograph shows the side view of a woman sitting in the prow of a small motorboat, the blustery sky as gray and foamy as the waves that slap the sides of her small vessel. Her hair is blown back, revealing her mottled profile of disbelief and at the same time tranquility. She has reached this inner peace, the sense of letting go, acceptance. Her outstretched arms sweep the vastness and her fingers, forever frozen in their uncurling, drop a single rose into the choppy waters. The caption underneath: *This woman has surrendered her husband's ashes to the bay.* On second glance I see tiny flecks of white dotting the waves, dust, grit, sand and the shell-like fragments of what was once bone and flesh: a life.

My mother runs her outstretched index finger under the words at the bottom of the page: *It's important for the survivors to have a ritual, to come together and air their grief at the passing of their loved ones.* I look back at the photos. There is something about the people, something tribal, unconventional at least, that makes them look familiar to me. They are people honoring death and grieving their losses openly, without apology. In doing so they have dropped the veils of the church, the pomp and circumstance, the empty prayers and palliatives about the deceased "going to a better place." The people in the photos do not carry wax-like lilies and cast their eyes down in the presence of the almighty.

They open their eyes and gaze up into the sun.

And down into the pit of their own grief.

They are alive even in the presence of death.

Even as I recognize this, I feel myself pulling away. The tears in my eyes are suddenly drying to anger, my nerve endings retreating into a safe, hard place. There is only one thing I know for sure about the mourners spread before me in the glossy pages.

They are not us.

We are surrounded by light. The walls of the rectangular examining room are covered with opaque white light panels that darken as the oncologist clips my mother's MRI films into place. The top view, side view, frontal view, rear view. The insides of my mother's body are displayed like the cross section of a diaphanous tree. Murky gray outlines swim in a translucent black sea. The oncologist stares hard at each panel and with a solid black magic marker circles the cloudy white spots, amorphous blobs and solid white masses, which he names as he moves around the room from panel to panel: *all throughout the pancreas; at the bottom of the liver next to the gallbladder; the top of the kidneys near the adrenal glands; a five-inch tumor in the abdomen; the long white ridge in her sternum deflecting into her ribs; the left pelvis where the bone has eroded.* My mother's face is as white as the disposable gown the oncologist has her change into in the adjacent dressing room. He asks if she'd like my father and me to stay. She nods and he helps her onto the examining table.

"It's definitely not breast cancer or colon cancer," he says, when he's finished examining her, pulling the rubber gloves off his hands.

When she is dressed, we file across the hallway to his office. The comfortable leather chairs that we sit on might as well be beds of nails. The oncologist sits behind his mahogany desk, the walls behind him lined with gold-framed diplomas. The afternoon sunlight filters through the window and flashes in his diamond pinkie ring as he lifts his hands and folds them under his chin. Deep lines are etched into his face. His cheeks are jowly, his forehead square and furrowed. He has the build of a man who watches what he eats, who exercises methodically, yet everything about him is massive: the cigar-shaped fingers folded under his chin, his elbows resting like tree limbs on his desk. His oversized coffee cup rests solidly on the desk that is hewn not from a single tree but a forest. Each word he speaks is ponderous.

"The next step," he says slowly, "is a biopsy of the tumor."

My mother stiffens. More tests, more pain, more climbing in and out of the MRI tube, overnight hospital stays, long needles poked into her frail body. "Couldn't the biopsy cause the cancer to spread through my body?" she asks.

He unfolds his hands, drops them from under his chin and refolds them again. His square knuckles are stacked in a slightly crooked vertical line. "There are no guarantees. But even though your condition is inoperable, it could be managed, controlled. Unfortunately, we're not talking about a cure. If the origin of the condition is ovarian, which I don't think it is, there's a fifteen percent success rate that it could be controlled for a certain period of time."

"How long?" The question blurts out of my mouth before I can stop it.

"With treatment, a year, at the most two years. Do nothing"—he picks up his hand, palm up, and drops it back down on his desk—"six months." His deep voice drops off, like a slab of rock sliding into a quarry.

The tears I have been collecting in the reservoir of my anger— shored up by the luster that the oncologist has surrounded us with, the deep finish of the mahogany, his glittering diamond pinkie ring, the polished gold globe that is his paperweight, his world, his gleaming tie tack, his tailored suit, his buffed, manicured fingernails—suddenly burst forth in an undeniable sob and stream down my face.

He reaches across his desk and hands me a box of tissues.

"You're an only child?"

I blow into the deep pile tissue and nod. At the age of thirty-four, I am reduced to a three-year-old who has lost her mother in a supermarket. I feel diminished not by the oncologist's age but by his status, his sacrifice of everything for his narrow education, his profession that slices people into categories and body parts without any thought of the whole, the glittering baubles that are his reward. I want to hate him. But when I hand back the box of tissues and look into the lines of his face, I see a deep sadness, the result of too many patients who couldn't be saved.

"I have these two to think about," says my mother, who is holding my father's hand on the armrest between them. "They're not ready to let me go."

He regards her with heavy silence.

"It's very important," he says, "to make this decision for yourself. The treatment can be invasive, trying on your patience. If you do it for someone else, you're bound to have some resentment."

"I felt a lump in my abdomen ten years ago when I was in the hospital. I told the doctor but he wouldn't look at it." A day after our visit to the oncologist, my mother and I sit in the back yard. The sky is an iridescent blue arc. The leaves of a nearby dogwood rustle in dark, shiny, maroon clusters. The dogwood is a volunteer, its seed dropped by birds in the middle of what used to be my mother's organic garden. Now the only things distinguishing it from the rest of the lawn are a few shaggy patches of oregano, rosemary, mint. My mother is remembering the week she spent in the hospital ten years ago, after she had gone to a doctor complaining of fatigue. He had taken an x-ray, found a dark spot in the intestinal area and put her in the hospital for a colonoscopy. It was the same year that Ronald Reagan had the procedure done. My mother found out later that the dark spot was just a shadow and her fatigue was caused by a mild case of anemia, cured by vitamins. After she was discharged from the hospital, she looked up the doctor and found long, unexplained absences in his medical practice. Then she ran into another patient of his who said she believed he was an alcoholic.

"I always say that the hospital is no place for sick people. If you're not sick already, you start to think you're sick. I was faint from all that sugar water they fed me all week. I had to fast for the colonoscopy and all I could eat was Jell-O. Jell-O! For a week! It's a wonder it didn't kill me. I took my walk, though, every day. I tried to time it so the nurses wouldn't see me. In the morning when they were changing their shifts, or later in the afternoon when they were taking their coffee break. I'd walk from my room to the patient lounge and then sneak out the fire exit and walk up and down the stairwell. The stairs were made from a metal grate, so you could look down and see the bottom floor. Your father came with me sometimes and other times I went by myself. Up and down those stairs, ten times each way before I was finished.

"At first the nurses didn't know what was going on, but then they started to catch on.

" 'What are you doing up there?' asked the nurse, just as I was going up my first flight of stairs for the day. She must have followed me down the hall.

" 'Nothing,' I said, 'just taking a walk.'

" 'There'll be no walking as long as you're in this hospital.'

" 'Yes ma'am,' I said, and started to come back down. Then she left and I turned right back around and finished my walk."

She snickers and then turns serious.

"I never saw the doctor, just his associates. He had every doctor in his practice stopping in to see me. And when I told one of them that I thought I had a lump in my abdomen, he wouldn't even look at it. All he was interested in was my asshole. Assholes were in that year. Ronald Reagan's was on the front page of every paper."

A gust of wind sweeps the laughter from us. Nearby a single brown leaf spirals from a neighbor's elm tree, its sideways fingers curled upwards like a small boat in a blue sky. My mother pulls the front of her gray sweater together until the two sides overlap.

"When I was in the hospital, I shared a room with a woman who was dying. She told me her life story. People do that when they're dying. The poor thing. I opened the window so she could breathe some fresh air. Her husband came to see her and sat there like a dummy and watched the football game. Her two daughters never showed up.

Then I woke one morning and her bed was empty."

It's time for us to go inside so my mother can rest and I can start making lunch. She leans forward on the seat of her chair and places the cane solidly on the ground between her legs. Before pushing herself up, she looks over at the garden.

"Your father won't know what to do with them," she motions toward the sprawling oregano patch, the stalks of mint, the bushy rosemary plant. "He might as well mow them down."

My mother has decided not to have the biopsy.

"But Mom, what if there's a chance?" I am talking to her on the telephone a week after our visit to the oncologist.

"I can't take any more," she responds. "No more hospitals, no more tests. It's too painful."

I am silent, wanting to respect her wishes, but at the same time needing to beg her to live.

"But the doctor I talked to told me a patient of hers had the same condition that you have. She had the treatment and surgery for a hip replacement. Two years later, she's still alive."

She is silent.

"What if I go ahead with the biopsy? What if they stick a needle into that tumor that's been there for God knows how long and the cancer spreads throughout my body? What if I die early? How would you feel then?"

"Good for her," says one friend, then another, when I tell them of my mother's decision. Both have watched parents die drawn-out painful deaths, two, three years, in and out of hospitals, the treatment so invasive it is unclear whether it or the disease killed them. I talk to more people and find several whose mothers, old women invisible to the medical establishment, were misdiagnosed and ended up in the hospital with fourth stage cancer. Both of them died almost immediately after going through the biopsy.

I come to accept her decision, but not the doctor's prognosis. With the urgency of saving my own life, I talk to the macrobiotic counselor morning and night, reporting on my mother's progress, listening to his advice: "It is a difficult decision for her to make, but studies have shown that people with macrobiotic lifestyles live the same amount of time as people who pursue traditional medical treatment, but with a higher quality of life." With held breath, I wait for him to say that she could be cured, like one of the macrobiotic success stories I have read about in the books I am bringing home to my parents: *The Macrobiotic Miracle; To Live Again; Recovery from Cancer.*

"Perhaps," is all he says. "Perhaps."

The counselor tells me about some natural remedies, some which work immediately. Buckwheat plaster for my mother's feet, which have been swelling. My mother, who was trained as a nurse, explains to me that the swelling is called edema, caused by water getting backed up when the kidneys aren't doing their job.

"This will never work," she says about the buckwheat plaster.

Then, forty-five minutes later, after we remove the oatmeal-like paste from her feet, "It worked. I can't believe it."

I grate ginger, squeeze out the juice and mix it with sesame oil, then rub it on her hips when they begin to ache.

"It's better than aspirin," she says with astonishment.

Other remedies I am not so sure of. Shiitake mushroom tea to shrink tumors. I go to the health-food store and buy several fresh shiitake mushrooms. They are twelve dollars a pound but the mushrooms are very light.

"Use dry mushrooms, not fresh," says the counselor when I talk to him. "Fresh too strong."

"Shiitake!" my aunt explains over the telephone. "That sounds too *yaan*. You have to find out whether her cancer is *yaan* or *yeen*. Bone cancer sounds *yaan* to me."

Yin yang. Yaan yeen. I don't know if I'm helping to save my mother's life or slowly killing her.

My mother sticks to her diet: a scoop of brown rice, adzuki beans to help her kidneys, fresh greens, organic collards, mustard greens for calcium, miso soup and wakame seaweed for special vitamins and minerals. With my mother I chew my food twenty times, remembering the counselor's words: "Drink your food and eat your drink." Before our meals, we hold hands, my mother, father and I, and chant "Suuuuu." I have a feeling my father is just mouthing the words, but he goes along with us. It may sound crazy, at best "new age," but the chanting before each meal works as a soothing vibrational frequency, a kind of grace, acknowledging that the food we are about to eat will form our bodies. My mother takes a walk around the block almost every day, nothing compared to the four miles she used to walk, but enough to get her outside into the fresh air.

"Isn't this day beautiful," she exclaims as we loop around the drive, next to the hill that leads down to the creek that runs between the two sections of tract houses. The creek is hidden behind the treetops that we look down on, magnificent in greenish reds and orange yellows: maples, elms, ashes, an occasional wrinkled beech. She stops walking for a moment, hangs on to my elbow and with her good arm points her cane up to the translucent bell of blue sky. "I'm so glad I didn't kill myself last winter when I woke up with this thing and felt like dying. If I had I never would have seen this beautiful day!"

She has stopped taking her painkillers, just extra-strength Tylenol, to allow her body to better heal itself. Some days are better than others. But still she is losing weight. And the pain is increasing. I start reading *The Tibetan Book of Living and Dying*, carefully outlining the Buddhist exercises in each chapter and come across one called *Tonglen.* With this exercise I develop compassion by putting myself in my mother's place. I breathe in her pain and breathe out tranquility. I don't know if it works, but it calms me down. A friend lends me *Many Lives, Many Masters*, a book written by a medical doctor about past-life experiences. I give it to my mother.

"It seemed so real. I could hardly believe it," she says, her eyes moist when she hands me back the book. "But everyone died a violent death in each lifetime. It doesn't seem worth it. Can't I sign up somewhere not to have to do this again?"

A day later when I mention the book, she says, "The woman was always a servant. Didn't you notice that? In one lifetime she was a servant and in the next one she was a secretary. I'm not coming back unless I can be a college graduate." Her voice is perforated with lost opportunities.

I don't bring up the book again.

Every afternoon when I come to visit, we put on a meditation tape and sing along with it. She sits in her gold velour rocking chair, me on the far right end of the sofa, next to her.

"I am whole. I am full of light."

We sing a few times, breath moving through us in a circular motion. When I close my eyes, light swirls up like colors dabbed on a palette, a chalky yellow, muted green and at the bottom a deep tranquil blue.

"That's good," she says. "It takes the pressure off my sternum."

And we breathe a deep breath to begin again.

Mother May Be the Death of Me

MARTHA K. BAKER

$\mathcal{M}$other won't die.

We've been waiting for her to die for a long time. The autumn of '93, we thought she was a goner. We planned to be sad. We planned a memorial, complete with "I Come to the Garden Alone." We planned to dance on her grave, a jig perhaps, nothing too choreographed, just a symbol of naughty joy and relief.

But she lived.

My husband says she will outlive us all, especially since staying alive means she can make the lives of all four of her daughters a living hell. What reason does she have to go? he asks snottily.

Mother has been in poor health ever since I've known her, which is almost fifty years. Mother didn't exactly "enjoy poor health," to borrow my father's father's expression. She suffered and not without complaint, rubbing her gassy stomach, noisily passing wind—oral and anal—wherever she stood, in public or private.

"There, that feels better," she would announce.

The whole time we were growing up, she told us about having

scarlatina as a child, about her liver after a bout with jaundice, about her need for a strict diet.

She took pills for what ailed her. Once, when I took my first husband home, he whispered to me, "You know your mother's half-stoned all the time, don't you?"

I didn't. Sometimes when I was dusting each pill bottle on her dresser, I would line them up. If I knocked one over, the whole row cascaded like dominoes. But, no, I did not connect her behavior with those prescribed capsules and tablets.

Why hasn't Mother died of an overdose?

Part of cleaning always meant wiping up coffee and sweeping up tobacco. Mother drinks coffee and smokes cigarettes. She is a child of her era, having been born in 1920 (six days before the bill passed giving women the right to vote). She smoked tobacco and drank coffee (at least she rarely drank alcohol—remember her liver?) all through World War II, all day and most of the night at work. She still does.

Mother is not a clean smoker. Little Mount Etnas of butts rise in ashtrays about the house; coffee rings mark her trail. One time when I drove the two hours to clean her house, I found dead matches carpeting the floor of the spare room. Barely a loop of the shag rug showed for the matches she had simply dropped to the floor after lighting up.

How come she hasn't burned to death?

When we were growing up in the fifties and sixties, Mother worked nights as a Linotype operator for a company that publishes medical texts. About two-thirty in the afternoon, she prepared her lunch. If we were home in the summer, she would have one of us daughters assemble it for her. A Thermos full of coffee, a fried steak, half a canned cling peach on small curds of cottage cheese, a slice of white bread. A pear half, the occasional variation. One fresh pack of Raleigh cigarettes and a full book of matches.

When Mother finally went on the day shift after I left for college, she would return home about three-thirty p.m., expecting my two younger sisters to have her hot supper waiting on the table for her.

She rarely returned the favor: When one of those sisters came home from eighteen months of teaching in Australia, she walked in the front door, expecting maybe a greeting in the living room. Not a sound, not even a streamer shouting "Welcome Home." Mary finally found Mother back in the kitchen, eating her usual steak dinner.

"I couldn't wait for you," Mother said. "I was hungry."

While in high school, this same sister had to grocery shop for Mother. The A&P used to sit two blocks from our house, so we could walk there through the alleys, but then it closed. Armed with the grocery list, my sister had to go to three stores for Mother. We didn't have a car, so Mary had to beg a friend to drive her. If the store (or all three) was out of something specified on Mother's list, Mary would try to make reasonable substitutions *in situ*, but Mother could be a stiff taskmistress—she didn't like Libby peaches subbing for Del Monte.

Why didn't she die of apoplexy?

During the school year, Mother would climb on the bus for work about the same time we arrived home on that city bus. The four of us, ages ranging over a dozen years, would fend for ourselves for dinner. Before my father left for good, he would make a meal, wash dishes while we dried and endured the snap of wet dish towels on our backs and legs, and then he would leave to be with his current doxy.

We rarely knew a time when we weren't alone at night. Only occasionally did living two blocks from the state pen bother us. Mother would call from work if she'd heard about a prison break to tell us to lock the door to our house (really, the bottom half of a two-story rental). Sometimes we would hear Mother coming home about twelve-thirty a.m. I don't remember feeling relieved to hear her key in the door.

Our meals weren't much more imaginative than Mother's—often we "spoiled" our dinner by downing a whole stack of Premium saltines waiting for Daddy to come home to feed us macaroni and cheese.

We were glad when Daddy left. I was eleven, my older sister was twelve, and our two younger sisters were six and one. We liked having the house to ourselves. We older sisters cared for the younger. Changing diapers evolved into monitoring homework as each sister left, one by one (the oldest to marry at age seventeen, three others to college).

Mornings meant we had to tiptoe in the dark to keep from waking Mother. If we needed clean socks, we knew to raid the hamper and turn yesterday's anklets inside out. If we needed money for the school picnic, we knew to mine under the davenport cushions. If we woke her, it meant fixing her coffee.

Find her crumbled-soft, brown paper lunch bag. Take out the Thermos. Pour cold coffee into the aluminum pan on the stove kept solely for reheating coffee. Stand on the cold linoleum floor waiting for the coffee to boil—just around the edges. Pour into a cup stained brown beyond the abrasive help of baking soda.

Return to the kitchen if Mother Bear found the cup of coffee too hot or too cold.

Meanwhile, Mother had reached for a cigarette. Her coughs rattled phlegmishly through our jack-leg apartment. At least after Daddy left, those god-awful morning cough-choruses dropped from stereo to monaural. When I watched the final scene in Ingmar Bergman's *Cries and Whispers*, I could barely tolerate the sound of the tubercular woman as she coughed to death: too loud an echo.

Why hasn't Mother died of lung cancer?

Mother still coughs. Only now when she hacks, she wets herself and soils whatever she's sitting on. Mother still drinks coffee and smokes cigarettes. A few years ago, I read a report that said people who smoke *and* drink coffee have a greater risk of heart trouble.

Why hasn't she died of a heart attack?

When Mother broke her hip two years ago, my sister Mary and I drove to our hometown to serve as her advocates. The prognosis was not good. We left early so we could wave her off to surgery; instead, we found her hooded in an oxygen tent. We knew Mother has about one-fourth of a lung left to supply her with oxygen, but we did not know that Mother didn't have enough oxygen in her blood to allow for surgery—at least, no doctor was willing to put her under anesthetic.

My mother, an anemic seventy-nine pounds, lay in that hospital with her broken joint for eleven days before her doctor would take such a risk.

We started planning on taking her to a "home," at least to convalesce. Mother would have none of it. She was going back to her second-floor apartment. (She had moved next door when our old house had been taken over by the landlady to house her business.)

How would she ever negotiate those steps? How would she ever get in and out of the bathtub for those two-hour baths she used to take—more selfish than sybaritic, what with five females living in a one-bathroom apartment?

A year after Mother broke her hip, she broke her wrist just leaning on it to weed, so why hasn't she died of a broken skull from getting in or out of the porcelain tub?

Mother is now hooked up to a fifty-pound air-cleaning machine. Sometimes when she gets cabin fever, we ferry her to the city where three of us daughters live. For her visit, we have to haul that machine down two flights of steps at her apartment and up two more at Mary's. (Mary is the only one of us she'll stay with because Mary lets her smoke inside.) Next, we haul up the emergency oxygen tanks.

"Is that heavy?" she asks between coughs as I struggle with a long green cylinder, the vein on my forehead bulging like Charles Boyer's. She's just being polite; she doesn't really want to know.

We asked Mother if she ever forgets and smokes around these air units. "I'm not that stupid," Mother says, as she lights up, the plastic tube to the machine barely out of sight.

Why hasn't she blown herself to smithereens?

My sister has a fantasy. One day, Mary will follow Mother into the kitchen where she smokes perched on the highchair we used as babies. The kitchen is relatively clean these days, not only because we pay for a maid service weekly but also because we come back "home" about once a month and remove the opened cans of Del Monte peaches, the ones with the blue fur on the fruit, wash dishes frosted in congealed grease and empty the ash trays. Anyway, in Mary's fantasy, she will step on the machine's umbilicus, cutting off Mother's clean air supply.

My sister swears that Mother will die happy, thinking of her cigarette.

We will be relieved when Mother dies. We will no longer have to run up and down steps doing her laundry as we have done for forty years. We will no longer have to fish for current bills to help her pay them; her system of robbing Peter to pay Paul lasted only until we began to earn salaries and could help. We will no longer have to feed her or clothe her or buy sheets for the window "treatments" she sees in slick magazines—she can afford neither the magazines nor the linens.

We will no longer have to mother her.

For a while, I tried to soothe myself with thoughts that God had a plan for keeping Mother alive past all good sense. I gave up trying to answer why. My husband's a philosophy professor; his only counsel: "Theodicy is a mug's game."

We will be sad when Mother goes—after all, caring for her has taken up years of our lives. We will be sad, too, when we finally realize that we will never have a mother, as the last vestige of infantile hope that Mother would one day assume the banner is ladled into the body bag with her. Maybe then, we will reckon at last that there will be no return on this investment.

When I went away on vacation this year, I told my two younger sisters that, if Mother died while I was gone, they could start without me. I meant, they could look in my desk for the telephone number of the funeral parlor I'd found that, for four hundred dollars, would keep Mother's bony, airless body for half an hour until folks arrived from the medical school twenty-five miles away.

My littler sister said, "Do you honestly think the celebrating will be over by the time you come home?"

Ten days later, Mother was still alive. I called to let her know I was back, but she didn't ask much about my vacation. She asked if I would come home to wash her windows. And the curtains need starching and ironing, she said.

Postscript: Marigold Harman Baker died March 28, 1996. Her courageous doctor wrote "cigarette abuse" in the blank after "cause" on her death certificate.

You Always Come Too Late and Leave Too Early

MARION FREYER WOLFF

As long as I can remember, there had never been any doubt that my sister and I would take care of our parents. It was simply assumed that our role was to nurture and protect them in their old age as they had sheltered us when we were young and vulnerable. We were a tightly knit unit and the roles in the family structure were clearly defined: Father was the undisputed "boss," Mother was the homemaker, nurse, seamstress, darner of socks and social secretary. Before marriage and motherhood she had been a portrait painter, a singer with a lovely mezzo-soprano voice and an occasional writer of essays and poetry.

What made our family special was the fact that we had been able to escape from Nazi Germany two and a half months after the Nazis invaded Poland and World War II began in earnest. It was truly a miracle that we managed to elude the ever-tightening noose of the Nazi henchmen. In those days, the United States limited the total number of immigrants to about one hundred fifty thousand per year. Great Britain and Ireland were assigned about eighty-three thousand places, most of which were never used, while Germany was allotted about twenty-seven thousand. Poland, with a Jewish population of over three million, had only six thousand quota places. American consuls in Europe were given the authority for assigning quota numbers and visas. Our relatives who held American quota numbers were too far down on the list to be issued visas and perished in the death camps. My mother's father was deported to Theresienstadt (Terezin) at age eighty-two and died soon after arrival. Aunt Kate, my mother's unmarried sister, was deported and died somewhere near Lublin. My mother's two brothers and their wives were able to get out. Aunt Kate could not bear to leave her aging father and sacrificed her life. She was not even given a chance to die with him.

A similar situation existed in my father's family: Aunt Paula, the unmarried daughter, gave her life to stay with her mother. She was gassed in Auschwitz; her mother died in Theresienstadt. There was absolutely nothing that my parents could have done to save their relatives. As sole survivor of his family, my father carried this "survivor guilt" to his grave. My mother surrounded herself with the portraits of her parents and sister that she had painted in 1920. When we arrived in New York City in December 1939 with a few suitcases, we were happy that we had been able to take boxes of old photographs with us to the New World.

Ulla, my older sister, went to work and I attended school, and soon we both married and moved away from Baltimore, where the family had settled in January 1940. Ulla moved to Chicago and I moved to a suburb of Washington, D.C., but we remained in constant contact with our parents by phone, weekly letters and frequent visits.

By the time my father had reached eighty, the family had agreed on a plan for my parents' future: As long as possible, they would remain in their apartment in Baltimore. When the daily tasks of living became too difficult, they would move to the Self-Help Home in Chicago, a retirement community for Jewish refugees. Ulla had made sure that their names were on the waiting list so that they could move in at once whenever the need arose.

Two years later my sister Ulla died suddenly and unexpectedly from a "silent" brain tumor, and my parents removed their names from the list of the Self-Help Home.

I realized that I was now the only daughter and that the responsibility for my parents' care rested squarely on my shoulders. I could sense that, in their grief, my parents needed me more. They were constantly on my mind and my friends started telling me that my preoccupation with the care of my parents was excessive and depressing. I, however, considered my behavior realistic and responsible. Perhaps refugee children are more committed to the care of their aging parents. I, for one, never forgot that my brave, intelligent father had given me a second chance at life. If it had not been for him, I would have been another Anne Frank.

Even before my sister's death, my husband John and I worked out a routine to take care of my parents' needs as efficiently as possible. On Thursday my father dictated a shopping list over the phone; Friday evening and Saturday morning were devoted to shopping; Saturday afternoon was spent cooking and on Sunday morning we assembled the grocery items in two large canvas bags that had wheels. The perishables went into two insulated picnic bags. John arranged the cargo in the trunk of the car, and other items, such as clothing, books and packages, went into the back seat. By leaving the house about ten o'clock we usually arrived at my parents' place about eleven, in time to set the table for dinner at noon.

My father would stand at the window and watch as we rolled the grocery bags along the concrete walk to the garden apartment. His hearing had deteriorated but the clatter of the metal wheels was loud enough for him to hear our arrival. He had always insisted that he was able to understand everything that he *wanted* to hear. Eventually, when one of his old-time friends threatened to stop visiting because the strain on her gentle voice became too painful, Father at last bought a hearing aid. "I can hear the birds now!" he admitted. "For years nature has been perfectly silent."

Now legally blind, my mother could no longer work in the kitchen. We arranged for Meals-on-Wheels to be delivered during the week. Our shopping trips and weekend cookery continued, but on a reduced scale. One Sunday on our trip to Baltimore we got caught in a terrible tie-up on the highway. There was no escape and no opportunity to notify my parents. I visualized my father standing at the window and my blind mother asking what time it was and why we hadn't come yet.

When we arrived about an hour and a half late my father remarked sarcastically that we needed to manage our time better. John tried to explain that traffic tie-ups were beyond our control.

"You always come too late and leave too early," my father grumbled.

The stress must have gotten to me, for I burst into tears. "All my life I've tried to please you, and apparently I can never do anything right," I said, wiping my eyes.

"I am sorry," my father said softly. "I would never do anything to hurt you. You know that you are all I have left." His dark eyes looked so sad; my anger melted. My father, a silent stoic, had never mentioned the many losses he had experienced in his life. In our home it was assumed that hard work and a spirit of acceptance would make bad times bearable. We had survived the Nazis and created new lives in America, hadn't we? It was Ulla's death that had shaken my father to the core. No matter how hard I might try, I could not fill the void.

I retired from classroom teaching to be more available to supervise both households. With my father's consent, we hired an architect to design an independent living unit to be added to our house. It was to have a separate, wheelchair-compatible entrance, a room for a nurse when needed, a living room/bedroom combination and a large deck for them to enjoy our lovely garden. My father agreed to the financial arrangements, but when the blueprints were ready, he refused to go along with the plan; he said he did not want to give up his independence. John and I paid the architect, cancelled our agreement and never mentioned our plans again. My parents remained in Baltimore.

The last seven years of my parents' lives were a constant challenge. I wrote out shopping lists—my husband did all the shopping for two households—cooked dinners, conferred with the part-time home aides who looked after my frail mother and occasionally spent the entire weekend in Baltimore to help my father with small typing jobs. I phoned every night, exactly at nine o'clock, and when I was unable to reach my father—he would take the receiver off the hook to avoid "crank" calls—I felt guilty and anxious until I got through the next day.

When my mother fell and broke her hip I rushed to Baltimore to support my father and to negotiate with the doctors. The morning after her surgery we got an urgent call from the intensive care unit. They were "having trouble" with my mother, claiming she was "totally uncooperative." When I reported at the ICU the nurses welcomed me with open arms. "We cannot deal with your mother," they said, pointing to the frail, bluish-pale woman.

"Mutti, what is the problem?" I asked as I rubbed my mother's hand. "Are you in pain?"

"No, not at all," she said. I was puzzled. My mother had impeccable manners and was kind to everyone. We used to joke that she would wear a hat and gloves to take out the garbage. I saw no reason for the defiant behavior the young intern described.

"They keep asking me what my name is," said my mother, gesticulating wildly and struggling to pull herself up. "I refuse to identify myself to my enemies. I'll never tell those Nazis who I am. I will not cooperate with my enemies," she repeated in a surprisingly strong voice.

"Mother," I tried to explain, "you are in Baltimore in a hospital, and there are no Nazis here. The doctors and nurses are your friends. They would like you to drink something so you can get your strength back."

"I will touch none of their poisoned drinks," my mother said adamantly. "They were so mean last night," she continued in a low voice. "They chased me into a swamp and I couldn't get my legs out. It was terrible." She sighed.

I threw the thin cotton blanket back and felt her cold damp feet. There were marks on her legs where she had been tied down on the operating table. "I'll get you out of the swamp," I said as I turned to a nurse and asked for two heated blankets. A few seconds later I wrapped my mother's feet in the warm covers.

"Ah, now I can move," she murmured. "How did you get me out of the swamp?" I succeeded in having her sip hot chocolate through a flexible straw. "You make me feel secure," she whispered before she fell asleep.

The nurses and doctors watched me in mute amazement. I asked them to follow me into the hall, and as they stood in a circle around me, I gave them a five-minute lecture on the Holocaust. I wondered how much these young people who were listening to me so earnestly knew about the Nazi era. In some history books, the Holocaust was mentioned as a brief footnote to World War II. Some school reading lists include *The Diary of Anne Frank*. I guessed that this was the staff's first experience in dealing with an individual Holocaust survivor, a confused old lady, a real human being. (In the eighties the Holocaust was not yet a familiar word. The opening of the U.S. Holocaust Memorial Museum in April 1993 and the release of Steven Spielberg's movie *Schindler's List* in the same year changed that.)

"My mother was never in a concentration camp," I said, "but her father and sister perished at the hands of the Nazis. In the confusion caused by the anesthesia, my mother imagined that she had been dragged to a camp and that you were her enemies. She'll be very cooperative as the effect of the painkillers wears off. You need not ask her who or where she is. She knows it very well."

It was very quiet when I finished. A young man in white stepped out of the circle. "Thank you for telling us about your mother," he said, placing his hand on my shoulder. "We'll take good care of her— all of us," he promised. As the nurses returned to their work, I looked back into the ICU: Mother was sleeping peacefully.

I hurried home to tell my father the good news.

After rehabilitation in a nursing home, my mother returned to the apartment. She learned to get around with a walker, but most of the time she sat in the armchair and listened to Beethoven and Schubert. Because of glaucoma that had been diagnosed much too late, her eyesight was fading rapidly, and toward the end of her life she lived in total darkness. My father had not permitted me to take her to another ophthalmologist. "Your mother is *my* responsiblity," he would bark at me. "Who are you to tell me what to do? You are only my daughter." I consulted a counselor who advised me to "tread a fine line." Legally my father had the final word.

When my father turned ninety, we hired a string quartet to come to the apartment and play chamber music for him. He was very pleased with the performance, although he admitted that he had heard better groups in his lifetime. My mother sat in the big armchair and looked happy.

Four years later my father was diagnosed with terminal cancer. I spent hours on the phone (long distance) trying to impress on the doctors that my father had a legal living will and did not want any heroic measures to extend his life. I spent more and more time in Baltimore in order to act as my father's medical advocate and to protect him against futile high-tech diagnostic procedures. It is perfectly legal to refuse treatment, but not many elderly people are aware of their rights. I had no difficulty calling the hospital to cancel the appointments for blood tests and scans that the doctors set up for my father. It saved him from sitting in hospital waiting rooms, lying on narrow gurneys in hallways and enduring unnecessary pain.

When I went back to my own family, my heart and thoughts remained in Baltimore. I no longer made any plans for social engagements, dinners out or tutoring sessions, anticipating an emergency call at any moment. A carefully packed suitcase was ready. My purse was bulging with "to do" lists and emergency numbers. Whenever the phone rang, I jumped, convinced that this was "the call." Nights were filled with anxiety dreams. My doctor prescribed sedatives.

The call came on a Saturday in late May of 1987. John and I rushed to Baltimore and took my father to the hospital, where emergency surgery was performed to ease his pain. We had inspected half a dozen nursing homes months earlier and had made arrangements for eventual admission for both parents into the best one. I took up residence in their apartment, transferred my mother to the home and had friends shuttle me back and forth between the hospital and the nursing home. Three weeks later my father moved into a private room on my mother's floor. The staff erroneously assumed that they were dealing with a rabbi or professor and treated him with respect. Yet my father was terribly unhappy there. It is heartbreaking to watch a man who has been the boss all his life become totally dependent on the mercy of others. He asked me to go to the street drug market in Baltimore to buy pills to hasten his death. I explained to him that I would do anything for him, but obtaining illegal drugs would land me in jail.

"Papa," I said, "your life is essentially over. You are ninety-four and very ill. I will see to it that you will not have to suffer."

My father looked at me with his dark sad eyes and said, "*Now* you make sense!" I consider it the greatest compliment he ever paid me.

He died the next morning. I was relieved that he did not have to linger.

We continued the weekly trips to Baltimore to visit my mother. Realizing that her health was deteriorating rapidly, I signed a formal statement requesting that my mother *never* be transferred to a hospital. (She did not have a living will.) She now slept most of the time and did not appear to suffer. I was unsure whether to mention Father's death, but the nurses said it would be better if I did not bring up the subject unless she asked. I am fully convinced that she knew. Two months later she died at the age of ninety-two. "I do not want to die" were the last words before her heart gave out.

I returned home physically and emotionally drained but content to know that my parents' suffering was over. It was good to be back with my husband, my daughter and my students. Yet I often wonder what I could have done differently to ease my father's pain and his anger at losing control. There are no easy answers. If I had to do it all over again, I would probably do things the same way. But this time I'd have a phone in the car and a beeper on my hip to stay in constant touch. Modern technology can be a great stress reducer.

In 1989, my autobiographical book *The Shrinking Circle: Memories of Nazi Berlin, 1933-1939* was published. It is dedicated to the memory of my parents, my sister Ulla and all the relatives and friends we had to leave behind.

My idea of immortality is that the memory of those who precede us continues to live within us. In that sense I never "lost" my parents. Their spirit remains alive.

Chocolate

MARY ANNE MAIER

$\mathcal{I}$ don't remember where we got the chocolates. They were fancy, Godiva maybe, in a tiny box. I was busy tempting my mother with any kind of food I could think of because she had pretty much quit eating by then. The doctors couldn't understand it: The tamoxifen had not only stopped the growth but was shrinking the tumor in her lung from the metastasized breast cancer.

We'd had five good years, plenty of time to swoon under the hypnotic sway of our ritualized denial. Cancer? Not us; not our family. Mom had had a lump in her breast and they'd removed it. OK, they'd removed it breast and all. She'd wanted no one outside the family to know about it before or during that initial surgery. I'd tried to talk her out of such silly secrecy. "There's no shame in being sick," I'd said. "People care about you, you know. I know they'd really appreciate hearing."

"I'd just as soon you strip me naked and lay me on the front lawn." Those were her exact words, so of course that was the end of that. After she'd found a place that could fit her with prosthetic bras, there was no reason to mention the cancer again on her account, although she wanted us girls to get checked regularly. She cooked fabulous meals just like before, and we ate and played cards and laughed whenever we all got together.

Here's what I remember: Since the beginning of time, my mother's body softens in the kitchen. The day revolves around dinner, with meat thawing early, vegetables washed and cut by noon. My brother and I hang around her legs when he comes home from school in the afternoon. She holds a potato in her left hand, pushes a paring knife up through it with the thumb of her right. We beg for slices of raw potato with their dirty-white crunch and smell of dirt, and she laughs in a way that opens her mouth and squeezes her eyes into a perfect squint as she hands them down to us. She glides around pets and children as she stirs, tastes, adds, wonders, invents. "How was school today?" She puckers to suck in the hot broth of Great-Grandma's little dumpling soup. "What's for dinner? You'll see. Will you run downstairs and get me a jar of tomatoes?"

After the first cancer, long after her four kids were gone, she kept the urgency of each day at bay by letting her heart flow into every new recipe, into the ongoing stream of dinners for two, into any feast she could find an excuse for creating. My favorite picture of her shows her gray hair still pillow-tousled, eyes focused on a cookbook with eyebrows raised in perpetual interest.

For five years. Until she gave up food. Until the tumor in her lung scarred the x-ray like an ugly germ amoeba magnified into a horror-movie creature under a microscope's glare.

But they'd faced it down, shrunk its fearsomeness with a drug. The specialist in Denver laughed the day he told her, "At this rate, you're going to starve to death before you die of breast cancer." It sounds cruel now, I suppose, but at the moment it seemed hopeful, at least to me, like, "We have the cancer on the run now, so all we have to do is get you eating again and you'll be set." The hope didn't catch in Mom's eyes, though. Her gaze had moved far off into the distance

Mary Anne Maier   195

since the cancer returned, somewhere out into the blue sweet air of Wyoming's prairie is my bet, where her eyes could have their own eternity, where even the most frightening storm is beautiful, and most of all, everything just is.

In fairness, she wouldn't let anyone stick a scope down her throat till near the end, and that's when they found the stomach full of cancer from esophagus to intestine, which of course explains why she'd quit eating. But the chocolates were before we knew that.

I'd made one of my treks up from El Paso to spend a week with Mom and Dad as I had every couple of months since we learned the cancer was back. It feels hollow, heartless, to admit how much I enjoyed those eight hundred miles of splendid solitude, the blessed emptiness that lay between my husband and my sick mother and wounded father, a straight shot north and south between my home and my home-home. The thirty-five miles on I-10 from El Paso to Las Cruces would be crowded with eighteen-wheelers, like a pack of mad dogs sweeping me along in their rage; but as soon as I ducked out of their dust and onto I-25, I was on a Franciscan retreat to a beautiful nowhere, meditating on yuccas glowing gold before the unlikely mountains that are naked giants sleeping forever on the hot sands of the Chihuahuan desert. In a couple hundred miles, the sharp edges of this landscape would soften into the gray-green sage of the high plains, then melt into the rolling ocean of grassland that laps at the toes of the younger, white-topped giants living where New Mexico and Colorado pretend to divide them by a border. I'd drive along, gorging myself on this beauty, and think about my mom. I'd wonder if I'd be able to talk to her this time, or if we'd just lie on the bed watching *Oprah* as we had recently—as she'd taken up once the cancer had crowded the energy to do anything else out of her body.

The big problem, of course, was food. I'm no cook and neither is my dad, really. I hated that part of it: coming up to help but being so bad at thinking of foods she might like. All my husband and I eat are things like bean burritos and pasta with green olives and capers. We have a hard time feeding house guests, let alone a dying mother. But getting food into her was clearly becoming a more desperate issue every day. My dad and I just had to do the best we could, though I could tell he was a little disgusted with me for not being a better help in the meal department as my sisters were. My mother, the food expert, never even nudged me in that direction, saying that women didn't have time anymore to devote their lives to cooking and sewing as she had. So there I was.

What I really wanted was to have that mom back, the mom who would say, "How do pork chops sound? I found a recipe in *Bon Appetit* for thick chops stuffed with mandarin oranges and whole garlic cloves, and I thought I'd try it out on you tonight." Or, "This chicken is Mimi Keenan's recipe. She brought it back from a trip they took to Thailand and served it to our bridge club. I'll write it out for you." I wanted to weep, and sometimes I would on those long, cold drives, because she couldn't take care of me anymore, and I couldn't take care of her.

Dad would ask me most mornings what we'd have for dinner that evening, and my head would feel stuffed with wads of cotton, that kind of spongy, suffocating cotton that stops medicine bottles, making it impossible for images to form, for thoughts to travel and combine into a meal. Hot dogs? That's ridiculous! How childish! Fish? The smell would certainly make her sick. Pasta? Where do I start? How do you plan a meal? Remember the 4-H class about meal planning? Or was that table setting? I won a purple ribbon for cookies, but cookies are all wrong, of course. How could I be struck by amnesia now, at this one moment in my life when it actually mattered? Why did I stand, not thirty-five but eleven again before my dad's innocent question, before my mother's unlikely need?

I think we made some Schwan's things out of the freezer that week, like some chicken breasts stuffed with ham and cheese or something. We may have had a roast from Kelly's Superette over in Torrington, which is easily the best meat market in a two-hundred-mile radius, a place my mom just loved. I'm reasonably good at potatoes and rice and vegetables, and Dad likes to make salads, so we always had the rest of the meal if we could just come up with meat, which I don't have a clue how to fix. A couple of times we brought in Chinese from a good little restaurant there in Cheyenne, and Mom seemed to enjoy their tangy hot-and-sour soup.

The thing about her illness was that her tastes in food didn't change; she just couldn't eat it anymore. She wasn't asking for Cream of Wheat or Malt-O-Meal, and I know she felt defeated, as good as dead, when in the end we brought in cans of that protein nutritional supplement suggested by the doctor. She'd never drunk milk; I bet the sight alone of that thick, sticky milkshake made her sick, although she only gave it a sideways glance and still managed a thin smile at me. I had to sneak the cans out of the refrigerator during her nap one afternoon and beg a neighbor to dump them at a senior citizens' center, to get them out of her sight and pretend we hadn't suggested that she'd come to that.

The last time we brought her home from the hospital I remember this: We were driving on the road that curves behind the mall, looking out at the prairie grass waving from the soft hill that rises there, just a few cattle grazing. She said she couldn't wait to get home and have some homemade white toast with sharp cheddar cheese and a glass of red wine. It was as if we'd just busted her out of prison and were headed for endless passion fruit in Rio; I could see that meal floating before her eyes like a little spot of heaven. She said she'd been thinking about it for days; this had been among her favorite feasts for a good thirty years, after all, something she most often ate leaning against the kitchen counter. This time we got her settled into a chair in the living room, which was odd in itself since she'd spent her entire life in the kitchen before moving up to bed. I got her a glass of wine while I toasted the bread (bread with a finer texture than mine ever had—she'd made it herself and frozen it) and sliced the cheese. She seemed to enjoy it, but I know she didn't hold it down long. It was her last glass of wine.

So what it came down to was that during this week, one evening I was half-lying near the bottom of their big, hard bed, catty-corner from her, careful not to jostle her dwindling frame, and as I recall now, I think the chocolate came in a fruit basket wrapped in yellow cellophane. It was a gift from a group, I believe, maybe church or her women's club. I'd brought the basket up for her to see, and she'd picked out the box of chocolates. (Was there a ribbon?) She wasn't too much of a candy eater normally, but she offered me a piece and had a piece herself. They were wonderful—maybe we had two. I was delighted that it tasted good to her, happier still that she hadn't lunged out of bed and hobbled bent in half to the bathroom to give it up again as quickly as it had gone down.

But the next morning I found spots of chocolate down the front of the deep rose top sheet and on the pillowcase. It was my fault: I should never have encouraged her to eat chocolate right before she went to sleep. I learned later (always later) that chocolate is a stomach irritant. I was startled when I found the stains, but I think I decided immediately to look at the whole thing as a laundry challenge because I'm good at laundry. My mind remained clear on laundry.

"Oh, no! You must have thrown up during the night," I blurted out. I'm thinking, I'll use cold water and a little Softsoap first, like I do with blood on panties. I wonder if she's got a fabric brush downstairs. Surely she does. So I'll scrub it a little before I put any stain remover on it, and I'll try to let that sit for at least half an hour before I wash the sheets. I wonder what sheets I should put on the bed now.

She said, "No, we must have left a chocolate sitting out last night when we were talking. It melted there." That was ludicrous. Completely crazy. We wouldn't have taken a chocolate out of the box and just set it on the bed for future reference. Besides, this was obviously a more liquid consistency than an uneaten chocolate. (I know my laundry stains.) What was she talking about?

"No, because remember we put the box back in the basket and moved it over to your dresser?"

"No," she said. "I would have remembered."

When I think back on it now, I'm amazed at the kinds of things I chose to talk about with my mother before she died. We both knew that the number of words to pass between us was limited, that we were winding down to the end of our life's conversation. I chose in this case, and in others before she died, to explain why I was right.

Later that week, while my father and I were out running errands, she must have teetered down to the kitchen where she made us a creamy, delicate custard the color of brand-new baby chicks. She told us that night how she'd spilled the bowl of eggs on the rug in front of the sink halfway through and had to start over after taking the rug out to hose it off. She'd had to lie down between attempts (shoulder bones protruding now, belly beginning to distend). When Dad and I got home, we found the custard in the oven, cooking gently in a pan of water as in a birthing bath. It was her last gift to us, a little bow to tie up so many years of nourishing our family.

Heading south out of Cheyenne, I saw three antelope bound westward across the flowing prairie toward a low butte, as if they might make it to the Snowy Range past Laramie by nightfall, floating on the crisp sage air. I'm almost certain my mother was with them. Only out in the eternity of those plains that are my home as surely as they are hers could I finally hear her heart speak. How could I have missed it? She was ashamed. (Head turned slightly to the north, looking back, but far away already now.) She was not the kind of woman to throw up on her bed sheets, cancer or no. And she was still my mother. I should have known better. I sometimes hear the echo even now when a white cloud, like thick cotton, bounces it back to me from the purest blue sky.

Life with Mom

FLORENCE LADD

"Florence wants to be cremated and have her ashes scattered on her land in Vermont. And I think we can arrange it for her," I overheard my ninety-one-year-old mother casually remark last year in a telephone conversation with someone, probably a relative or close friend. I was stunned. I dashed to a mirror to examine my appearance. I looked healthy and felt quite well. Until that moment, I thought I was in very good condition for a woman of sixty-five. Then it dawned on me that Mom, who has survived her brother and sister, two daughters and a husband, has calculated the odds of outliving her next of kin, sole surviving offspring and major source of support: me.

I meditated on her longevity and began to consider my own. "Did you know how long Granny was going to live when you arranged to have her come and live with you?" poignantly asked my son, Michael, then approaching his twenty-fifth birthday. That was in 1995, when Granny turned eighty-nine. It was her third year in our household. She had moved from Washington, D.C., in the winter of 1992, having suffered a series of strokes. It appeared that she was, as she phrased it, "at journey's end," and would not be able to continue living independently. Her doctor told me she would never recover the level of abilities she had before she became ill. Because of severe rheumatoid arthritis in both hips, her mobility was already limited; and with paralytic effects of bilateral strokes, she was certain to be an invalid.

Thanks to a congenial real estate agent, Mom's home, a northwest Washington townhouse (where she had lived alone since my father's death in 1975), was sold almost immediately to the perfect buyer: a grandson of Mom's next-door neighbor. Sold with the house were many of Mom's treasured possessions: furniture, dishes and appliances. Even now, as if reminiscing about deceased old friends, she speaks of the handsome dining room set, a flattering mirror in the foyer and her piano. I think she experienced more keenly the loss of her material objects than the loss of her physical abilities. What I learned from my ruthless sorting and selecting of Mom's household effects is that one generation's treasures are the next generation's trash, and that I should begin to dispose of my eclectic treasures so that Michael will not have to trash them. My sense of loss of my childhood home recurs whenever I return to Washington, with a hotel or a friend's house as my destination rather than our Quebec Place home.

When Mom had recovered sufficiently to travel by air, I went to Washington to accompany her on a flight to Boston and the drive to our home in Cambridge, Massachusetts, where a decade earlier we had prepared a room on the first floor with Mom in mind. My husband Bill, an architect, had enlarged a modest room and improved its bath facilities. We regarded the room as hers even before the move. When Mom visited us, it was the room she occupied. There was no question that Bill and I were prepared to *house* my mother. But were we prepared to *live* with her?

When the moment of moving Mom to Cambridge arrived, Bill welcomed the opportunity. His relationship with his own mother had corroded because of mutual neglect; her recent death had left him with a legacy of guilt and bitterness. He was ready to accept my mother in our household and to explore the possibilities of filial fellowship with her.

Committed to having Mom live with us, I systematically surveyed the array of Boston-area home care support agencies and interviewed their representatives. In turn, I was interviewed by them, and our home was inspected from the point of view of its correctness for an elderly invalid using a walker. I found several agency reps intrusive and opinionated. "Those oriental area rugs will have to go!" (They did not.) "You'll have to rearrange the kitchen entirely." (We did not.) "The lighting level needs to be increased throughout the house." (It still does.) The agency that best suited our situation and that deemed the environment appropriate was the Erikson Home Care Program based in Cambridge.

In discussions of my plans for Mom's care, mental health professionals and friends inevitably asked, "Have you considered placing her in a nursing home or assisted living residence?" I explained that Mom and I shared, as African Americans, a tradition, cultural expectation and custom of caring for one's own—kin care for kin until the very end. Institutional care, from her perspective and mine, was the last resort. Besides, I reasoned, she took care of me when I was too young to care for myself; it was my turn to care for her.

Mom arrived happy to be out of the rehabilitation center but not pleased about winter in a snow-covered New England neighborhood. It looked cold, so she was cold. With the thermostat in her room set at seventy-five degrees, she shivered. Before long she had symptoms of a minor stroke, spent a week in a Cambridge hospital and, subsequently, a long stay in a Cambridge rehabilitation facility, where she recovered, rejoiced and returned to live with us happily ever after—so far.

The Erikson Center assigned a gifted, young home care aide to Mom. Karen came to our home on weekdays, and in four hours—eight o'clock to noon—performed paramedical miracles and cosmetic wonders. She also organized excursions to cultural events and found transportation to shopping malls. (Mom returned from a shopping trip with her ears re-pierced: two holes in one ear lobe, the other conventionally pierced with one.) Karen introduced an exercise routine. Using her walker, Mom did several laps daily through the living room and dining room. When weather permitted, a walk to the playground on our street was a source of exercise and entertainment. Karen encouraged Mom's use of lipstick and blush, and she manicured Mom's nails. She renewed Mom's interest in baking; together they baked bread weekly and cookies for special occasions. On her own, Mom resumed playing hymns on the piano, and she initiated correspondence with relatives and friends. Karen provided constant inspiration, support and her unique manner of therapeutic companionship.

Replacing Karen on weekends, I attempted to perform the tasks that Karen did. The breakfasts I prepared, however, were never as good as Karen's. When I selected outfits from Mom's closet, I made reasonably good choices, but somehow blouses and pants didn't match as successfully as those Karen selected. I made her bed, but never as smoothly and quickly as Karen. I laid out her medications and steered her wheelchair, but not as well as Karen. Mom seemed to enjoy her outings with me, but they would have been more pleasurable if only Karen had been along. I was grateful for Karen's enterprising service and its benefits for Mom's health and well-being, but I recognized my severe case of Karen-envy.

After two years of incomparable assistance and companionship, Karen left home care work to attend graduate school. She left Mom in better condition than she was prior to her initial strokes! A retired elementary school teacher, Mom takes pride in Karen's decision to embark on a career of teaching English as a Second Language.

Since Karen's departure, there have been several other home care aides whose educational aspirations have become a topic of Mom's conversations and a focus for her motivational efforts. With Karen as an example, she urges each to acquire "more education and to find work that is more challenging."

What could be more challenging than spending those morning

hours with Mom? With patience and genuine interest, the home care aides—seven in the years since Karen's departure—follow her daily monologues about her teaching career; they hear her repeated attacks on Jesse Jackson and Jesse Helms, her disapproving commentary on Anita Hill and Monica Lewinsky, her series of mean mother-in-law (my beloved grandmother) stories and her ceaseless celebration of the life of her only grandchild, my son Michael. (He's a very good poet and promising performance artist, but for God's sake, he's not the second coming of Christ!)

What I find most unsettling are her versions of life with my father. From their forty-five years of marriage, she selects moments that reflect unfavorably on his character: his daily visits to his parents' house, evidence of being overly attached to his mother; and his fondness for bourbon, with a drink before dinner and a nightcap as signs of excess. She takes full credit for family stability, home ownership and their relatively comfortable lifestyle. Her recitation of my father's flaws undermines my memories of Dad as a supportive, engaged, generous family man. I closely identified with my father. Physically, I resembled him. As the first-born, I claimed his special interest, and with the birth of two more girls (one who died in infancy and the other, Ethel, my mother's favorite, who died of cancer at sixteen years), my father turned to me with the energy and attention he had reserved for a son. When Mom begins her attack on him or, more accurately, her memory of him, I turn away or simply turn off. I leave the room, find a quiet corner and read, fleeing in the same way that I did as a girl when Mom's outbursts of indignation about something my father had said or done incited her. I hid behind books, while Dad escaped to his basement carpentry workshop.

Mom's entry into my adult life revived my memories of our family's dysfunctional moments. She confronts and is judgmental, while I, like Dad, avoid conflict and am reluctant to criticize others. Her standards regarding proper dress (gloves are essential in all seasons) are more formal than mine. She inspects what I wear for special occasions and offers her approval or disapproval. When she disapproves, I feel reduced to an unsteady stage in my girlhood and become confused and agitated, like a fifth grader who cannot solve a simple riddle. Fortunately, Bill generally intervenes with a light-hearted observation or a comic analogy that diminishes the tension. When I complain to him, Bill attributes her behavior to old age or the pain of her arthritic condition. I recover, my annoyance subsides, I take a walk or a nap, and we carry on.

Games, television and small talk provide a means of mediating tensions. Karen introduced Mom to Scrabble. An intense, highly competitive player, Mom claims the game prevents mental decline. Home care aides spend several hours each week bent over the Scrabble board. For those who have never played, she offers instruction, after which she takes pride in their Scrabble skills. A neighbor visits weekly, expressly for two games. And believe me, Bill and I have put in Scrabble time, too. Do we *let* her win? No. She is a strong player and wins without assistance or deception. Mom keeps a mental record of wins and losses, and she has a scheme for rating players and a set of indicators that predict ability at the game. While reading the newspaper or magazines, her search for seven-letter words for the game is a major preoccupation. She regards defeat as a challenge for a better performance; winning gives her a sense of accomplishment and satisfaction.

Television is Mom's major source of contact with the world beyond our home. She prefers legal programs with court scenes. Crime shows with violent episodes also fascinate her, as do sordid news stories. She watches *Jeopardy* and answers questions, occasionally with Bill at her side, while I prepare dinner. (On weekdays, she dines alone, earlier than our dinner hour. Sunday dinner is a ritual that brings us together.) Televised football games bring Mom and Bill together on winter weekends. With Mom, I sometimes view the evening news and weather forecasts. Local weather conditions interest her; she also follows the Washington weather, Florida weather (she used to visit a nephew's family in Palm Coast) and weather in New York, where Michael lives.

We continue to be astounded by Mom's interests and abilities. Her prodigious memory is remarkable. In early September, anticipating the visitations of neighbors' children on Halloween, she recalled the names and ages of those who visited in the previous year and described their costumes. She recites poems that she memorized during her childhood and adolescence, and she knows the lyrics of songs she has not heard for decades. She remembers details about the lives of relatives and friends. Disappointed when I fail to recollect an incident that happened perhaps forty years ago in the life of a relative, she rolls her eyes with resignation about my unreliable memory.

When my novel, *Sarah's Psalm*, was published, Mom read it over several weeks. Throughout her reading, she reported her interpretation of characters and their actions. Her appreciation of the work and her liking it mattered to me more than critics' comments. I was pleased by her effort to read it. She has a copy in her room that she proudly shows to the medical professionals who make house calls and others visiting for the first time.

Mom reads the Bible and the *Boston Globe* daily. She scans magazines, lingering over human interest and gossip articles, and listens to books on tape. And she studies merchandise catalogues. A compulsive catalogue shopper, she receives approximately six catalogues per week. She orders gifts for relatives and friends, and household items that she decides we need. Most of her orders, however, are for clothing for herself. The UPS driver delivers at least three packages a week. She receives pants, blouses, dresses, pajamas, slippers, shoes and an expensive type of thermal underwear. Her closet and drawers are bulging with her old clothes and new acquisitions, enough for another decade or more. She regards catalogue shopping as a hobby, and she feels she needs variety in her attire. With the help of an aide or with my weekend assistance, she dresses for the day in a fashion suitable for receiving guests or going shopping, adorning herself with make-up and jewelry.

On weekends, we usually have lunch in a restaurant, take shopping trips, visit a greenhouse or go to a museum. For those occasions, she wears her better outfits—often something new. She usually wears pants for outings, because it is easier to climb into our Jeep and slide into the wheelchair (faster transport than her walker) dressed in pants.

In Washington, church-going was an occasion for dressing up and participating in a social scene as well as in the services at the Second Baptist Church. Now that she is physically limited, it is difficult to dress Mom in time for Sunday morning services, although it is not impossible. On a few occasions, we have been sufficiently organized to take her to an eleven o'clock church service or to an evening program of carols at Harvard's Memorial Church. Recently, however, religious worship has been brought to her over the airwaves—the early morning televised "Hour of Power" and sermons broadcast from Memorial Church during the academic year. I wonder what religious practice means to her, but I do not ask. I am afraid she would regard such an inquiry as an attack on a belief system that somehow sustains her. I am curious, but not curious enough to risk her disapproval of my irreligious way of life.

From time to time, we bundle Mom up and take her to our house in southern Vermont. The trip is not a chore in spring and fall, but in winter, we dress her warmly enough to endure the cold wait in the car while we shovel a path in the snow for her entrance. When it is too treacherous for her to use her walker on the path and up the four steps to the door, she sits in the wheelchair and we push and lift her. We treat the transport as if it is a winter sport.

❧

When Bill and I leave for our summer vacation in France, we engage a house sitter/companion for Mom. In this capacity we have had Toby the filmmaker, Richard the minister and tennis coach, scholarly Mary Esther from Ghana and Gem, a versatile teacher from Australia. Summer 1998 was spent with Wambui, a minister and aerobics teacher. Each year has brought a different companion with different qualities and skills. Mom enjoys getting acquainted with the summer resident, learning about the personal history of the newcomer and exploring scenarios for his or her future. She offers advice and prayers for their ambitions and, through phone calls and correspondence, follows their progress after they have gone. Mom claims that she misses us, although she is reluctant to part with the summer companion on our return. With transatlantic calls and correspondence, I keep in touch and follow Mom's summer program and inform her of mine. The summer respite is mutually refreshing.

In the tableaux of episodes with Mom, particularly when there is tension between us, I step out of the frame to look at my behavior and hers, and from a psychological perspective, consider our relationship. I remind myself that I was trained in psychology, and that early in my career, I specialized in gerontology. I recognize our moments of regression, denial, acting up and acting out. I believe that my professional training allows me to view discord from a certain distance. I discuss incidents, after the fact, with Bill or an aide, who points out that I often concentrate on our dysfunctional moments and tend to disregard or take for granted the cordial nature of life with Mom. In general, our days are tranquil and congenial.

Our relationship would not be as decent, heartening and mutually respectful as it often (but not always) is without the home care aides, summer companions, the diversion of Scrabble, visits and telephone calls from relatives and friends (especially Michael), and Bill's sound advice, good humor and intervention. I am grateful for the financial resources and support that make it possible to have Mom in our midst. Her retirement fund covers the cost of home care services; health insurance and Medicare cover medical expenses. We have plenty of separate space in our home, and the Vermont house offers a change of scenery from time to time. If the arrangements appear to be managed easily, it is because ample financial resources make it possible to create conditions and acquire services that foster compatible coexistence.

Life with Mom is our only choice. Assisted living facilities do not appeal to her, and the mythology she has collected about nursing homes render even the best of them unacceptable options. Given her relatively sound health and mental abilities, I am unwilling to consider another living arrangement for her. Besides, she is often interesting and entertaining, and her living with us has enriched our family life and brought to our household more structure, routine and vitality.

I am living out the experience as her only surviving offspring—an only child observed by her own only child. The tradition of caring for our elderly at home continues. Michael is pleased by the situation we have created for his Granny, and he offers his support by being in contact by telephone and by frequent visits. He inquires about how our differences in personality and values influence the quality of our lives. He is learning from our situation and developing expectations about my old age. Already, he insists that I must be a more active elderly woman than Mom is. I hike, take yoga classes and do aerobics with my best interest and Michael's hope for prolonging my independent life in mind. I try to enhance my longevity; however, my mirror shows the genetic dominance of my paternal side, which is not exceptionally long-lived.

In a recent session with an attorney regarding my will, he asked, "Do you have plans for your mother should you predecease her?" I thought about her plans for my ashes, her engagement in life, her aspiration for longevity: She wants to see ninety-five, and perhaps one hundred in the year 2006. I expect she will be around long after my ashes have been scattered across a patch of land in Vermont. I contemplate her future and mine with a measure of satisfaction about living out life with Mom.

The Manila Envelope

LINDA-MARIE

On May 3, 1997, I went to see Mother. After years of therapy and confusion in hating and loving her, I have finally resolved to accept the past. I don't know if it is possible to be with our mothers without blending the past with the present.

The old house she has lived in for over forty years is showing wear and tear. Wildflowers fill the cracks in the cement steps left by earthquakes. They are a bright yellow and die each year to be born again in spring. Mother pays a gardener who barely touches anything. He has offered to remove cardboard boxes and rotting pieces of wood that are propped against the house, but she won't allow it because she feels she might need them someday.

On this particular evening she is sitting at the dining room table shredding papers. She was at one time an excellent artist. Some of her paintings are propped up in corners while others hang askew on the walls.

Each room of this rather large house is filled with cardboard boxes of papers, of clothes, of gadgets and whatnots—many purchased from

TV. Nothing seems to be ordered or to follow a pattern. It is like so many pieces of so many jigsaw puzzles scattered around the rooms.

There is a room just off the dining room where she keeps her cat confined so he won't get away. The cat is desperate to get out while I'm here. The smell from the room is overwhelming. I peek in a crack in the door and see piles of kitty litter inches thick. This is the same room I once had as a child. I am no longer affected by the drama of the past. I do, however, feel sad for the cat.

Mother has always been a small woman who is a collage of European and Native American. Her face is clear and comely. Her once dark hair is white and her eyes are green. She doesn't look at me when she talks.

"I want you to decide what happens to me if I get sick," she says. "Look over there on the buffet. There's a big yellow envelope. I got a lawyer to make it all up for me."

The buffet is stacked with everything. I see a number of manila envelopes. I also come across note pads that are filled with biblical concordance: row after row of shaky writing, *John: 4, 7; Mark: 11, 25* and so on for pages and pages. I don't know what these scriptures say. Mother writes down scripture the preacher shouts out in church.

I sigh. "Does the envelope have writing on the outside? What's the lawyer's name?"

She is shredding junk mail. The shredder is a new toy. "I don't know what his name is," she answers me in her three-year-old voice.

I want to shake her and scream. *Look! If you want me to help you do something, then you need to help me! And don't give me that shit about Jesus will take care. . . .* I would never, never talk to my mother like that. *There is a limit to my patience.* But we are locked into the same story and cannot leave until the end.

We have an ongoing discussion that goes like this:

"Linda, do you know anyone who helps pack rats?"

"I could call someone, but you know you will have to throw some things out?"

"Never mind. Goodbye." At that she either hangs up the phone or leaves the room.

I finally find the envelope. Inside is a Durable Power of Attorney. It gives me the right to look after Mother's affairs if she is too sick to do it herself. I already hold a conservatorship for my mentally ill sister.

How sick do you have to be before you let someone clean out this firetrap? Don't you know I freak every time I hear news about a house burning to the ground, killing everyone?

"What will you do if the house catches fire?" I ask carefully so as not to offend. She reminds me that when the Oakland firestorm destroyed thousands of houses and many acres of land, her house didn't burn. She is convinced it is because her sisters prayed for her. *I hope there is a heaven.*

I find a photograph of me on the floor that fell out of one of the photo albums stacked in a corner. In the picture I am eleven years old and in the cat's room. I can remember the stench from the body cast that was used to keep my broken hip in place. Strangely enough, the photo doesn't affect me. It was from some other planet or some other girl, one in a Dickens novel maybe.

I show Mother the picture and ask her what album it belongs in.

"Oh, just set it on the table. Umm, I remember this," she says, looking closely at the photo and turning it over in her hands. "Joe gave me the film. That's when all the flowers were blooming in the yard and we got watermelon."

Her memory is so different from mine: another confirmation that this is our story—not just my story.

In 1956, our next-door neighbors were Mr. B., the chief probation officer of the county, and his wife. They had no children and lived with Mrs. B.'s mother. During the heat of the summer that year when we had all the windows open in our house, Mother and I were arguing about the television. At some point she jumped on me and pummeled my face with her fists. I screamed and screamed. She felt awful later when she tried to bring down the swelling with ice packs. I had two black eyes, one swollen shut. That night she went out and left me with her husband, who used me to masturbate. The next day Mrs. B. sent a county social worker to investigate. The social worker asked me to sit on the steps with her, and then she came right out and asked me if my "father" molested me. I answered, just as casually, yes.

Within a matter of days my stepfather was in jail, my siblings were in separate foster homes, I went to a school for delinquent girls, and Mother was left in shock alone in her big empty house, the house right next door to the chief probation officer.

In 1977, a book about my life, thinly disguised as a novel, was published. I began writing it after I'd been to a few women's liberation meetings. I knew I felt a rage, but at the time women were just beginning to create a language defining our lives. I rarely heard stories of the child abuse that must have been deeply buried in our souls. *I Must Not Rock* was added to other books that made the personal political. I felt compelled to write my personal experiences and hoped we would find a common language.

But I didn't want my mother to know about the book after it was published. When she and her sisters asked me about it, I lied. Of course, she found out anyway and was hurt by my words. When my brother went to pick her up one day in the locker room of the city college where she worked, he heard her shrieking and crying out so loud he called an ambulance to take her to a hospital. I'd turned into that awful busybody, Mrs. B.

I told and now I am afraid to speak. I have taken responsibility for her hurtful behavior because I'm stronger than she is. Today she looks so small in her little pink dress with the flowers on it and her hair like feathers moving with the slightest breeze. When I lived with her, she made my dresses with underwear to match. She cooked all the meals carefully, following food plans of the day. But the state took all of her children away and assigned them to institutions and foster homes. She never drank, swore, smoked or used drugs.

In 1955, my mother had three small children and me. I was disabled from a fall and spent nearly a year in a body cast. She used her hands to remove impacted feces from my rectum after someone told her I would die if I didn't move my bowels. Before we lived in the nice house on the nice street, we lived in housing projects near a shipyard and naval base in Oakland. It was an accepted fact that Navy planes were allowed to swoop down and drop fake bombs on the buildings, playgrounds and schools. The projects are crowded places with angry people. On hot days, Mother would sit outside and talk with the other "ladies," and I spent hours alone in a dark room in a body cast.

"How's yer car runnin'?" Mother asks me today.

"Great! Thank you again and again," I say. "I don't know what I would have done without your help. Now I can visit the kids and your little great-granddaughter." I am not only glad she bought a car for me but because acts like these confirm our relationship to one another. It was expensive and a financial sacrifice—one she was not obligated to make.

I live alone in an apartment in San Francisco that is arranged just the way I like, with a computer as the dominating motif. When I drive home I leave the past behind. It wasn't always that way. I had help from friends and therapy. Some may ask, at what point did I stop obsessing about the misery of my childhood and come to the reality of my maturity? I don't know.

I once allowed these memories to torment me. Now when I'm alone in my apartment, the dawn moves me to my balcony with a cup of tea where I enjoy pine trees full of songbirds. I watch people with their dogs in the park below, and way off in the distance, past a body of water, is the land my mother occupies. That is her land and this is mine.

Tonight in Mother's land, I open one of the albums and see a picture of me in the projects. I seem happy enough, with cut-out pictures of dogs on the wall. Mother and her mother documented everything with photographs. Now she gets up and hands me a collection of snapshots of my little granddaughter. "Those are for you," she says.

"You sure are a good photographer." I am not only impressed with her artistry but also fully warmed by this loving gesture. It is moments like this one that remind me of the time her neighbors complained about the colors she painted her house. She called the painters only six months later and asked them to paint the house more compatible tones. *I hate those busybodies. I swear if I outlive you I will paint the house many shades of green, just like you wanted.*

I love the stories my mother tells about her childhood. She has told me the story of her birth many times, but I want to hear it again.

"So Mama wouldn't stop cannin' food when she was having me. The midwife kept saying, 'Go on an' lay down, Missus, or yer gonna have that baby in the kitchen.' So when I was borned, Mama was too tired to give me a name. 'Sides, she wanted a boy. She was tired of having girls. So then my sisters named me." She looks up at me as I rest my elbows on the table and my chin on my hands. "And when you was borned the nurses named you—yep, named you for that soap opera star on the radio."

I could see her in my mind's eye—that young woman giving birth in the home for unwed mothers, asking the nurses for help in naming me.

She named my older brother, Mickey. I barely remember him growing up. The first time the state "stepped in" to save Mickey and me, our clothes were stuck to the sores on our bodies; we were hungry and frightened. He had filled my bottle with his urine and fed me so I wouldn't cry. The police saved us and we wept because we missed our mommy.

Mother's grandfather sexually abused her as a child. She was considered to be "a little slow." She was also considered morally corrupt. *What kind of a goddamn mother would leave her little children starving in a room alone? What awful mother would leave her daughter with a man she knew was sexually abusing her while she was out carousing? What kind of a woman lets her husband beat her kids bloody and even holds them down so he can?*

After I was grown, I ran away to marry, then to leave my husband, then to leave my children and then to leave lovers—to leave and leave until I felt too tired and wounded to run anymore.

I stopped talking to my mother for three whole years. It was a time for pulling away and redefining myself. It is what people do when they leave the area where they were raised. Only for me, I stayed here—nearby. I could look out of my window and see Oakland, where Mother lived. I could drive down the street with friends who left their birthplaces and imagine what it was like for them.

I watch my mother shredding the junk mail. "Whatja gonna do with the stringy paper?" I ask.

"I don't know," she says playfully. "Guess I'll have to get more boxes to put it in."

I finally stopped asking if I could help her clear out some of the junk in the house. Other family members have offered to help. Sometimes when I take care of her house when she's away, I bring garbage home with me to dispose of it; otherwise, she'll recover it from the trash bin and carry it back inside. A nurse at the clinic called it a "hoarding syndrome."

Occasionally she will put the boxes haphazardly on the front porch. One of my brothers will sneak up the stairs and throw stuff out before she realizes it's gone.

Part of me believes this collection of little value is meant to fill the void left when we were rescued from her. Bad people took her kids because of something I said to Mrs. B.'s social worker. If only I'd kept quiet. Now I must fend off any other bad people, like the fire department and the health department. This responsibility for her care should she become ill is a large weight on one hand and a way of showing her I care on the other.

Yes, Mother, I care enough not to throw anything away without your permission. You can trust me to keep this one more secret sacred.

She stops shredding when the shredder sticks. I don't know where to put the papers from inside the manila envelope, so I balance them on my lap.

These papers give me an incredible amount of power. I can dissolve the trust, sell the house, put Mom away—on and on. I don't think my younger brothers will like this. When their father—my stepfather—was alive, he set up the trust to exclude Mickey and me. The power his widow is handing me while she pulls the junk mail from the shredder is overwhelming. I have also been made executor of her trust should she die before I do. The money does not add up to millions; it is possibly only a few thousand at this point. It is the trust in my ability to love and be fair that she is giving me. Is it from guilt? I would like to believe we have now forgiven one another.

When I was twelve and lived in an institution, I could hear my mother call me, "Linda, Linda." I heard her voice in the wind calling mournfully, and I'd feel a terrible longing. I wasn't allowed to love her. She was a bad mommy, so I was assigned other mommies in foster homes and institutions to take her place.

There is something no substitute mother or caregiver could give me, and that was a common history. Regardless of how difficult the stories may sound—or even fanciful—I had only one past, mine, and that past was shared with Mother, my siblings and our ancestors. Because of Mother, I have a love of history, writing and mystery. Because of Mother, I also have a fear of failure, speaking out loud and being discovered.

She never missed visiting her children, even when we were scattered to the winds. She was burdened with loss, and I was responsible. It was my duty to comfort her. Our drama was written into forms, page after page, by the State of California.

"Nobody understands how it is when your kids get taken away," she says as though I was someone else.

Why did you have to say that now, you idiot! You know you blame me, so what the hell are you, some kind of masochist? Aren't you damn afraid of what I might do with this power?

"I know, Mama, I know how hard it must have been for you." I tell her this and kiss her forehead. I love her. When I was a little girl I was afraid of her. Now I am afraid *for* her.

The last time her kids were taken it was my fault, but not the first time. Not when Mickey and I were three years old, but after, later on, when I was eleven. I told on her husband. I told about his violent rages and about his sneaky sexual proclivities that included me. Now I am afraid no one will love her as much as I do, and I am limited in what I can do for her. I am middle-aged and still afraid of her. I am afraid she will abandon me, wound me or expose me for loving a bad mommy.

Nobody understands how it is when you get separated from your mother, no matter what she's done. I never told Mother this. It is not like being abused as an adult. Parents are our very arms, legs and brain cells. After the first time the state "stepped in," I went back to her and her husband, and my big brother Mickey disappeared through a door and wasn't seen again for seventeen years. Then it was an awkward meeting. He had come back from the dead and was on his way to Vietnam.

In 1948, Mickey was taken by his father to live in Florida. Mother and I mourned his loss. He may as well have died of some dreadful disease. We shared this hurt. I remember when a small picture arrived to confirm that he had not died. After all, he had been a sickly child. I was the strong one, the one Mother leaned on. We looked at the photograph with a magnifying glass. We studied every bit of the *not-dead* boy's face.

"Please don't ever call anyone Mommy but me," I remember her asking me. It hurt her so much that Mickey called his stepmother Mommy.

Last year, Mother sat next to Mickey's hospital bed with his wife and watched him die a slow, agonizing death. He was wounded in Vietnam and left with serious lung damage that he had never overcome. She told me it hurt to see him suffer so much. But his actual passing affected us less because we had already mourned his death for years.

There is a large photograph of Mother's husband on the wall. He looks mild, half-smiling down at us. He is wearing a gray sweater with a bow tie. He has horn-rimmed glasses that don't disguise the blind eye. Because of attacks from a brutal father, he was blinded in his right eye and lost the hearing in his right ear. There is no excuse for bad parenting. While I don't believe being abusive is genetic, it can be hereditary if not caught in time.

"I wish he was here," Mother says, looking longingly at the picture.

She had four other children by her husband, my half-siblings. She was married to him for nearly fifty years. He was autocratic, cruel and abusive to all of us. But what is remembered is this: I told. I talked, exposed the family in the big house on a quiet street in a respectable part of town. I told about the raging woman who chased me with a knife and left bruises on my younger siblings. I told what her husband did to me while she was out dancing.

"I dreamt about him last night," she says to me. "He was never very handsome, but he was sure good-looking in my dream. Isn't that funny?" She chuckles and the feather hair bounces on her head.

I had a dream for many years. I was standing on a hill and I saw you in the distance. I could mouth the word, "Mommy!" I could feel the blood rush from my neck to my head. I was screaming and no sound came. If only you could hear me you would run back and save me. But you couldn't hear and then you disappeared into the distance.

In 1943, my mother was an unwed teenager, and I was her second child. She sat in the reception area of the adoption office, waiting to fill out forms to hand me over—but she didn't. I cried because I wanted to nurse, so she left. She nursed me and the story began.

She was there with my husband when my daughter was born in 1966. She cried and said she couldn't stand to see me in so much pain.

Now when I bring her a pile of new and old mail from the basement, she says, "Naw, whatja bring this old stuff for? I just want the new stuff. Here, you throw the rest back down there."

I obey.

"Would you like to put the shredded things in a bag?" I ask, trying to be helpful.

"No, but I could put them in that box over there. See. No, not that one, the one with the blanket sticking out. Yes, yes, that one. Just throw the stuff out."

My sister walks in the back door. She has been to the park, walking the dog, and just put him in the pen in the yard. She grunts hello and goes up to her room. I hear the door close. I know better than to take it personally.

My sister brought Mother and me back together. R. had been roaming the streets for years as a bag lady—you know, the kind of person you step over and laugh at. I couldn't bear it. If anyone thinks there is no such thing as mental illness, walk a mile in my moccasins. A dear friend helped me get R. into a hospital. Now she and my mother live together. I put my sister first for several years until she was stable. It was my duty. And now it is good for both of them to be together. R. can pay bills and Mother takes her to church, as R. is unable to socialize on her own.

I stopped going to Mother's house when my children were very young. I refused to go while my stepfather was alive. Then, in 1980, I moved and changed my phone number and tried to imagine I was without a mother. I was getting in touch with the fear I had of my stepfather and realizing that Mother chose him over me. One image that haunted me was Mother in the courtroom sitting next to her husband while I sat on a cold bench with a stranger. I was twelve years old.

It was during the time I removed myself from Mother that I decided to go into therapy. Then, when one of my brothers called me to say our sister was mentally ill, I went to support him and help. Mother was there, and when she saw me after three years we hugged and cried, and I was left feeling I had abandoned her.

A few months later my stepfather died and left my mother money enough to see her through decades. She misses him, and I must accept that. She cannot allow herself to feel the damage he created in her children's lives. She was a child of the Depression. And he inherited money.

Some want to know how Mother could live with her husband after what he did to her kids. In my version of her life, she had no choice but to return to him after he got out of prison. After all, not everyone is a hero. There are some who take what life gives and others who challenge and fight back.

We go over the power of attorney papers.

The Gift

SUSAN L. FELDMAN

A great love goes here with a little gift. — *Theocritus*

I'd always been a planner. Half the fun of any trip, I believed, was the carefully prepared itinerary and packed suitcases. But I applied this logic to every aspect of my life, keeping lists, diaries and artfully worked out agendas for not merely my day-to-day but for the decades ahead. I believed I needed to know exactly where I wanted to be at any given time. Yet when the early morning call came to my New York apartment that my mother, having suffered a massive stroke, had been taken to the hospital by ambulance from her Florida condo, I was on board a flight to her in two hours' time.

As the plane gained in its ascent, I downed half of an unaccustomed midmorning stiff drink as I tried to get my bearings, find my place. Yet I know now that it is only as I look back on these events that I can see how the circumstances of the previous twenty-two months had propelled me to that airline seat. The vague fevers and infections and chronic inflammation that I'd begun to experience shortly before my twenty-ninth birthday had turned into a constancy of disease, leaving me at age thirty unable to continue teaching or to carry out many of the activities I ordinarily counted upon. I had finally been given a diagnosis of sorts by the time my mother had her stroke: an autoimmune disease of unknown etiology (its name, lupus, would not be bandied about for yet another year).

Had I expected my domineering, powerful, resourceful, incredibly witty and delightful mother to be there continually for me? To take care of me always and especially now that the rug I hadn't known existed—that of our precariously precious good health—had been yanked out from under me? Of course I'd held fast to that belief, the perquisite of being someone's beloved child. But that was before the routines of illness had become my own norm. On the day I resigned from teaching, as I checked off my schedule, I became conscious that this was also the end of everything that had come before—that time in which plans and expectations could always be counted on and fulfilled. And as I opened my calendar that next day, I knew that everything written down for the hours ahead—and every day thereafter—could simply be listed under *All bets are off.*

To say that the hospital corridors, diagnostic centers, consulting rooms and labs in which I'd spent the nearly two years of my life before that precipitous flight to Florida had prepared me for my mother's illness would perhaps be an oversimplification. It was rather the very fact of my *being* in those places at all—out of the planned existence I had always expected to have—that enabled me to put the phone down after the hospital's call and get the hell out of bed and into a cab on my way to Kennedy Airport that morning before I'd even considered what day of the week it might be.

I arrived at the hospital and immediately made my way to my mother's gurney-side in the emergency room. From the distance of ten feet I recognized the figure that was surely my mother—her famously heavy, lush hair spread out like mounds of whipped cream on the pillow. But once I stood next to her, I saw the paralysis on her left side, the mouth twisted down. I took her right hand in my own and she opened her eyes. For a moment my heart stopped as I was met by only a dull gaze. Then recognition filled those sharp green eyes and she squeezed my hand. "Hey, Rosie," I said. The right side of her face began to twist up into what I recognized would now be her smile.

I began quickly to fill her in, knowing that having all the answers was what she always wanted. My eldest brother, a doctor living in another southern city, was making arrangements to come; the other one would be flying down from Chicago in the next few days. When my brother arrived he would be able to see the scans and talk with the specialists and get us the full picture. Then we would know the extent of the damage and what her prognosis might be. All we had to do now was wait.

The moments, so precious in that most immediate of knowing that she was still alive and her spirit intact, now stretched into hours. And I began to recognize that change in her expression: the lines of surprise and fear that form on a patient's face as medication wears off and the pain begins its grip once more. I stood outside her room and called out several times to staff passing by, but was always told that someone would be down in a moment. My own hospitalizations had already taught me that this reply translated into *We are not going to pay the slightest attention to you right now.*

Finally I came back in and told my mother that I was going to the nurse's station to see about her medication and being moved onto a floor. Then, on automatic—having lived in New York City my whole life—I put my bag down at the foot of my mother's gurney and said, "Ma, watch my purse." And as I turned to hurry from the room I heard my mother say, her voice coming out thin and reedy, but the intonations completely recognizable as her own, "Don't you worry, Susan. If someone tries to take it, I'll beat the hell out of 'em." I turned back to her, my mother the Zinger Queen, always getting one better than her so-smart college-educated kids. I looked at her, began to laugh and then walked out. But I paused outside her room for a moment and put my head against the wall and wept. I knew then I didn't need to wait till my brother's arrival to hear about the scans: I knew she would be all right. I wiped my face dry and rushed to the nurse's station, where I unleashed upon their Dixie sensibilities the full weight of my Brooklyn moxie till several people scrambled to get my mother a shot and shut her daughter up.

We soon learned my mother would need extensive rehabilitation; not for a moment did anyone, including me, question into whose purview this would fall. I was the youngest, the only daughter, the one who hadn't gone out of town to college and begun a life elsewhere— the one who had, as everyone so clearly expected, stayed close to her mother till her mother had turned everything on its head by announcing at sixty-five *she* was moving to Florida. After conferring with her doctors, I put into motion all the plans for my mother to be flown on a stretcher back to New York and moved into one of the country's best rehab facilities about an hour north of my home. Their initial assessment was that her prognosis was excellent, but it would take about two months of intensive rehabilitation for her to be functional again. And they informed me in no uncertain terms that a vital and mandatory part of their program required active participation of family members—did I understand what this would entail?

I suppose in everyone's mind this seemed perfectly natural at the time. My older brothers were both professionals with heavy schedules and had children to raise and lives to pursue. They had previously settled down in those other cities knowing that I was just a subway ride away from my mother, and when she'd moved to Florida, well . . . wasn't I still the daughter? It seemed perfectly reasonable to them that my time and energies were, and had always been, completely expendable and that of course my mother's care, my mother's well-being, was totally mine to consider and handle.

The doctors I saw, however, did not quite reckon the situation that way. My no longer being able to teach meant that I had the time to take the train up to my mother's hospital several days a week and work with her in physical therapy and occupational therapy and art therapy and then meet with her specialists. But I had in fact left my job because I hadn't the health nor well-being to work a full day. I'd been told by my doctors that I needed to live a more "conservative" existence, carefully managing my activities, treatments and time. But during the first weeks of my mother's hospitalization, I looped back into the early stages of Kübler-Ross's grieving as I denied the reality of my own situation. And certainly I was fully aided and abetted in this by nearly everyone around me as they assumed I would scramble to do what was best for my mother's recovery, not taking into consideration what might be the cost to me.

Soon I was exhausted all the time and in more pain. I attributed both of these to the constant worry and concern for my mother, ignoring the fact that I spent many hours on trains, and then standing, stooping and working alongside her. I did not ask myself if I should be pushing one hundred and fifty pounds of wheelchair bound patient around the rehab center's extensive grounds. Sadly, no one else asked that either.

However, I couldn't help but notice that in spite of the ever-present fatigue, I now found myself constantly wired, going repeatedly to the candy machine at the center and snacking on incredible junk. I chided myself for this bad case of nerves that made me consume Milky Ways and chips like a teenager living in a dorm for the first time. It was only during the third week of my mother's hospitalization that I followed up with a visit to my own doctor and he noticed that I'd put on weight. Concerned, he discussed in greater detail the new medication regimen I'd begun just days before the call had come about my mother. This medication could make a patient hungry, tired and speedy, and he cautioned that I'd best watch my diet. I immediately reduced the dose, the well-being the drug may have given me not worth the side effects at the time. I already had too much to worry about and manage in my mother's care.

As the weeks went by, my mother became increasingly difficult to deal with. Though I'd been warned that stroke patients cry easily and can be very emotional, my mother repeatedly lashed out at me, castigating me over and over for the tiniest of things—crimes certainly never committed, only anticipated or imagined. Each day with her became one in which I constantly gritted my teeth, held my tongue and tightened every sinew in my frame as she picked over what little was left of my self-esteem after two years of my own illness, watching my life and youth and dreams all slip away.

There were several other patients my mother's age on her floor, and I began to talk each night with their children. One woman in particular, who had grown up quite near my mother in New York and then also retired to Florida, had two grown daughters who came on alternate days and then together on weekends. I began to compare notes with them and found they did not report their mother experiencing the rage and fury that my mother constantly directed at me.

During an appointment with her neurologist in which he assured me that my mother was doing great, I hesitantly raised the issue of her nearly constant anger at me. He smiled. "There are two kinds of stroke patients," he said. "One kind is like the woman down the hall from your mother. They are placid, easygoing and accepting of their situation. They don't fight back. And as a result, they are invariably wheeled out of here in about eight weeks' time. The other kind are patients like your mother. They are very angry and find it incredibly frustrating to try and get their bodies to work in a whole new way. They fight and curse and shake their fists. But they *walk out of here* in that same time frame. Your mother will be one of the ones who walks out, I promise you that. But she will make your life hell in the process." I thanked him for his candor and for that vision of my mother, her arm in mine, walking out of the hospital. I knew it was only this that could sustain me.

After some time, I was required to bring my mother home on

weekends so she could practice her newly acquired skills with a three-prong cane. I'd spent weeks learning how to help my mother maneuver through her new life, but more importantly, learning how *not* to help her—learning to let her deal with the sometimes agonizing slowness of everything that she undertook to do, learning to let her ride out her frustrations and failures, learning to hold back my deepest instincts to instantly reach out and do for her what was so very difficult for her to do on her own, learning not to cry along with her, but patiently say, "Let's try it again, Rosie. Let's try it again."

She walked well with the cane, excelled at it as she had excelled at everything she put her mind to, instilling in us, her children, that of course an *A* was fine for everyone else but an *A++* was something we should always aspire to. I was certainly well schooled in how to handle her walking with the cane around my apartment and saw no cause for alarm as she, talking with a visiting friend, was rounding the turn toward my kitchen and faltered. Waiting for her to right herself, I only jumped to my feet when I saw her legs go out from under her, and then watched, as in one of those slow-motion horror sequences, my mother's head hit the corner of my forty-gallon fish tank as she fell to the ground. Her white hair was suddenly drenched in blood and her eyes rolled back in her head; she seemed to be choking. I put my fingers into her mouth, trying to clear her airway, amazed at how much blood was pouring now over us both. Suddenly she looked up at me and started breathing on her own. "Don't go anywhere," I said, trying to smile down at her as I got to my feet.

Medics, stretcher, ambulance, the trip to the ER. I waited in the corridor as the hospital staff did scans and then made calls to the neurologist at the rehab center to discuss these in light of her previous films. Two police officers approached me, introducing themselves. They asked about my mother's fall, and I gave cursory responses to their questions, my attention riveted on the doorway to my mother's room through which the neurologist would eventually emerge and tell me if my mother would survive. They continued their questions, some repeated again and again: "Where were you *exactly* when your mother fell?" "Did you and your mother have, let us say, any words today?" "Were you perhaps a bit short of patience with her and maybe . . . ?"

It was at this juncture that I tuned in and finally caught the point of the questions that I'd thought were merely a routine result of my calling 911 for an ambulance, something I'd never done before. "You want to know if *I hit my mother?* You want to know if I hit my mother and she fell?" To this one of the officers nodded. I looked at him in complete astonishment and nearly began to laugh. "Hit my mother? Officers, you don't understand. When I turned thirty just over a year ago, it occurred to me for the first time that I might be able to tell my mother I wasn't happy with her line of conversation, for heaven's sakes. *Hit my mother?*" They resumed their questioning, and I heard the term "elder abuse" for the first time. No, I assured them, I hadn't hit my mother. I couldn't even imagine winning an argument with her much less initiating one.

At that moment the neurologist came out and told me that my mother had apparently experienced a seizure that had brought on another stroke. All the doctors agreed that it was likely a seizure had also precipitated the first stroke, though no one was with her to witness it. They would now treat her for this seizure disorder. "Please don't blame yourself," the neurologist explained. "You couldn't have prevented this in any way. When she had the seizure she lost consciousness. Even if you had grabbed her, you couldn't have held her— she was then a hundred and fifty pounds of dead weight being pulled by gravity to the ground. All that would have happened is that you would have toppled down with her. Her head wound is just a bad gash—head and face wounds bleed a lot and so look pretty awful. We've just cleaned it and taped it. This stroke hit right near the original one, so while she has lost some ground she hasn't suffered any substantial new deficits." I shook his hand then and that of the two police officers and went in to see my mother. She was drifting in and out, so I just stood there silently crying, waiting for her to know I was there.

My mother had been one of those people blessed not merely with perfect health but a cast-iron stomach ("I can digest nails," she'd proudly proclaim, sticking another piece of herring in cream sauce in her mouth) and extraordinary stamina. She'd been hospitalized only to deliver three babies and once in her fifties to take care of some uterine polyps causing intermittent bleeding—a brief stay that had been a real annoyance to her. She'd taken good care of herself, giving up her thirty-one-year habit of chain-smoking after the Surgeon General's report came out, though by then it was too late to undo the damage to her arteries that would finally lead to those strokes more than fifteen years later. Though all three of her children would be suffering from chronic disease by their forties, the gene for this passed only through her to them. She was "healthy as a horse" her whole life, a given I assumed as a child, like clean water from the tap and excellent public schools nearby.

When I was fifteen, my mother and I were already living alone, my brothers having gone off to their own lives in other parts of the country, my father having died when I was a child. She was as usual preparing our dinner that weekday night and I was in the living room studying when I heard her cry out. I ran into the kitchen to find my mother holding her hand as blood spurted from a large cut. I slid to the floor, the room having gone spotty and black almost at once. My mother splashed cold water on my face, but when I looked up and saw the blood on her hand I got all woozy again. After she cleaned up the cut, wrapping it expertly in a bandage, she helped me up to put my head between my knees. Finally she said, "I didn't think you were squeamish, Susan."

"I'm *not*," I said. "I've visited friends who are ill . . . you remember Eileen had that surgery and the boys got into a fight in my room and there was a head cracked open and blood all over the place right in front of me . . . " As I spoke I could feel the color returning to my face.

"I know. I certainly didn't think the sight of blood would bother you," my mother said, "but obviously it did."

"No," I said. "It wasn't the sight of blood, Mom. It was the sight of *you* bleeding." She nodded and then, like so many other times, we left the *I love you so much* unspoken between us. Instead, we prepared dinner together, my two hands pinch-hitting for her injured one and not much good at it.

My mother's weeks in rehab stretched out as she tried to regain the ground she'd lost with the second stroke. It was summer now, and unlike many of the others on her floor, she had only her daughter and son-in-law as regular visitors. When I called my eldest brother and suggested he come to see her, he couldn't fathom the point of his leaving his practice at the hospital. Didn't I have everything in hand? When I broached this with my other brother, he patiently explained that he and his family had visited my mother *last* summer and so this year they were of course taking the kids to visit his wife's parents.

"But last summer your mother was living in Florida and you could take your kids for a vacation to the beach to see her. This year the situation's changed and your mother is now in a rehab hospital following a stroke. Maybe it would be a good idea for everyone to visit for *her* sake," I suggested. Why was I being so obtuse, he said. This summer he *had* to take the kids to visit their other grandparents. Wasn't that obvious?

By then, I was so accustomed to this pattern in our lives that my only thought was for my mother's pain and embarrassment in having to explain to friends and staff at the hospital how it was that her sons couldn't come to visit her that summer—and that of course she understood. That they also wouldn't come to help their increasingly ill sister take care of their mother was something I had by then tentatively begun to consider.

Late one night, I was waiting for the cab that would take me to the train station from the hospital. I was sitting on the floor of my mother's room, trying to find some position in which all of me wouldn't ache quite so much. My mother looked over at me and said, "I'm sorry. I'm sorry this is so hard on you. Is there anything I can do to make it easier?"

"Too late, Rosie," I said.

"What could I have done before that would have made this easier then?"

"I should have been twins," I said.

"Sorry," she said. "I didn't think of that at the time."

The cab came and I kissed her goodnight, assuring her I'd be back the next day with the things she'd asked for. She watched me leave, calling out some last minute instructions. Exhausted, I slumped into the cab.

With the lulling sway of the Harlem line that night and on so many many nights to follow, my thoughts would wander from the lists for my mother's care to the phone call we'd had shortly after she moved to Florida. Though it had been a time of celebration not crisis, my brothers' participation in my mother's retirement—the party, the planning and purchasing of her condo and then the move itself—had been minimal and grudging at best. One night after she'd settled in, I'd sat on my kitchen floor with my cats playing around me, listening to my mother from her kitchen in Florida. Her fingers drummed on the table in lieu of those cigarettes she had given up as she discussed her sons' distance and what she now recognized as their frequent self-absorption. She had given so much of her best to them that her youth and energy were used up by the time I came on the scene. When I was growing up, she was a widow in her forties coping with a full-time job and older children who needed to be sent through colleges and graduate schools. Her pride in their achievements had been as unstinting as her generosity of spirit and care.

Perhaps it was the lateness of the hour or the new geographic space between us that emboldened me to put into words for once what was usually left unexpressed in that pact of mother-daughter absolute trust. "I think, Rosie," I said across the distance, "you put a lot of your eggs into the wrong basket."

There was a long silence. Finally my mother replied, "Yes, I know."

Those nights on the train, it was not the image of my mother walking out of the hospital on my arm—which she did weeks after her second stroke, returning to her life once again until another series of strokes eighteen months later finally felled her—it was those words, *Yes, I know*, that kept me going, sweeter to me than any endearment might have been.

And as my own frailty increased and the demands of my illness grew, I took those words deeply to my heart. I began to ask how best to take care of that child so cherished by her mother. I began, slowly at first, to learn how to set limits for myself, to say *No, I am not well enough for you to count on me now*, to extend to myself the kind of care *she* would have given and thus honor that faith she'd acknowledged in me. I learned at last—though not without great pain and at great cost— to choose wisely into which basket I'd put the love my mother had shown me, carefully tending it, recognizing always how precious and fragile that gift might be.

Sheer Grace

BONNY VAUGHT

$\mathcal{F}$rom childhood, I knew that someday I would take care of my mother. My father was ten years older than Mother. They had no surviving brothers or sisters; one niece lived nearby. I was their only child. Mother's care would fall to me. It was a fact. I didn't think of it as a privilege, but I knew it would be my duty.

In the midst of moves that crisscrossed the country, my husband and I talked fleetingly of difficulties her care might present. She was in relatively good health, and so was Dad. Like most children, we were not eager to think of our parents' final days. One thing was clear: Mother would never leave Clinton, Iowa, nor would John and I ever live there again. She would need long-distance caregiving.

A single phone call from my father changed every expectation. He'd summoned an ambulance for Mother in the middle of the night. "It's her heart," Dad said. "A heart attack. It's serious, but you don't have to come home. Everything's under control."

Her doctor told me firmly, "Don't fly a thousand miles for nothing. Come in three weeks when your mother goes home from the hospital." (Three weeks! How bad *is* this heart attack?) "She'll need a lot of help when she goes home. You'll be useful then."

I flew back the next morning. My cousin met me at the airport; we went straight to the hospital. Dad choked up when he saw me. His own heart was breaking.

In intensive care, Mother whispered a few words at noon. At one o'clock they let me see her for another five minutes. "Take your father home," the nurses urged. "Make him get some rest. Come back this evening."

As we drove to the house, Dad and I talked about Mother's seventy-first birthday. Only a week ago, they'd had a fine time; she sounded happy when I called.

Dad was utterly bewildered. How could this awful thing happen? She had high blood pressure, but not *this*, he said over and over. Nothing like *this*.

I went back to the hospital late that afternoon while he rested. Sitting there, talking quietly with my cousin Donna—a caregiver indeed—we began to hear horrible, shuddering gasps for breath. We thought they came from intensive care, but neither of us connected them with Mother. Then a nurse appeared. "Your mother's nearly gone," she told me. "You can go in, but don't be surprised by the way she looks."

Donna raced to call my father and was running down the hall before the nurses let me into the intensive care unit.

I watched my mother die. Even now, years later, I cannot bear to think about it.

Dad reached the hospital just after she fought for her last breath. "I think she was waiting for you," he told me. He began to cry. "It's just the two of us now."

In that instant, I became responsible for him.

We did all the things families do when a loved one dies. The pastor came and we called a special friend, Anna Marie, who joined us. What struck me that night—and struck hard—was the pastor's flippancy.

He was new, leading what was once my home congregation. It appeared he'd barely have time to bury my mother.

Dad, grateful for any pastoral attention, responded humbly. I backed off from confrontation. The pastor could help my father through the loneliness to come.

In retirement, Dad and Mother had bought a small house, an easier house to maintain. Dad, going on eighty-one, meant to stay in the house and live alone. He wouldn't need any help, he assured me. Well, meals might be a slight problem. And cleaning, too, now that we talked about it. But I was not to worry; he'd handle everything.

In fact, my father had always been in the care of women. His mother, his sister, his wife: a line of women who established and maintained homes for him. He'd been in the Army during World War I and lived in the YMCA after his mother died, but those were short breaks. Essentially, he'd had eighty years of tender loving care from the women in his life.

Dad had once been five feet five inches. "Five foot five *and a half*," he liked to say. During his seventies, Dad's vertebrae crumbled, and he lost several inches in height to Paget's disease. He looked frail and vulnerable when he stood alone.

After Mother's funeral, I sprang into action. By the time my husband and I flew back to New York, I'd arranged for Dad to have visiting nurse checkups at home, Meals on Wheels delivered five days a week and a woman keeping the house clean.

Within a week, my father canceled everything.

He didn't need any visiting nurse. The food they brought was so bad he couldn't eat it. No woman could keep a house the way his wife had.

I was so busy being Miss Dutiful Daughter, I forgot how my father operated. For years and years, Dad had listened politely to every suggestion and agreed with whatever idea was offered. Only later, when the planner or suggester was gone, did he say what he thought. He was often scathing. And then he'd do what he intended from the beginning.

I had to admire his gutsiness, but he sure made it hard to give him a hand.

Donna and Anna Marie were wonderful about keeping me informed. Donna raised six children, and she can lighten problems with a wry sense of humor. Anna Marie knows everybody in town. She sizes up a situation and knows where to get answers. We consulted about my father. We fretted over him. And Dad, being Dad, calmly went his own way.

He'd always been a loner. He was skillful at his job and had once been a leader in our church, but my father faced the world with a stern, unyielding manner. (I heard his frequent, admiring comments about tall people and wondered if six more inches in height would have made him more comfortable in the world he knew. Maybe he'd have metamorphosed into the witty, engaging person we glimpsed momentarily.)

After Mother died—as before—it was impossible to get him out of the house. He hated to be with people. I remember one shining moment when, after much coaxing, much urging, he went to an anniversary party. Dad came home so pleased with himself he called me before he'd taken off his coat. "I went and I talked to people," he said proudly. It was the last time he ever tried that.

His driving became problematic. It was hard for him to turn the wheel and see the road now that he'd lost height. Nevertheless, he made daily trips to the cemetery, saying he talked to Mother and could also feel her presence at home. I was shaken when he had his own headstone carved and installed. He had it fully engraved with the last two numerals left blank, to be chiseled in the year he died. I couldn't imagine seeing my own headstone every time I visited Mother's grave, but Dad felt he was taking care of things.

He did keep the house in order; everything stood stiffly in place. He just didn't do any cleaning. The whole house grew a layer of dust— a serious layer of dust. He invariably asked visitors what they thought of his housekeeping. They murmured polite approval, and he let the

dust pile up some more. Neither Donna nor Anna Marie dared suggest cleaning; he would have been deeply offended. Every time I visited, I'd stay up for hours cleaning after Dad went to bed. He was
trying so hard, nobody wanted to hurt his feelings.

Twenty years ago, I don't remember hearing much about "women
as caregivers." I drew support from friends who were in the same situation. We shook our heads and commiserated over mothers and fathers getting more stubborn by the minute.

I had watched my mother care for her mother at home while Nana
died of cancer, but I couldn't give direct care. My caregiving had to
span a thousand miles. I had to find a thousand ways to compensate
for those miles.

Many trips I made to Clinton were painful. My father disdained
greetings and farewells. It hurt me to fly back for a visit and not even
be greeted at the front door. He'd mutter an abrupt "Come in" from
across the room, and I'd wonder why I made the trip.

At the end of a visit, Dad might not walk as far as the door to say
goodbye. In fact, he might turn his back and pick up a newspaper
before I left. I thought maybe it was hard for him to see me go. I
reminded myself he'd never been demonstrative. Yes, he'd treated me
shabbily. Wasn't it "just his way"? I wondered. In a parent-child relationship turned upside-down, might I help my dad be a gentler father?
I wrestled again and again with these questions.

From the East Coast, I wrote and phoned often. Dad, in turn,
set up a portable typewriter on a little table in the middle of the
living room. Every visitor saw a letter in progress in the typewriter.
Dad, it seemed, was constantly writing to me. One problem: He
seldom finished or mailed a letter. When he did, they were crisp
and to the point. They were so brief he'd add a piece of cardboard
in the envelope. "Ballast," he called it. He was afraid his letters
might be too insubstantial to reach me. He had no idea what weight
they carried.

For three years, thanks to Donna and Anna Marie, Dad got along pretty well. He could be quite self-sufficient when he stayed within the world he'd set up for himself. From time to time, Paget's symptoms flared up, and he was in agony. Gradually, as his spine adjusted, the pain would ease and he'd declare himself fine again. I learned how to get information from his doctor; Anna Marie and Donna were alert to his needs. Perhaps because of geographical distance between Dad and me—a safe distance for him—he occasionally expressed feelings.

Those three years were a revelation. While I was doing long-distance caretaking—and not as much as I wanted to do—this shy, reluctant father of mine started showing a softer side. He *wasn't* all sternness and bristling standoffishness.

I signed a contract to write an industrial history and explained to Dad that the book would involve nine months of travel. Some trips were easy; I'd drive to Philadelphia and spend the week researching and interviewing. Other trips were more strenuous. I had to go west to California, north to Toronto, cover a number of places in between. I was careful to supply my father with an itinerary and phone numbers where he could reach me at any time. Things were going well.

Suddenly a call came from Donna. My father had checked himself into the hospital. "He said there was no way to reach you. He didn't know where you were." I was stunned.

The doctors never did find anything wrong while he was in the hospital, not anything new. Dad's emphysema was increasingly troublesome, and Paget's disease was a trial for him. But basically, he was getting along pretty well. Evidently he took my travel as a sign of abandonment. Was the tie between us closer than I realized?

My own physical problems abruptly put everything in a new light. For nine months doctors tested and guessed and dithered while I was in excruciating pain from—they finally got it!—a herniated cervical disk. During those months, my main goal was to get dressed by four in the afternoon. I tried not to worry Dad, but I couldn't write to him very often. I couldn't hold a receiver, so we learned to talk back and forth on a speaker phone, cutting in and out like a CB radio.

Shortly after I committed to a rigorous treatment, Dad was badly frightened. He woke up one morning without sight in one eye. Donna happened to visit and found him curled up on the couch. She got him to the hospital.

The diagnosis was never clear. Doctors thought he'd probably suffered an aneurysm, though his loss of sight could have been caused by a stroke. The experience was compounded by fresh pain from his crumbling vertebrae. It became clear that my father could not go back to his house and live alone. He needed to be cared for in a residential facility. "A nursing home," Dad said bitterly.

John and I flew back to help him make the transition. After all the years when I loved to fly, I found myself wiped out by pain from the pull of acceleration and braking as our planes took off and landed. By the time we reached Clinton, I was in worse shape than my father. Neither of us wanted the other to know how bad things were.

I saw my father fumble angrily with his wheelchair. I watched him flinch from a dining room where all the residents wore bibs. I heard this formal, private man, not called Mr., not even addressed as Lewis, but casually called "Louie." It was dreadful. This new life would be very hard for a man so intensely private.

More trouble. The place was terrible. That was Dad's word: *terrible*. Any place else in Clinton would be better. We arranged for him to be transferred to another facility. It, too, was terrible. Maybe, he said, more terrible than the first place. Soon he was sure: The first place wasn't as bad as this.

Back he went to the original residence, and there my father carved out a place for himself. Proving the statistics, he was the only male resident on his floor.

My father started smoking cigarettes when he was in the sixth grade. For seventy years he smoked, never trying to quit. Now, when his doctor told Dad he must stop, my father amazed everyone. He quit cold turkey.

"How in the world did you do it?"

"I opened a new pack of cigarettes, took one out, broke it in half and threw it in the wastebasket. Then I threw the pack away. I haven't smoked since." I thought what he'd done was remarkable, but Dad was nonchalant. "I really don't miss 'em too much." He never smoked another cigarette.

His doctor told me Dad had about six months to live. My father didn't know the prognosis, and the doctor insisted he not be told. (Much later, I realized how uncertain the doctor must have been.) I could hardly get the words out when I informed Donna and Anna Marie.

Dad settled in. With ferocious willpower he tried to wrest control from the staff and director of the nursing home. He hated the dining room. He wanted to eat alone, so he tried bargaining: "If I go to lunch, can I eat by myself at night? Have supper on a tray in my room? That wouldn't be any work for you. Couldn't you do that for me?" The staff, adept at yielding or holding firm, timed their responses to give Dad the greatest lift. Sometimes he won.

My parents had always lived modestly, but Dad was paying his own way in the nursing home. Not covered by insurance, he declared he was paying "full price." When all other ploys failed, he reminded the staff of his status. He never understood why it didn't gain him a thing.

Residents were encouraged to personalize their rooms, but Dad wanted only a few things brought from the house. He flatly refused one essential: He wouldn't have a phone in his room. No amount of persuading or pleading moved him. "Too much bother. I don't want people calling all the time." You can point out how inconvenient it is for his daughter, or his niece, or a friend like Anna Marie to reach him. But you don't remind an elderly man—a man already deeply distressed about being dependent—that he's outlived or alienated almost anybody he ever knew. You swallow hard and hope the nurses will understand.

And those blessed women did. They encouraged Dad to call me

from the nurses' station. They were cordial when I called and quickly helped him wheel his chair to the phone. I never understood how he balanced his fierce need for privacy against having the world hear his end of the conversation. Yet somehow the setup worked for him.

On certain issues my father was a realist. He no longer wanted to pay monthly bills and dues—even in a nursing home, responsibilities go on—so Dad asked me to get a power of attorney to handle his affairs. To my dismay, Dad's attorney brushed me off, said it was impossible. I lived too far away; it would never work. I found another lawyer.

Dad knew it was time to sell the house. I was in too much pain to travel, but I could phone the realtor Dad chose, work with him by phone and make plans with an auctioneer. With great help from my husband, we took care of the sale of the house and its contents.

Dad always had a flair for numbers. I'd worried about his sense of loss when the auction was held, but he turned out to be intensely interested in the price each item brought. When we talked on the phone for the next few weeks, he wanted to go back over the lists, telling what each thing had cost when it was new. He remembered prices paid in '35 and '40 and just after the war. Adding up columns in his head, he played with the numbers.

After he lost the sight in one eye, Dad feared going totally blind. He thought if he used the remaining eye too much, he might lose it as well. He reasoned that if the doctors couldn't diagnose the problem, they couldn't be sure it was all right to use his good eye. Television in his room occasionally caught his attention, but Dad scorned activities in the dayroom on his floor. He wouldn't watch TV there, and he certainly wouldn't participate in activities planned for the residents. But then, Dad always was a loner.

He was a third-generation railroad man. His grandfather worked on a construction crew for the Chicago and Northwestern Railroad, and his father was a conductor on the same line. Dad himself, for forty-four years, was a clerk in the C&NW office in Clinton. Three generations, each moving one step higher. But my father hated his job. For most of those forty-four years, surely in all the years I saw him there, he was angry and resentful. His competence never faltered, but he didn't hide his scorn.

Dad handled the retirement applications for railroad personnel, so he was able to calculate—without a word to anyone—the exact day he could retire with full pension. The morning of that day, Dad walked into his boss's office, tossed retirement papers on the desk and announced, "This is my last day in this place." His boss and co-workers were astounded. Dad walked out the door at four-thirty and never went back. He took pride in the way he ended all those years. Was this a man who would turn gregarious in a nursing home?

A nursing home chaplain visited him, but the pastor of Dad's own congregation was "too busy" to come regularly. I smarted as the minister gave me excuses and neglected my father.

Finally, an intern came to the church for a year's training, and the pastor assigned her the nursing-home visits. Dad was delighted to have "Pastor Jan" visit every week. Indeed, he was so delighted it began to eat away at me. She was on the scene; I was far away. But I was the faithful one, the dutiful daughter. Confounded Jan was a fly-by-night.

On Father's Day, of all times, the florist garbled the message on the card with the flowers I'd sent. Dad thought Jan had sent them. I went ballistic. How many daughters did he think he had?

I can look back now and—almost—laugh at myself. He found comfort in her visits. Of course I wanted him to have that. I just didn't want him to get so caught up in a stranger's *assigned* visits. I did have enough sense to keep this struggle to myself. Only my husband knew how I felt about the interloper.

All his life, my father was a struggler. He didn't expect life to be easy. Both of us were staunch Midwesterners, raised to be reticent, so we didn't quote Scripture to each other. Never had, never would. We missed something, I think. We could have reminded each other of that stirring passage in Hebrews: "Let us run with patience the race that is set before us," and recognized our mutual problems with patience. I hope my father pictured himself running a race. I wish we'd tried to talk about *being* as well as doing. That's an opportunity we missed.

Rhythms of a nursing home are imposed upon the residents, and everyone, including my father, comes to rely on them. One day, I heard cold fury in Dad's voice. His favorite sweater had been sent to the laundry instead of being dry-cleaned. It was ruined. He was enraged about the sweater and felt captive in his wheelchair. The incident so riled him that he went on at great length about a blizzard that had left eight-foot snowdrifts all over town. (He'd discovered how much news came from the local radio stations. Nothing got by him now.) I tried to sympathize about the sweater, but he went over the blizzard three more times.

As soon as we finished talking, I called the owner of a men's clothing shop in Clinton. Muffy, a kind man who understood Dad's distress, said he'd be glad to go to the nursing home and see that my father got a new sweater. We conspired to give Dad a selection of colors—and *two* new sweaters. Navy blue was his favorite color, so Muffy would take a dark blue and a light blue, and he'd add two others so Dad would have a choice. We laughed because I knew exactly which ones would stay with my father. Muffy agreed to take trousers, too, and provide Dad with several new outfits. True to his word, he got to Dad through the snowdrifts the next day.

What did my father like best? The light blue? The dark blue? Neither. They both went back to the store. Dad picked a bright red sweater and a bright yellow one. So much for navy blue. I'd never have thought to get him such bright, cheery things. (It was a good lesson. I brightened up what I sent him in the future.)

Muffy, like so many others who dealt with my father, wondered if Dad appreciated what he'd done. The roads were barely cleared, and ice made them dangerous. "Your father must not know how bad the storm was," he said, trying to figure out the curt reception Dad gave him. I didn't tell him how up-to-date and aware my father was, thanks to the radio.

A lifetime of protecting my parents came into play. I'd spent years interpreting and reinterpreting their coldness and isolation; I could do it from a thousand miles away.

Yet this became a time of change for Dad and me. If I had been nearby—say, twenty minutes away—all his old defenses would have prevailed. But if a man's daughter lives a thousand miles away, and if that man controls his phone access and can read and reread his daughter's letters in his own good time, a man in his eighties can change.

My father thawed. He truly did.

After twenty-five years of keeping my husband at a distance—a lot farther than arm's length!—Dad started to talk to his son-in-law. Each time John flew back to Iowa, we asked Dad to think of places he'd like to go and things he'd like to do. Dad usually wanted to get a hamburger and ride around town to see what had changed. Their rides always included a stop at Mother's grave. My father began to make conversation with my husband. All of us had to adjust.

Dad's emphysema suddenly worsened, and he had to be taken to the hospital. This time John rushed back, bracing himself for the worst. But there sat Dad, alert as could be. Nurses told John, with considerable amusement, that my father had started buzzing them at six o'clock that morning. He had to be shaved and ready for his son-in-law! That was the trip when Dad told me, "I'm beginning to understand what you saw in this fellow." John, standing at his bedside to help him hold the phone, began to laugh. "Dad!" I protested. "It took you twenty-five years?" I was laughing, too, as the tears welled up.

We three, my mother and father and I, had never been demonstrative. There were no hugs in our family. Never a quick, easy "I love you." That made it all the sweeter when my father actually said those words. "I love you, too, Dad," I said. Over the phone, for the first time in my life, I said those words to him.

It is extraordinary to see an eighty-four-year-old man change.

Meanwhile, when company headquarters relocated, John and I had to move to Stamford, Connecticut. Dad thought brick buildings were solid and substantial, so he was pleased to hear about the brick condominium where we'd be living. He looked up information about Connecticut, told me it was the Nutmeg State, rattled off statistics over the phone.

He wanted us to take a check drawn on his account and find something for our condo. By coincidence, we'd just seen a stained-glass shade that would be perfect in the new place. It was a wonderful gesture from my father, and he took pride in showing the pictures we sent. (Sending him things to talk about, hoping he'd connect with a few people, I'd learned snapshots were invaluable.) This time, I'm not sure who was more touched: John and I in Connecticut with the stained-glass piece, or Dad in Iowa, basking in satisfaction over a generous gesture.

There were times when I felt I was on a short leash. I could no longer drive and Dad knew I was immobilized. He assumed that meant instant access. I was supposed to be at the other end of the line whenever he decided to call. However, he called at random. If I wasn't there to answer instantly, he was agitated and worried.

My great ally was a nurse named Mary. She grew fond of my father and sensed what he needed throughout the day. Donna and Anna Marie sang her praises, and I began to know Mary as we talked on the phone. She said that for her, as a nurse, no illness seemed more frustrating than emphysema. She longed to give relief, yet could only stand and watch as the terrible struggle to breathe went on and on. Maybe her great compassion for my father stemmed from his medical problems, but I think there must have been qualities in him that drew her. Whatever the reason, she was a godsend. I counted on her for honest, detailed reports on Dad's medical condition. Equally important, she watched out for his emotional stability. If he looked despondent, she suggested he call me. If he was weary, she suggested he watch television or she wheeled his chair to the windows at the end of the hall.

Mary often wished she could be a volunteer instead of an R.N. "So many times, I'd just like to make a piece of toast for your father and talk to him while he eats it." Her nursing duties were heavy; volunteers handled the lighter, more rewarding tasks. Without a doubt, the Marys of this world, watching over our elderly parents, are saints who walk among us.

After eighteen months in the Stamford condo, John and I moved again. He had a new job—my father had a bank vice president in the family—and we needed to be closer to New York. I loved the place we found on Long Island. Dad caught the excitement in my voice, and again he pored over pictures. He savored the charm of the Dutch colonial house where his stained-glass shade glowed in the dining room. He sounded happier than in years.

Three weeks after we moved to Long Island, my father died of a massive heart attack. The end was quick. It was merciful, people told me. I tried to listen to their condolences.

My father had lived far beyond the six months his doctor predicted. In fact, he was in the nursing home for a full three years. His mind was clear to the very end.

When I called the pastor—that ever-so-busy man—to arrange the funeral, I learned that Dad had made him promise one thing: The pastor was to make a tape of the funeral service and send it to me. Dad had explained that I wouldn't be able to travel to Clinton for his funeral. As we went on with funeral arrangements, I could hardly speak.

My father—the loner, the man who did not want to be around people—for years and years paid American Legion dues and Masonic dues. Not that he'd gone to a meeting in fifty years. Quite simply, he wanted Legion and Masonic rites at his funeral. Dad got what he wanted. Listening to the tape, I heard the pastor wonder if my father had been a saint. I knew how Dad would have answered that one.

The final years of my father's life were an enormous gift to the two of us. We needed all those days and nights, weeks and months, to begin to know each other. I met a father I'd never known. He discovered a whole new daughter.

Today, I treasure a picture of my father and his sister on a carousel at the turn of the century. Dad is twelve. Lillian is three. She's a dark-eyed little beauty, a winsome child. Dad looks jaunty. He's wearing a white shirt and tie with a spiffy suit and a straw hat tipped back on his head. He's smiling at the camera, beaming with pleasure. I smile back at him. It took a lot of years, but I was—at the very end—blessed to know the boy within the man.

Never mind the duty, the responsibility, the tangle of caregiving.

Set aside the no-win situations and the constant worry.

Give up the old hurts.

We had the gift of time. We shared his final, fruitful years—and I saw duty transformed into grace. Sheer grace.

Today, I smile back at my father.

The Dress

MARIAN MATHEWS CLARK

*U*gly or unique—I couldn't tell. But it caught my eye immediately on the July sale's $29.50, ten percent off rack. I pulled out the size eight from where it hung, baggy and limp, mashed between two other dresses. It was rayon; I wasn't the rayon type. And where would I wear it? Maybe to an occasional ballet? But I wore peasant skirts and blouses, even to those. So I passed it by, but those rust-colored suns of various sizes on the black background summoned me back. I lifted it off the rack, put it back, lifted it off, put it back, lifted it off, then carried it quickly, without thinking, to the dressing room where I tried it on. I had to be at work five blocks away in fifteen minutes.

In the fitting room, I stood up straight and looked at the color against my skin. I'd been wearing a lot of black, and that rust orange was striking. But those huge shoulder pads, the high neck and straight skirt? Was it ugly or unique? I still couldn't tell. I needed time.

"Could you hold this for twenty-four hours?" I asked the clerk.

"Eight," she said. "It's on sale. And if you sign up for our credit card, take off an extra fifteen percent."

"I don't want a credit card," I said, then realized with all the discounts, it could end up being a twenty-dollar dress. In my price range. "Eight hours should be enough," I said.

And it was—to decide that, after all, the dress wasn't me and to remember my grandfather's warning that, "A bargain isn't a bargain unless you need it." I'd made a wise decision.

But in the middle of the night I awoke, startled, and wondered how I would feel if someone bought the size eight before I could return. I tried to chalk my worries up to menopausal anxiety and repeated, "A bargain isn't a bargain isn't a bargain," for five minutes. But when the last of the bargains slid through my mind, "What if it's gone?" reappeared. So I flipped on the light and worked crossword puzzles until four, reminding myself that a friend had gone through these middle-of-the-night menopause worry fests for two years. This dress obsession was, of course, physical.

The next day, I called my mother in Oregon for our twice-a-week chat. "I've been looking at a dress," I told her. "An elegant but inexpensive one. At least I think it's elegant. Or maybe it's ugly. I can't decide. But it may end up costing only twenty dollars."

"Sounds like a bargain," she said, out of breath. "You deserve something new."

"Are you out of breath?"

"Oh, I was just taking a nap and had a hard time getting to the phone. Did you ever think you would see the day your mom took naps?"

"Why are you so tired?"

"It's just that darned fibrillation," she said. "I'm OK. Now what color is it?"

"Color? Oh, the dress. It's not a big deal," I said, scribbling *fib, fibrill, fibrillate* on a note pad.

"Come on," she said. "You think I'm going to pass up a chance to hear about my daughter buying a dress?" Her voice sounded stronger.

I stopped scribbling. "Black and an odd sort of rust. It's rayon and has to be dry-cleaned. It's not me, really. I don't know where I would wear it."

"Home at Christmas?"

"Instead of jeans?" I said and laughed.

"You said it. I didn't."

Five years before, I wouldn't have been able to joke about our different dress habits. I would have been irritated at her saying things like, "I'd like to see you in a suit, just once." But after her second heart surgery, my resistance had waned. "I'm afraid you're stuck with seeing me in jeans," I said. "I'll probably be buried in them."

"You could wear the dress over them. Like mother, like daughter."

"Not this again," I told her. My last trip home she'd taken me to her closet and pointed out a blue silky dress. "That's what I want to be buried in," she said. I must have gasped because she assured me she was feeling OK.

"Yeah, it sounds like it," I said, staring at her instead of the dress. Had she looked this pale for some time, or was there a change?

She reached up into the closet to pull out the dress.

"Here, I'll do that," I said, taking it from the hanger. "The doctor said you weren't supposed to raise your arms above your head."

"Good heavens," she said. "I'm fine. I just wanted to clarify a few things to make the funeral arrangements easier—when the time comes." She lay her chin over the neck of the dress. "What do you think?"

I nodded slightly then reminded myself she'd always been a planner. She wasn't hinting she would die tomorrow. I pointed to a bone-colored jersey dress and tried to sound enthusiastic. "I've always liked that one on you," I said.

"Well then," she said, "maybe I'll just wear one over the other."

We both laughed.

"We're not talking about the funeral again," I told her on the phone and drew hilly lines through *fib, fibrillate, fibrillation.* "I wish I could make up my mind about this dress. It has these huge shoulder pads I can't stand."

Marian Mathews Clark   253

"Oh, I hate those things," she said, sounding tired. "I thought they went out in the forties."

"If I do buy it, I'll bring it home at Christmas so you can see it," I told her. "That'll go fast. It's only a few months away."

That weekend, a friend came into town and agreed to go with me to look at the dress. I was relieved to see there was a size eight left on the rack. In the dressing room, I wiggled into it—the elastic at the waist a bottleneck—then smoothed it around me and belted it up. I stood straight for her inspection. When she was quiet, I felt self-conscious.

"Look at these absurd shoulder pads," I said.

"They don't bother me," she said. "I like it. It's just that the neck looks baggy." She examined the collar. "I'll bet you could press it. This material irons up really well. Or maybe you could move these buttons over."

"I'm not good at altering things," I said. I pushed the shoulder pads back. "Does it hang funny on this side?"

"Um—maybe a little different from the other side, but not noticeably. What about a six?"

I nodded, tired of the whole thing, but asked the pushy clerk I'd never liked if there was a six. When she said, "No," I was glad to be done with it. But then she volunteered to call all the stores in the area on Monday. She didn't seem to remember me from a year before when she'd followed me around the store oohing and aahing over everything I took off the rack. And when I'd finally chosen something to try on, and she'd chirped, "Oh, that's so cute. Are you buying it for a certain occasion or just for fun?" I snapped, "I don't buy things just for fun." When I'd emerged from the dressing room, she was nowhere to be seen.

That week when I'd called my mother, I'd told her about the sales clerk. "I don't like strangers pretending to care," I said.

"Oh?"

"Yes, like bank tellers handing you your money and saying, 'Have a nice day, Marian.' They don't know me from Adam. They're so phony."

"Or friendly," she said.

"Uh huh," I said, reminding myself she and my father banked in a town of fifteen hundred where bank tellers really did know everybody. How could she possibly understand?

Now, as this phony-friendly clerk smiled at me and said she would let me know if she found a size six, I wondered if my mother had been right.

"I've settled it," I said when I called home that week. "No six, no dress."

"A six?" my mother said. "You're the littlest thing." My mother had gained fifty pounds her freshman year in college, had spent ten years losing it and had been fighting to keep her weight down ever since. She was full-figured, big-boned and had always said she was thankful I was built like my father, tall and lanky. And she hoped I had his heart, too. At eighty-three he was chopping thistles, building windmills, cutting down an occasional tree.

"I'm a size ten now," she was telling me. "Only one hundred twenty-five when I weighed this morning. It's kind of nice not to have to worry about weight after all these years."

"Why are you losing?"

"I'm just not as hungry as I used to be. It's all that sitting around. You know your mom isn't used to that. After eighty-one years of doing things, I don't like taking naps and sitting, but I'm doing OK."

"But are you eating?"

"Oh, yes. I don't have your dad's appetite, of course. But then nobody does. In fact, I'd better go. I can hear him in the kitchen unloading the dishwasher. He's a Mathews. When it's five o'clock, it's time to eat. I hope you find a six," she said. "I love you."

There was no six, the clerk said, when she called on Monday. She'd phoned Cedar Rapids, Des Moines, Davenport, all the stores in the area. She seemed to be in a rush. After all, I realized, the sale was on. She had customers waiting. As soon as I hung up, all I could think of was, "Customers—waiting to buy that size eight, the last eight in Iowa City, probably the last eight in Iowa. The eight that wasn't that much too big with that lovely tailored look, that was, after all, not ugly but exquisite. Shoulder pads were in. The suns were stunning."

I didn't have to be at work until one but took an early bus into town and rushed into the store, hoping, praying the dress would be there. I rifled frantically through the rack and found it. I snatched it up and hurried to the dressing room to try it one more time. It would look much better with my black heels instead of the blue loafers that stuck out beneath the midcalf skirt, I assured myself. And when a customer said, "I didn't like that thing on the hanger, but it sure looks good on you," that cinched it.

I filled out the credit card application and waffled only temporarily when the clerk said, "That'll be $39.50."

"Thirty-nine fifty?"

"With the discounts." She showed me the original $69.99. "It was on the $29.50 and up rack."

"Oh. And up," I said and continued filling out the application, more slowly now, trying to ignore the woman behind me who shifted from foot to foot. As I wrote my address and phone number I reminded myself I'd been suspicious of the low price. This was a quality dress, and the higher price legitimized it. My five-dollar shirts at resale shops had spoiled me. I was making the right decision. And that night when I awoke at three a.m., thinking that I paid twice what I'd originally planned, the customer's voice saying "It looks good on you" lulled me to sleep.

But the next morning, when I saw it hanging among my jeans and flannel shirts and gauze skirts, I touched the huge shoulder pads and felt scared. I called another friend. "This dress is driving me crazy," I said. "I thought I was finished with it, but here it hangs, out of place, and I feel I have to take it back. It was nearly forty dollars. A twenty-dollar dress I'm iffy about didn't seem so bad, but forty dollars?"

"Don't panic," she said. "You can still return it."

"But what's wrong with me?" I said. "Maybe this wavering is fibrillation of the brain."

"I think that's only of the heart," she said. "But don't worry. Last year, I bought and returned a red vest four times over a two-month period."

"And they kept taking it back?"

"It got so bad that when they saw me coming, they just nodded. They were kind enough not to say, 'Oh, it's the vest woman,'—to my face anyway. This dress must be a metaphor for something."

"For what? I'm indecisive sometimes but never this bad. I've just bought a dress that hangs funny, isn't really me, definitely costs too much and might not fit."

"Exactly," she said.

"Exactly what?"

"The cost, the size, the fit? I don't know." She laughed. "But remember, you'll have to take it back five times to top my record."

When I hung up, I felt better and pondered metaphors and clothes. I thought about the two-piece, short-sleeved outfit I'd picked up a few years before while shopping with my mother. It wasn't quite a suit, but as close as I'd been to one for a long time. I'd held back, hesitant to buy something I had little occasion to wear. And it needed minor alterations. But it was on sale, and as I stood before the dressing room mirror, my mother looked so pleased (she knew enough not to say how pleased) that I decided I could surely find someplace to wear it. She insisted on paying for it, her unspoken compensation for my unspoken compromise.

I'd paid ten dollars for the alterations, worn it once that year, then hauled it out each year after that—at first with the intention of wearing it again, then with the notion that maybe I wouldn't and finally with the realization that I never would and, after the first wearing, hadn't intended to.

On the other hand, there was the green wool coat that I'd loved at first sight and had grown more attached to each winter. My now ex-husband had told me to pick out anything for my Christmas present. He usually didn't have an opinion about my wardrobe, but he wanted this to be special. When he saw the green coat I'd chosen, he frowned and proclaimed I looked like a Christmas tree.

"It's my constant dilemma," I'd told my mother when I visited her a few days later. "If having integrity means doing what you believe, how do you please somebody else and yourself at the same time? Maybe when husbands say, 'Do what you think is best,' they really mean, 'If you loved me, what you think is best would coincide with what I think is best. Or if it doesn't, you would consider my opinion strongly, especially when it's so important to me.'"

"You analyze everything so much," my mother said. "I would have died a long time ago if I thought about things the way you do. If he says, 'Get the coat you want,' I assume he means, 'Get the coat you want.' If he doesn't like it, you can't feel guilty."

"But there'll be a price to pay," I said. "Because underneath he'll be hurt. You see . . . "

My mother, who'd been standing, moved to a chair, sat heavily into it and put her feet on a stool.

"Is it making you nervous to listen to this?"

"Not as nervous as this coat thing seems to be making you," she said. "The doctor said when I sit I should put my feet up. That's all."

"OK. Well, it's this way," I said, sitting on the edge of the couch and leaning toward her. I wanted her to understand what I was up against. "To honor his intention—to get what I like—is to not value his taste. That's what makes it so hard."

She nodded and looked at me for a minute. "I wonder," she said, "if there's a way to find a coat that you both like. There are lots of coats."

I told her that would be caving in somehow, not dealing with the issue.

"I suppose so," she said. "It's just so complicated that I can't figure out what the issue is."

I hadn't taken the coat back. I liked the way it hung, slightly A-lined, over dresses and pants, above heels or flats. The big square pockets held my gloved hands or head scarves or small books. Wearing that coat was the one good thing about winter each year. Even after my marriage dissolved, I'd still had the coat.

Maybe I would become as attached to this dress as I had to the coat. But I seriously doubted it, and I tried it on for yet another friend when she came to spend the night a week later.

"I like it," she said.

"But the shoulder pads," I said. "They make me look like a football player. And don't you think it hangs a little baggy on this right side?"

"It's made to look baggy," she said. "Take it off and let me look at the shoulder pads. I used to sew a lot for the kids."

I struggled out of it and stood as I'd often stood in front of my mother while she did last-minute alterations. My mother had been a home economics major in college. Except the last time I was home and needed to make a couple of seams in a blouse, she said she couldn't help me, that sewing made her nervous these days. She'd sat in bed by the sewing machine and watched while I struggled with the seams, and she'd cheered me on when I grew discouraged. "I feel so bad I couldn't help you," she said when I finished. "All the home economics training wasted." But then she sat up straighter and assumed the determined look I'd seen the day she decided she would recover from her second heart surgery. "I shouldn't complain," she'd said. "I can still get around. Your poor Aunt Myrtle has diabetes so bad she can hardly walk."

My friend inspected the dress. "Well, no wonder it hangs funny," she said. "One shoulder pad's in backwards. But I don't think anyone will notice. You could take it out and turn it around, but it's sewn oddly, so I'm not sure it'll help. A different eight might have the shoulder pads sewn in right."

"It's the last eight in Iowa City," I said, tired of the ordeal. But I was obsessed by a demon that wouldn't let me go. "I wonder if there might be an eight in Cedar Rapids."

So Monday I called the Cedar Rapids store and asked if they had an eight. "This one's shoulder pads are irregular," I said. The clerk disappeared for a few minutes. When she returned she said, "You're in luck. We have sixes, eights and tens."

"Sixes? Are you sure?"

"Yup, and eights and tens. Do you want me to hold it? If I do, I'll need to put it on your credit card."

I'd caved in to obsession. "Yes, and put one of the eights on there, too," I told her. "In case the six doesn't fit."

"They're $49.50," she said. "That'll be . . . "

"But mine was $39.50."

"Well, let's see," she said. "We'll still have to put them on your card, then remove the ones you don't want. I'll make sure you only end up paying $39.50. So for now, I'll hold a size six and eight and add $90.00 to your card."

"OK," I said feebly and sat, numb, for a few minutes after I hung up. I now had $137 worth of ugly or elegant dress on my credit card, a steal I'd planned to buy for twenty.

I finally bought the six. The shoulder pad was in backwards—on every dress—but I decided my friend was right, that no one would notice.

On the drive home, I didn't feel joyful about purchasing something I loved, only mildly relieved to have done something. This decision felt similar to the one I'd made about not moving to Oregon several years earlier. I had a job and friends in Iowa, an ailing mother with no other offspring in Oregon. I wavered between leaving and staying for several years. And I couldn't think of a compromise. Moving to Wyoming, halfway between the two, wouldn't accomplish anything. When I finally decided to stay in Iowa, I realized that some decisions didn't solve the problem; they just put an end to the uncertainty—for the time being.

In my apartment I hung the dress in the closet in its bag, which to my relief covered it entirely. I couldn't see even a hint of the suns.

I was finished with it. Except, of course, to tell my mother when I called home that week. "That clerk was a phony and I should never have trusted her to call around for a six," I said. "She lied to me."

"Unless there was some mistake," my mother said. When I didn't respond, she said, "Well, you're probably right. I don't see why sales people can't just tell the truth."

"Beats me," I said. "All I know is that when the bill comes, I'm paying it and canceling that credit card immediately."

"Does this mean you're keeping the dress, then?"

"I guess so," I said.

"Well, don't you like it?"

"It's fine. Yes, it's fine. I'm too tired of hassling with the stupid thing to care. And now I'm not sure why I bought it in the first place."

"So you can wear it to church at Christmas," my mother said. Then she laughed. But her voice sounded weak and tired.

I laughed, too. "You're pushing your luck here, Mom," I said. "I'm just getting used to having a fancy dress hanging in my closet. I think that's about all my system can stand." When she didn't say anything, I said, "Are you all right?"

"Well . . . sure, I'm OK," she said. "Just a little tired."

"Come on now. Tell me the truth," I said, bracing myself against the living room wall.

"I just had a bad night," she said. She sounded out of breath. "About two I woke up and couldn't find a pulse. I felt myself slipping away."

"Slipping away?" I said, hearing panic in my voice. I cleared my throat. "What do you mean, 'slipping away'?" I tried to sound calm.

"Letting go, I guess. It was kind of a relief. . . . "

Marian Mathews Clark   261

"Don't say that," I interrupted, stretching the phone cord to its limit and pacing between the television and the couch. "It sounds like you're . . . well, like you want to . . . "

"I don't want to die," she said. "I'm just tired of feeling tired. Anyway, your father got up just then to go to the bathroom, and you know he watches me like a hawk. I guess he said my name a couple of times and when I didn't answer, he slipped a nitro under my tongue. I'm fine now. Just tired."

"Do you think I should fly home?"

"Heavens, no. I probably shouldn't have told you, but you made me promise not to hide things."

"I'm glad you did," I said, half-lying, drawing squiggly lines in the dust on the face of the television. My mother's television would never be so dusty. "Will you see a doctor?"

"They'd just give me more pills," she said. "I'm taking twenty a day as it is. Besides I don't have those spells often. I probably won't have another one for a while. I wish I knew why my fool heart acts that way."

"I'll call you tomorrow, just to see how you are. About ten your time." I wiped the screen clean with my sleeve. "You think you'll be all right through the night?"

"Of course," she said. "Don't worry."

"Get a lot of rest."

"Rest is what I do best these days," she said and laughed. "Rest, rest, rest. I'm a rest expert."

After I hung up, I walked into my bedroom and stared into my closet. When I spotted the bagged dress, I shivered. I knew why I'd bought it. When the call came, I wouldn't have time to buy anything in Iowa City. And in my parents' town, the only purchasable clothes were hunting hats and sweatshirts that read, "This house supported by timber dollars," or "We like spotted owls. We eat them for dinner." Yes, when the call came, it would be up to me to make plane reservations, pack an overnight bag with a dress that hopefully wouldn't wrinkle and make a quick exit. It would be up to me to enter the house that would now be too quiet, the one my parents had lived in for fifty years. It would be up to me to open my mother's folder she'd been compiling since her second heart surgery where I would find all the instructions about the songs she wanted, the minister to call, names of people to contact.

She was ready. I hadn't been.

But now I had our dress—for her, something respectful, maybe even elegant; I still wasn't sure. For me, something not so expensive that after wearing it once I would feel guilty tucking it to the back of my closet where I would pull it out occasionally, at first assuring myself that I could wear it again, then toying with the notion I probably wouldn't and finally acknowledging I never would and had probably never intended to.

Even though she wouldn't say it, I'm sure she would be thinking I've made this far more complicated than it needs to be. But she knows by now that at times like these there's not a thing she can do with me but listen while I analyze and kick and squirm; help me see the humor when she can; then let me go.

Her Hair

WENDY W. FAIREY

$\mathcal{I}$ remember my mother lamenting the change in her hair. She was eighty-one, three years away from dying, though that was not my worry then and perhaps not even hers. She put the tips of her fingers to her tousled gray curls. "I used to have such lovely thick hair," she said. "You can't imagine how lovely and thick it was."

"But your hair is lovely now," I said. "And I don't see that it's not thick."

I meant what I said. I liked how she looked as an old lady, the way she had grown lighter in body and spirit. Especially I liked her hair. Short, unstudied, just a touch unruly, it added to the gamin look that seemed new and that quite charmed me. Whether to hide her hair, or as a purely practical matter, to keep her head warm, or both, she almost always wore a hat, a little navy blue straw hat with an upturned brim. The hat, the cane, the image of her as she hobbled along in her Reeboks, the only shoes, she said, that accommodated her bunion—these are things I remember.

Certainly I liked her hair better than all those years in which she had dyed it blond—then it could look like straw. And thank God she no longer wore that terrible blond wig, reminding me of an artichoke, that she had insisted on donning for social occasions throughout her sixties and even into her seventies. I found the wig in her closet when she died, stashed on the shelf above the bag of diapers. I'm sure they're not called diapers. Some euphemism surely has been devised to mask their sad necessity.

Now, though, it's my hair that's the problem. I noticed the other day that I can see through it. It had seemed off for some time, but I had thought this just the drying-out effect of winter. Then suddenly, seeing right through it, especially on top in front, I understood that I had suffered what my friend Hannah calls a *coup de vieux*, one of those dramatic capitulations to aging from which there is no rebounding or reversal. I stood there peering through my hair, as if continuing to look at it might make it sprout again. Of course, I only saw through it all the more clearly, no matter what I tried to imagine and believe. Not that its sorry thinness is something that leaps out at you like the hair of a person on chemo. To others, I probably just look a little older, a little more worn down. They might not know why. But I do. My awareness made me shudder at my image in the mirror.

I used to wish for fine, straight hair, so I could grow it long down my back and flip it casually with my hand or a toss of my head. The hair I was actually endowed with—dark brown, in contrast to my mother's natural blondness—was thick, sometimes unmanageably thick, and somewhere between wavy and curly. In my forties, I cut it short and chic and went gray more gracefully, so my friends said, than many other women. I'd have ranked my hair right behind my eyes and my bosom in my list of good features. I wasn't a great beauty as my mother had been. From something she once said to me, I realized that she had an absolute confidence in her beauty every time she walked into a room. This is what came into my mind when she lamented the thinning of her hair: her beauty and her knowledge of it, the self-assurance it had given her in facing the world. My mother had always told me it was inner beauty that counted—something, I've noticed, that very beautiful people often say. I don't mean to imply a note of insincerity, but I think outer beauty counts for them too. I felt for my mother, mourning her lost golden hair; yet the quality of this loss seemed something I would never share. In a strange way, this seemed to offer me a chance of greater contentment.

Yes, I hadn't been a great beauty. My looks had always been perfectly fine, at least not something to worry about. Perhaps my vanity lay precisely in that: in knowing I didn't have to worry, knowing I passed muster, that I was pretty enough and to some even quite enticing. When I was forty-four and single again after seventeen years of marriage, a young man asked me to go away with him for the weekend. "Why would you want to do that?" I laughed.

"So I could profit from your wisdom and beauty," he replied, a bit hurt, I surmised, that I should laugh at him. Now, ten years later, it turns out he's living on my street. I felt ashamed when, recently, dashing out in old clothes from my building to buy the newspaper, I ran directly into him, almost colliding, before recovering enough to stammer his name. *He* looked all right, maybe a tad heavier and with a little less hair, but I felt as though I'd turned into his grandmother. I tried to tell myself I was only fifty-five and still only nineteen years older than he is. But I knew in my heart of hearts that everything had changed. In our earlier encounter I had been bolstered by a pleasant sense of myself as *une femme d'un certain âge.* Now, though, I couldn't imagine that a younger man might still want me. Hadn't I joined "the near old"? On a recent date with a man who is my contemporary, we had talked about our grown children, our aches and pains, and our pension plans.

I think it's a sign of my weakened self-confidence that I've started sneaking into movies as a senior citizen. A friend told me she had done this, and I was sure I looked as old as she. Usually there's a young person selling the tickets, and how does someone young tell the difference between fifty-five and sixty-five, especially when I push my glasses a bit down my nose, squint and add a little quaver to my voice in making my request? "One senior for . . . " I've gotten in this way now maybe ten or twelve times. No one has questioned me, though it's poignant that I still expect to be challenged, or you might say it's more poignant still that I feel the need to *feign* decrepitude in order to have the scam succeed. Facing the second hurdle of the person collecting tickets at the door, I try to hunch over and maintain my squint as I hand over the ticket. My heart pounds as I glance into the ticket collector's face, afraid, yet also half-hoping, to detect in it signs of disbelief. Sometimes, too, back when I'm purchasing the ticket, I act a bit befuddled about the time of the movie I want to see and even its title. Sometimes I am befuddled. Just as other times, coming home from work, I walk heavily up the steps from the subway platform, my knees stiff and uncertain, while young men bound by me three steps at a time.

I used to bound. As a child, I climbed over the breakwater rocks at the beach like an exuberant antelope. As a woman, into my thirties and forties, I still felt like Hermes, a fleet-footed tomboy. I called myself an athlete, even when, increasingly, I felt sore; my feet ached, my knees hurt; I had twinges of bursitis in my elbow. Even now, I can still manage to get beyond the aches and pains to something I cautiously call transcendence, the moment when limits stretch, almost melt away, and the body, so extended into motion, no longer exists as a contained, containing object. It has become imagination.

But I don't still feel like a tomboy, even in those transcendent moments. The tomboy pulled up stakes along with the temptress. Both stole away a year or so ago when I wasn't paying attention.

I sometimes think I am lucky that I wasn't older when my mother died, that I wasn't the age I am now.

"I feel so old," said my friend Hannah, who is fifty-eight. Hannah's ninety-two-year-old mother, Rose, is now in a nursing home, and Hannah visits her every day.

"It's not you who are old," I told her. "It's your mother."

"Isn't it the same thing?" she answered plaintively.

Before Rose went into the home, when her crisis of health and confidence was first upon her, she stayed for a month with her daughter and son-in-law, and of course, she drove them both mad. I went over to help Hannah entertain her and to pay my respects.

A small coiled figure with gnarled hands gripping the sides of an armchair that seemed too big for her, Rose not so much sat in as emanated from a corner of a room. "I used to wish my daughter long life," she confided to me in her accented English. "But nooow," she drew out the word, "I'm not so sure." She peered into the middle distance, intense, an ancient sibyl. "I was all right until I was ninety. And then . . . and then *something happened.*"

What does one say in response? "You'll be fine." Isn't that a lie? Or, "I'm sorry." Do you offer condolences to someone for growing old? I think I said, "That sounds hard."

Rose nearly died after that—they said she couldn't last a week—but she rallied in the nursing home and is going amazingly strong. She's a spirited, relentless old lady, subtle in the battle with her daughter. Or is this only a daughter's perspective? Hannah feels her own life is over.

My mother, born two years before Rose, would be ninety-four now if she were still alive. A holy terror, I'm sure. She hated to be at a disadvantage. When she had her heart attack, she agitated against the nurses in the hospital, accusing them of trying to kill her. I went to visit her right after the attack. Her hair was limp and lusterless. I remember thinking she looked like a dying cat whose fur has lost its gloss.

"I think I could eat some smoked salmon," she said to me, prone in her hospital bed, in an only slightly stagy whisper. "I would love it if you could go up to Fraser Morris on Madison Avenue and buy me some of their delicious smoked salmon."

It was very hot out and I was rushed, needing to get back to my own house and children. When I saw Gristedes right up the street, only one block from the hospital, I reasoned that their smoked salmon would surely do. My mother spat it out and called it salty. "Is this really Fraser Morris smoked salmon?" she asked me. In truth, she could eat nothing. Her heart was half destroyed. In the months before her death she grew as light as a sparrow.

Children see you as spoiled or imperious, and you're really only trying to get a little comfort. I've come to understand that. I also understand that it's hard to be relegated to the corner, to be expected to sit like Rose in the armchair, with all the ravages of age upon you, and graciously keep in your place. It's a place our culture has so ill defined. I'm sure Rose felt peripheral, yet for Hannah she took up all the space.

Last month I went to Paris to see my son, who married young and has two little girls. He and his wife have many friends who visit together over bottles of wine, laughing and telling funny stories. My daughter-in-law was telling about her orthodontistry, a wry inconsequential tale. When she was young, her mother had accused her of sticking out her chin on purpose, but the problem was really her protruding bottom teeth. Then there were years of braces. And still she has a big chin.

As people laughed in response, teasing her about her chin, I thought of telling the story of *my* bottom teeth—of how I had worn braces for years and then my wisdom teeth undid the work, pushing my two front bottom teeth out of place. They had remained crooked, all my life. "See," I would have said, opening my mouth. "See how crooked they are."

I didn't say any of this. To do so seemed intrusive. But more than that, it seemed to me that my teeth didn't really count anymore. Why would anyone be interested in what I had done to fix them as a girl, when all they could be expected to do now was to fall out?

My mother would have shown her teeth, but I would have gritted mine while she was doing so, whether I was twenty or forty-five.

She died when I was forty-six, and that released me. In the eighteen months or so leading up to her death, I had felt not old, like Hannah, but in some profound way without a future. It had seemed wrong to be thriving when she was failing. It had seemed impossible that my life could continue after hers ended.

I say this. Yet it is equally true that I always resisted her, wary that if I didn't hold her off, she might consume me. So I wasn't one of those daughters who took infinite tender care of her old mother. I tell myself that she really didn't want me to. She was a woman who always took care of herself, right down to the end, when she went down to Florida, hired round-the-clock nurses and declared herself ready for death. But I didn't get the Fraser Morris smoked salmon. I would have liked to have done that. I would have liked to have done more.

She died, I missed her terribly. And I was free—in ways I had not been when she was alive. Exuberantly free of her scrutiny, I wrote a book, I had adventures. At fifty I boasted that aging couldn't dent me; I had just begun to have a fuller life. And then, and then, as Rose said, "Something happened."

Now I feel I'm on the other side of some great divide, where much of the time I live among echoes and shadows. I am death-brushed, a bit bewildered and, above all, haunted by my mother. If I and this ghostly intimate were still at odds, this might be terrible. But we're not. I don't altogether know why, but the relationship has softened. My resentment of her, so strong in her life, has lifted like a blanket of fog that startlingly clears away. I can vaguely remember all those stories I used to relish and recount about her selfishness, her unmotherliness; but they seem both distant and petty, no longer worth the indignant telling. My mother has become like an old friend whose follies are known but with whom it's pointless to be exasperated. That is not what's interesting. She also seems in some ways less like a mother than an older sibling, someone, as she returns to me at one age or another, who is really almost my age. Or rather, she can never be older than eighty-four, and I keep creeping up on her. It no longer seems contradictory that she adored her grandchildren but also found them tiring. I can fathom how she cared what her children did, what opportunities they had and mistakes they made, and how that caring also had a limit, as she resisted feeling responsible for their lives. I understand how she could console herself for aging with greater material comfort and order in her life: For to my surprise, the other-worldliness I speak of notwithstanding, I perceive how I, too, can find pleasure in a neater house in which all the cooking utensils and stray magazines are in place, in little and not so little purchases from Bloomingdale's, in vacations where the thrill and even danger of distant places is buffered by luxury accommodations.

And I understand that vanity, and even desire, can survive in an aging body.

I have run into my young neighbor Peter several times. After the first couple of encounters, I began to think twice before dashing out of the house in rags. Once I saw him when I was on my way to the theater, and I knew I looked good. That gave me satisfaction. We have talked about getting together for a walk or a drink.

I try to deflect my residue of lust—or is it just vanity?—by thinking of him as a candidate for my daughter, who is on her own with a young child. It both satisfies and chagrins me to think of handing him on to her—not, of course, that this is a transaction occurring in anyone's head but mine. He seems very nice and, I trust, would be good to her. A strong part of the fantasy is also that he would be good to me, that as my son-in-law, his devotion to me, right down to the end of my life—and not just as his wife's mother but as a woman he once found attractive and always liked—would be steady and heartfelt. I am confident he would even come to the nursing home. His visits would be very cheering.

But I can only think of being in a nursing home in this way, lightly, as a joke. Recently I consulted with a financial planner to get a better sense of my resources. "If you go into a nursing home at seventy-eight," she said, "do you agree that your discretional expenses would decline by eighty percent?"

"Excuse me," I said. "Why are you putting me in a nursing home?"

"It's a standard part of the exercise," she said.

"At least make it eighty," I said, my life seeming over, my heart full of dread.

My mother never went into a nursing home. She kept her wits. Her insurance covered her home care, she died quickly.

At my thirty-fifth college reunion (which it seems important to note was held in a cluster with the two classes above us, so it was really only our thirty-*fourth*), the women in my class talked more than anything else about their mothers. Nine years earlier, at our far better-attended and more buoyant twenty-fifth reunion, the talk had been of career aspirations, fulfilled and thwarted, of children going to good colleges or resisting this route, of marriages, divorces and remarriages.

Now, sitting in a circle, peering into one another's faces and drawn to tell some central truth, mesmerized by the double vision of our twenty- and our fifty-five-year-old selves, we forty women talked about our mothers. Alive, dead, dying, remembered, our mothers still had us in their grip.

Some were shocking ghosts. "I never told anyone then," said Mary Watkins, "but my mother committed suicide when I was a freshman here."

Another woman had been raised by her younger aunts. Her mother was in and out of psychiatric institutions. There she sat, fifty-five, with thinning gray hair and a beautiful gaunt face—I remembered a plumpish, rather homely dark-haired girl, whom I hadn't known well—speaking with intensity of how her younger aunts had really been her mothers, how she had only come to see this quite recently.

Other mothers were failing now, and doing it peacefully or badly. Their daughters were finding new channels of love for them, or they were wearily or warily—I had been one of the wary—doing whatever blood and complex feelings defined as necessary.

I took the plunge and introduced my particular ghost. "I'm better friends with my mother since she died," I said. "She used to be very difficult. But she's now so much more reasonable."

The group laughed. Someone agreed that this could happen. Still, the mood was somber. There we were, at fifty-five, all dwelling in the shadow of our mothers, which was a shadow touching and tinging the future as well as the past. Sitting in that circle, talking about our mothers, we dramatized our own aging.

Later in the dorm lounge, nestled in the window seat where as an undergraduate I used to read while a woman two classes above me played Rogers and Hart on the piano, I was nagged by the sense of something false. I had been sitting and talking with Peggy Carley, whom I hadn't seen since 1962 when she went off to marry nice Steve Edelman. They lived in Texas; she was a patent lawyer. We both had grandchildren and showed our pictures.

"My grandchildren give me such pleasure," I said. "Particularly my little curly-headed grandson, whom I get to see all the time."

Yes, life is still fun, I thought. How can we have been thinking that it is over?

I looked out the bay window through the high maple trees of the college grounds and saw three men sauntering up the path to the dorm. One of them, the slight one in the middle, had a familiar loose-limbed gait.

Eagerly I rose from the window seat and went up to the group as they entered the lounge.

"Danny Parker!" I said. "It's you."

The person I had addressed looked toward me. Beneath a somewhat wizened countenance, he exuded an entrenched assurance of boyish charm.

"We heard the classes of the early sixties were in this dorm," explained Danny, amidst hugs and hellos. "So we came to see who was here." The trio was from the nearby men's college, where their class was also having its reunion.

Paul McKee, sporting a gray ponytail, spoke of remarriage and a two-year-old son.

"That's the age of my grandson," I laughed.

"You're a grandmother," said Danny. "How fantastic."

Wendy W. Fairey   273

"And you," I said, "I hear you're a tycoon."

Grandmother, tycoon. It all seemed like make-believe, the overlay and camouflage of our young true selves. In college Danny had been a charming, wistful drinker. We had been in a play together. One evening he had gotten me to dance for him in his room, the way you normally dance only for yourself in front of the mirror. I think he was the first person who ever made me feel sexy.

"I'm a mini-coon," said Danny.

"Danny's a wonderful family man," said Joe Pearson, the other man. "He's wonderful to his wife and children."

I turned to Joe, a large man with soft brown eyes, whom I vaguely remembered. He had a picture of his younger self around his neck, which, slightly abashed, he drew out to show me. I looked at a heavy-set young man with a low hairline. "Oh yes," I said. I thought but didn't say that he looked better now.

"Joe's a calligrapher," said Danny.

"You know what I remember about you?" confided Joe. "Your smile. And you still have it."

Joe and I talked for some time in earnest flirtation, until he was merrily swept off by his friends. After he left, I fingered the piece of paper in my pocket with his address. He lives in Philadelphia, but says he often comes to New York.

I like to think it wasn't only the men who cheered me that day. Cheer beamed in the flickering afternoon light of the leaves of the high trees. It lay in the eagerness with which I showed off the pictures of my grandchildren. It resonated in my admiration for Linda Solomon, who has had lupus for a decade and still travels all over the world and copes and does not feel life is over. She and I took a walk together before dinner, past familiar and unfamiliar buildings, laughing when we called one building "new" and then realized it had been there for twenty-five years. And the more I thought over the events of the day, the more I rebelled against the mood of our earlier conversation in the circle of women. Not that we had been consciously distorting the state of our lives, but I was sure we were not as sad as we had been making ourselves out. A reunion is an intense and dizzying affair, inviting you, as it foreshortens a lifetime, to feel at once eighteen and eighty. Perhaps our declarations about our mothers, at the end of *their* lives, had been a way of admitting time's awesome power, of talking about our destiny in time as women, bound within our women's bodies. But our ritual regathering at this interval of years also had a more generative aspect. We looked deep into one another's faces and spirits and could see that we were still ourselves, recognizable both within time and despite it. The force of that recognition was palpable. It helped us to build the strength we needed to survive our mothers and then to carry with us their persistent ghosts more joyously and lightly.

When I got back to my own home in New York, I sat out in the little square across from my building where a couple of years ago the statue of Eleanor Roosevelt was installed. The Eleanor of the statue is not young, but she doesn't give the sense that age bothers her. Clad in her serviceable coat, leaning on a rock under the pin oaks, she rests her chin on her fist in pensive contemplation and clearly has a lot on her mind. The whole world is still out there. Her capacity to contribute is not in doubt. It was my mother who taught me to admire Eleanor Roosevelt, and I heard her speak once in the fifties when I was a girl. She seemed then a formidable figure—a large woman with awesome diction lecturing from behind a stage podium. The Eleanor under the pin oaks is a softer presence, subtly engaging the onlooker. In one of my reveries I imagine sitting near the statue with my mother, old but sprightly, beside me. We gossip and catch up on things. Eleanor's company puts us in good humor. Then my mother peers at me closely. "Your hair," she hazards, reaching out her hand, "I think it looks very attractive. But if you would just move this one strand . . ."

Resources

ORGANIZATIONS

American Association of Homes and Services for the Aging
This national association publishes free brochures with advice on how to choose a nursing home or assisted living facility.
901 E Street NW, Suite 500
Washington, DC 20004
phone: (202) 783-2242
website: www.aahsa.org

American Association of Retired Persons (AARP)
This nonprofit membership organization is dedicated to the needs of people age fifty and older and provides publications on a wide range of topics related to aging.
601 E Street NW
Washington, DC 20049
phone: (202) 434-2277
email: aarp1@aol.com
website: www.aarp.org

American Self-Help Clearinghouse
This organization lists national and local self-help support groups for any type of illness, disability or bereavement.
25 Pocono Road
Denville, NJ 07834
phone: (973) 625-7101
email: afhc@cybernex.net
website: www.cmhc.com

American Society on Aging
This professional membership association provides education and training for individuals and organizations that work with and on behalf of older people.
833 Market Street, Suite 511
San Francisco, CA 94103
phone: (415) 974-9600
email: info@asa.asaging.org
website: www.asaging.org

Children of Aging Parents (CAPS)
CAPS assists caregivers of the elderly by providing reliable information and referrals, a network of support groups, publications and programs that promote public awareness of the value and the needs of caregivers.
1609 Woodbourne Road, Suite 302A
Levittown, PA 19057
phone: (800) 227-7294
website: www.careguide.net

Children of Parkinsonians
COPS is a volunteer organization that serves the Parkinson's community through informational meetings, support groups and a monthly newsletter.
73-700 El Paseo, Suite #2
Palm Desert, CA 92260
phone: (760) 773-5628
email: copsca@gte.net

Eldercare Locator
Eldercare Locator provides a national guide to finding community assistance for seniors, with particular help with long-distance care.
927 15th Street NW, 6th Floor
Washington, DC 20005
phone: (800) 677-1116
website: www.aoa.dhhs.gov

Family Caregiver Alliance
This nonprofit organization addresses the needs of families and friends, providing long-term care by developing services, advocating for public and private support, conducting research and educating the public.
425 Bush Street, Suite 500
San Francisco, CA 94108
phone: (415) 434-3388

email: gen-info@caregiver.org
website: www.caregiver.org

National Academy of Elder Law Attorneys (NAELA)
This professional association of attorneys is concerned with improving
the availability and delivery of legal services to the elderly.
1604 North Country Club Road
Tuscon, AZ 85716
phone: (520) 881-4005
email: info@naela.com
website: www.naela.com

National Alliance for Caregiving
This new national resource center provides information on family
caregiving for older persons.
4720 Montgomery Lane, Suite 642
Bethesda, MD 20814
phone: (301) 718-8444

National Association of Professional Geriatric Care Managers
This association provides referrals to care managers who assess the health,
living conditions and needs of the elderly. They arrange and supervise in-
home help and services for long-distance caregivers.
1604 North Country Club Road
Tucson, AZ 85716
phone: (520) 881-8008

The National Council on the Aging (NCOA)
Founded in 1950, NCOA is dedicated to promoting the dignity, self-
determination and continuing contributions of older persons through lead-
ership, service, education and advocacy.
409 Third Street SW
Washington, DC 20024
phone: (800) 424-9046
email: info@ncoa.org
website: www.ncoa.org

National Family Caregivers Association
NFCA is the only national, charitable organization dedicated to making
life better for all of America's family caregivers.
10605 Concord Street, Suite 501
Kensington, MD 20895-2504

phone: (301) 942-6430 or (800) 896-3650
email: info@nfcacares.org
website: www.nfcacares.org

National Hispanic Council on Aging
This council promotes the well-being of Hispanic elderly people through demonstration projects, research, policy analysis, training and educational and informational resources.
2713 Ontario Road NW
Washington, DC 20009
phone: (202) 745-2521
email: nhcoa@worldnet.att.net
website: www.nhcoa.org

National Hospice Organization (NHO)
NHO promotes quality care for the terminally ill and provides information about hospice services in your area and the different types of hospice programs that are available.
1901 North Moore Street, Suite 901
Arlington, VA 22209
phone: (800) 658-8898
email: drnsho@cais.com
website: www.nho.org

National Indian Council on Aging
Since 1976, NICOA has been the nation's foremost advocacy organization for American Indian and Alaska Native elders.
10501 Montgomery Blvd. NE, Suite 210
Albuquerque, NM 87111
phone: (505) 292-2001
email: nicoa@swcp.com
website: www.nicoa.org

WEBSITES

Caregiver Survival Resources
www.caregiver911.com
This site provides an abundance of useful links to other caregiving resources on the Internet.

Caregiving Online (*Caregiving Newsletter*)
www.caregiving.com
This online support service, an off-shoot of *Caregiving Newsletter,* provides a wealth of information and resources for caregivers.

BOOKS

An Alzheimer's Chronicle: Letters to My Aunt
Penny A. Petersen
Desert State Publishing, 1997

Another Country: The Emotional Terrain of Our Elders
Mary Pipher
Riverhead, 1999

The Caregiver's Companion: Words to Comfort and Inspire
BettyClare Moffatt
Berkley, 1997

Caring for Your Parents in Their Senior Years: A Guide for Grown-up Children
William Molloy, M.D.
Firefly Books Ltd., 1998

Caring for Yourself While Caring for Your Aging Parents: How to Help, How to Survive
Claire Berman
Henry Holt, 1996

The Comfort of Home: An Illustrated Step-By-Step Guide for Caregivers
Maria M. Meyer
Care Trust Publications, 1998

Compassionate Touch: Hands-On Caregiving for the Elderly, the Ill and the Dying
Dawn Nelson
Station Hill Press, 1993

The Fourteen Friends Guide to Eldercaring
Joan Hunter Cooper and The Fourteen Friends
Capital Books Inc., 1999

Gifts from the Heart: Meditations on Caring for Aging Parents
Bonni Goldberg and George Kendall
NTC/Contemporary Co., 1997

A Good Enough Daughter: A Memoir
Alix Kates Shulman
Schocken Books, 1999

How to Care for Your Aging Parents . . . and Still Have a Life of Your Own
J. Michael Dolan
Mulholland Pacific, 1992

Learning to Sit in the Silence: A Journal of Caretaking
Elaine Marcus Starkman
Papier-Mache Press, 1993

My Turn to Care: Affirmations for Caregivers of Aging Parents
Marlene Bagnull
Thomas Nelson Inc., 1994

Rough Crossings: Family Caregivers' Odysseys through the Health Care System
Carol Levine
United Hospital Fund Publications Program
to order call: (212) 494-0776

A Very Easy Death
Simone de Beauvoir
Pantheon, 1965

With a Daughter's Eye: A Memoir of Margaret Mead and Gregory Bateson
Mary Catherine Bateson
HarperCollins, 1994

About the Contributors

Martha K. Baker, a writer and editor living in St. Louis, has written for national publications, such as *Glamour* and *PieceWork*, and for many local periodicals. She won the 1996 Thanksgiving essay contest on NPR's "Sunday Morning Edition." She has been a film critic since 1976. Her mother and father could not have passed a parenting course (they didn't even study for the midterm), but they did give her a love and respect for words.

Sandra Butler is the co-author (with Barbara Rosenblum) of *Conspiracy of Silence: The Trauma of Incest* and *Cancer in Two Voices*. Her writing, teaching and political activism focus on all forms of violence against women as well as the politics of women's health. Butler's seminars are attended by therapists, trainers, organizers and grassroots women interested in the intersection of personal growth and social change advocacy.

Cathleen Calbert's work has appeared in a number of publications including the *Best American Poetry 1995*, the *Nation*, the *New Republic* and the *Paris Review*. Her first book of poems, *Lessons in Space*, was published by the University Press of Florida in 1997. A second collection, *Bad Judgment*, was published by Sarabande Books in February, 1999. She is an Associate Professor at Rhode Island College.

Marian Mathews Clark grew up in Mist, Oregon, attended Graceland College in Iowa and graduated from the University of Iowa's Writers Workshop in 1987. She has been writing and working as an academic advisor at the University of Iowa since that time and has taught in Iowa's Summer Writing Festival. Her fiction appears in *Poets and Critics, Cottonwood Magazine,* the *Sun* and *Story Magazine.*

Korean-born writer **Maija Rhee Devine** is the winner of the Wyoming Arts Council's Doubleday Prize (1996) and Literature Fellowship (1998). Her essay "In the Lap of War" appeared in the *Michigan Quarterly Review* (Summer 1997), and a short story, "Crane's Grace," was published in the *Kenyon Review* (Fall/Winter 1999). She is completing a book-length memoir about her childhood in Korea. She lives in Wyoming with her husband and five children. During the 1998–99 academic year, she taught English at Nanjing University in China.

Wendy W. Fairey teaches literature and creative writing at Brooklyn College, where she is Professor of English. She is the author of a family memoir *One of the Family* (W. W. Norton, 1992). Her essays and stories have appeared in the *Virginia Quarterly Review,* the *New England Review, 13th Moon* and *Season of Adventure: Traveling Tales and Outdoor Journeys of Women Over 50,* among other journals and anthologies.

Susan L. Feldman's stories and essays have appeared in *Creative Nonfiction, A Room of One's Own, Tikkun, Reform Judiasm* and in anthologies published by Exile Press and Harcourt Brace Jovanovich. She lives in San Francisco.

Patricia A. Gozemba lives on the North Shore of Massachusetts and longs for an affordable old-age lesbian compound on the North Shore of Oahu. She teaches English and Women's Studies at Salem State College and is currently working on a book, co-authored with Eileen de los Reyes, called *Pockets of Hope: How Students and Teachers Change the World.*

Martha Henry is a poet and essayist. She works at the Knight Science Journalism Fellowships at MIT. She has a B.A. from Bowdoin College and an M.F.A. from the University of British Columbia. She lives in East Cambridge, Massachusetts, with her husband and a black Lab who once ate an entire basketball.

Caroline Jackson is a native of upstate New York and has lived in a Hudson River village for the past twenty-five years. She has worked as an editor and copywriter, but "Taking Leave" is her first published work. She has three grown and, she hopes, dutiful children.

Sheila Golburgh Johnson is a freelance writer whose work has appeared in many literary journals, commercial magazines and anthologies. Her novel, *After I Said No*, won the Sydney Taylor Award from the Association of Jewish Libraries in 1995 and will be published in 2000 by John Daniel. She has also edited an anthology of bird poetry, *Shared Sightings*. In 1998 Johnson won first prize in an international poetry competition sponsored by *Voices Israel*. She was recently featured in an article in *Santa Barbara Magazine* with two other nature poets.

Florence Ladd is the author of *Sarah's Psalm* (Scribner, 1996), which received the 1997 Best Fiction Award from the American Library Association's Black Caucus. Her short stories have appeared in the *Golden Horn* and *Wragtime*. Educated at Howard University (B.S.) and the University of Rochester (Ph.D.), she has worked as a teacher and administrator. Ladd has taught at Simmons College, Robert College in Istanbul, the Harvard Graduate School of Education and the Harvard Graduate School of Design. From 1989 to 1997 she was the director of the Bunting Institute at Radcliffe College. She lives in Cambridge, Massachusetts, and in a Côte-d'Or village in France.

BK Loren's work has been published in various periodicals including *Orion Magazine, The Sun, Alligator Juniper* and *Parabola*. She was the 1999 recipient of the Roberts-Rinehart Fellowship, and the 2000 recipient of *Alligator Juniper*'s national non-fiction award. She is currently at work on a book of literary non-fiction and a novel.

Mary Anne Maier is coeditor of the anthology *The Leap Years: Women Reflect on Change, Loss and Love,* forthcoming from Beacon Press (October 1999). Maier's essays and articles have appeared and are forthcoming in such varied settings as National Public Radio, *Journal of the American Medical Association,* the *Christian Science Monitor,* and *Southwestern Art.* A Wyoming native, Maier is a book editor for Texas Western Press.

Linda-Marie makes webpages. She can be reached at www.playink.com. She has lived in the San Francisco Bay Area all her life except for a short hitch in 1970 in Connecticut. Her book *I Must Not Rock* was published by Daughters, Inc. in 1977. She believes hippies were great and women should control the world.

Debra Marquart's poetry collection *Everything's a Verb* was published by New Rivers Press in 1995. For seven years, Marquart was a touring road musician with rock and heavy metal bands. She continues to perform with her jazz-poetry, rhythm & blues project, The Bone People, with whom she released two CDs in 1996: *Orange Parade,* acoustic/alternative rock; and *A Regular Dervish,* a jazz-poetry spoken word companion disc to *Everything's a Verb.* An assistant professor of English at Iowa State University, Marquart teaches creative writing and edits *Flyway Literary Review.* Her work has appeared in numerous literary journals and has three times won the Dorothy Churchill Cappon Essay Award sponsored by *New Letters.* In 1997, she won the Capricorn Novel Award sponsored by the Writer's Voice at the West Side Y in New York City for her collection of short stories about road musicians, *Hunger in the Bones,* which will be published by New Rivers Press in the fall of 2000.

Janet Mason is an award-winning poet, fiction and creative nonfiction writer. "Somebody" is an excerpt from her recently completed creative nonfiction work *Tea Leaves: A Memoir of Mothers and Daughters.* She lives in Philadelphia and is the author of *When I Was Straight,* a poetry collection published by Insight to Riot Press.

Sandell Morse has recently moved with her husband to York, Maine, from New Hampshire, where she lived and wrote for many years. Her short stories have appeared in many literary magazines including *Iris, Green Mountains Review, Bridges, Plowshares* and the *New England Review*. Another is included in the anthology *An Intricate Weave: Women Write About Girls and Girlhood*. A nonfiction piece is included in the anthology *Surviving Crisis*. She has been a Tennessee Williams Scholar at the Sewanee Writers' Conference (1996) and a finalist in the *Ploughshares* Robie Macauley Fellowship Award (1997). Her work has been nominated for inclusion in *Pushcart Prize XXIII: Best of the Small Presses*. She is currently working on a novel.

Kathryn Morton left a filing job at the *Virginian-Pilot* newspaper at age twenty-three to take a freighter to Europe. Her articles about that trip and about biking across Holland sold to *Mademoiselle* magazine. Returning to the *Pilot*, she married a reporter and had three children, while for fifteen years she wrote the paper's book review column, and occasional features and editorials. During the terminal illness of her middle child, she quit the paper and began freelance reviewing for the *New York Times Book Review*. After her son's death in 1986, Morton led her family into conversion to Judaism (described in an interview in *The Search for Meaning* by Phillip L. Berman, Ballantine Books, 1990) and became involved in Jewish education, including heading the Hebrew studies and bar and bat mitzvah training for a local synagogue. She is now finishing a book on artists who create Jewish ritual objects. She is confident that none of her children will ever write about her since she is herself perfectly normal.

Diane Reed lives in a small town on the coast of California and works as a technical writer for a project-management software company on the San Francisco peninsula. She holds a Master's Degree in Counseling Psychology. The mother of two sons and one daughter, she has five granddaughters. She lives with her dear friend, Phil, and her dog, a Boston terrier named Rose.

Bonny Vaught has written three nonfiction books, and now concentrates on essays and short fiction. She has been, in order of appearance: a Navy wife, a seminary wife, a pastor's wife and a long-term corporate spouse. When physical limitations kept her from teaching, she learned accounting. She is the treasurer for Crossroads Ministry, and anti-racism organization. After seventeen moves, she and her retired husband live in Hadley, Massachusetts—where she is free of wifely titles.

Marion Freyer Wolff was born in Berlin, Germany, in 1925, and came to the United States in December 1939. After obtaining B.S. and M.L.A. degrees from the Johns Hopkins University, she taught mathematics for many years. Now retired, she tutors math at home. Her book, *The Shrinking Circle: Memories of Nazi Berlin 1933–1939*, was published in 1989 by the Union of American Hebrew Congregations Press. A sequel, *The Expanding Circle: An Adoption Odyssey*, was published by the Fithian Press in spring 2000.

Tomasz Adach

Jean Gould is the author of the novel *Divorcing Your Grandmother* (Morrow, 1985) and the editor of *Season of Adventure: Traveling Tales and Outdoor Journeys of Women Over 50* (Seal Press, 1996). Her work includes poetry, short fiction and essays, some of which have been anthologized in *Another Wilderness* (Seal Press, 1994), *Grandmothers: Granddaughters Remember* (Syracuse University Press, 1998) and *Two in the Wild* (Vintage, 1999). For many years a college teacher and mental health professional, she is currently a visiting scholar in Women's Studies at Northeastern University.

Selected Titles from Seal Press

The Adoption Reader: Birthmothers, Adoptive Mothers and Adopted Daughters Tell Their Stories, edited by Susan Wadia-Ells. $16.95, 1-878067-65-6. With eloquence and conviction, more than thirty birthmothers, adoptive mothers and adopted daughters explore the many faces of adoption.

All the Powerful Invisible Things: A Sportswoman's Notebook, by Gretchen Legler. $12.95, 1-878067-69-9. Filled with a deep respect for wilderness, this beautifully written memoir traverses Legler's decade-long journey of self-discovery and reveals the ineffable grace of an outdoor life.

Blessed by Thunder: Memoir of a Cuban Girlhood, by Flor Fernandez Barrios. $22.95, 1-58005-021-2. In this evocative memoir, Flor Fernandez Barrios tells the story of her childhood during the Cuban revolution and the irrevocable changes it brings to her family and hometown of Cabaigüán.

Gifts of the Wild: A Woman's Book of Adventure, edited by Faith Conlon, Ingrid Emerick and Jennie Goode. $16.95, 1-58005-006-9. From the spectacular mountains of Patagonia to the mossy woods of the Pacific Northwest, *Gifts of the Wild* explores the transformative power of outdoor adventure in the lives of women.

No Mountain Too High: A Triumph Over Breast Cancer, The Story of the Women of Expedition Inspiration, by Andrea Gabbard. $16.00, 1-58005-008-5. The extraordinary story of seventeen women who battled breast cancer and then took on the challenge of climbing the Western Hemisphere's highest peak to raise public awareness about the disease.

Parting Company: Understanding the Loss of a Loved One: The Caregiver's Journey, by Cynthia Pearson and Margaret L. Stubbs. $18.95, 1-58005-019-0. A compassionate and revealing look at caregiving for the dying, including firsthand accounts of the dying process from a diverse group of caregivers as well as hospice and health care professionals.

Season of Adventure: Traveling Tales and Outdoor Journeys of Women Over 50, edited by Jean Gould. $15.95, 1-878067-81-8. Whether birdwatching in the Galápagos, camel-touring in Egypt or exploring the Pacific Cascades, these women display an uncommon *joie de vivre* and a keen awareness of their surroundings.

The Single Mother's Companion: Essays and Stories by Women, edited by Marsha R. Leslie. $12.95, 1-878067-56-7. The single mothers in this landmark collection explore both the joys and the difficult realities of raising children alone. Contributors include Barbara Kingsolver, Anne Lamott, Linda Hogan, Julia A. Boyd and Senator Carol Moseley-Braun.

Seal Press publishes many books of fiction and nonfiction by women writers. If you are unable to obtain a Seal Press title from a bookstore or would like a free catalog of our books, please order from us directly by calling 800-754-0271. Visit our website at www.sealpress.com.